THE NEW AVANT-GARDE IN ITALY:
THEORETICAL DEBATE AND POETIC PRACTICES

JOHN PICCHIONE

The New Avant-Garde in Italy

Theoretical Debate and Poetic Practices

UNIVERSITY OF TORONTO PRESS
Toronto Buffalo London

© University of Toronto Press Incorporated 2004
Toronto Buffalo London
Printed in Canada

ISBN 0-8020-8994-1

Printed on acid-free paper

Toronto Italian Studies

National Library of Canada Cataloguing in Publication

Picchione, John, 1949–
    New avant-garde in Italy : theoretical debate and poetic
    practices / John Picchione.

(Toronto Italian studies)
Includes bibliographical references and index.
ISBN 0-8020-8994-1

1. Italian poetry – 20th century – History and criticism.
2. Experimental poetry, Italian – History and criticism.
3. Avant-garde (Aesthetics) – Italy.   I. Title.   II. Series.

PQ4113.P43 2004   851′.91409   C2004-900740-8

This book has been published with the help of a grant from the Humanities
and Social Sciences Federation of Canada, using funds provided by the
Social Sciences and Humanities Research Council of Canada.

University of Toronto Press acknowledges the financial support for its
publishing activities of the Government of Canada through the Book
Publishing Industry Development Program (BPIDP).

University of Toronto Press acknowledges the financial assistance to its
publishing program of the Canada Council for the Arts and the Ontario
Arts Council.

Contents

Preface

The debate on literature and the arts provoked by the Italian neoavant-garde is undoubtedly one of the most animated and controversial that the country has witnessed from the Second World War to the present. Indeed, it embodies the last theoretical attempt to draw a general map of literature within the context of late capitalism and in the process, to offer a radical subversion of conventional aesthetic canons. Comprising roughly the period between the late 1950s and the end of the 1960s, the phenomenon of the *neoavanguardia* involved key writers, critics, and artists, both as insiders and as adversaries. Yet the critical attention the *neoavanguardia* has received outside Italy is rather scant. The theoretical positions represented by its major protagonists, such as Edoardo Sanguineti, Renato Barilli, Alfredo Giuliani, and Angelo Guglielmi, among others, remain virtually unknown beyond a restricted circle of Italianists. Even Umberto Eco, a prominent participant in the debate and an internationally acclaimed author, is seldom identified with the neoavant-garde. Likewise, the involvement of opponents such as Pier Paolo Pasolini, Italo Calvino, or Alberto Moravia, whose work has stirred substantial interest abroad, is not even acknowledged let alone given the attention it deserves.

The objective of this book is twofold: to provide a comprehensive analysis of the theoretical tenets that inform the works of the Italian neoavant-garde, and to show how these tenets are applied in the poetic practices of its authors. The decision to exclude other genres, namely fiction and theatre, is dictated by the view that it would have been inadvisable to explore a vast number of authors, poetry collections, novels, and plays within the same volume. Furthermore, the decision rests on the conviction that poetry is the area in which the neoavant-garde was able to obtain its most remarkable results.

As will be argued, the *neoavanguardia* cannot be defined as a movement with a unified program expressed in the form of manifestos or
shared theoretical principles. It experiences irreconcilable internal conflicts that are explored as a split between two main blocs: one is tied to
the project of modernity, the other to postmodern aesthetic postures.
The first identifies literature's formal ruptures with a subversive social
and ideological function. The second, considering literature as an integral part of the culture industry of late capitalism, embodies the belief
that there exist no pragmatic possibilities of antagonism – through aesthetic discourses – to the specific socio-political conditions of our times.
This study suggests that some of the contentious views expressed by the
neoavant-garde anticipate a wide range of issues that are at the basis of
literary and art theory in the 1970s and 1980s, when North America in
particular experienced an explosion of aesthetic ideas predominantly
mediated by French thought. The claim here is not that the theories of
the Italian neoavant-garde exhibit an unsurpassed degree of autonomy
or an unparalleled spirit of innovation; indeed, as will be underscored,
the *neoavanguardia*'s theoretical positions and literary practices cannot
be disengaged from a number of aesthetic models that include the
American avant-garde (Pound, Olson, Cage), the Frankfurt School,
Abstract Expressionism, post-Weberian music, and the *nouveau roman*.
Rather, the book's intent is to show that the neoavant-garde was able to
produce a rich and complex theoretical orientation and a body of creative works that have contributed to questioning, in a radical way,
received notions of poetry and literature.

In the context of the aesthetic perspectives of the second half of twentieth century, the *neoavanguardia* represents one of the most courageous
attempts to evaluate the specificity of literature within the structures of
our social and cultural institutions and, at the same time, to locate possibilities for re-stablishing a connection with the project of the historical
avant-garde (Futurism, Dadaism, Surrealism) which had been totally
abandoned by the literary movements of the preceding decades. It is
hoped this study will also serve as an incentive for further investigations in North America and the English-speaking world as a whole.
Undoubtedly, the neoavant-garde deserves much more critical attention than it has received thus far, both as a phenomenon in itself and as
a significant point of reference for comparative studies in literary theory
and practices. Even though over three decades have passed since its
demise, the issues it addressed continue to be fundamental and pressing for understanding the possible functions of literature in our age.

Acknowledgments

I would like to express my gratitude to the Social Sciences and Humanities Research Council of Canada and to the York University Faculty Association for the financial assistance they granted to this project, assistance that was vital to my carrying out research in Italy on several occasions. I also wish to thank York University's Faculty of Arts for a fellowship that released me from teaching responsibilities and thus provided precious time for writing this book; Dr Ron Schoeffel, editor-in-chief, and Anne Laughlin, managing editor, at the University of Toronto Press, for their kind support; and my copy editor, Curtis Fahey, who provided many valuable suggestions. I am grateful, too, to Achille Perilli for giving me permission to reproduce on the book's jacket two of his lithographs. Finally, I owe special thanks to the anonymous readers of the Press for their positive comments and constructive recommendations.

THE NEW AVANT-GARDE IN ITALY:
THEORETICAL DEBATE AND POETIC PRACTICES

1 Poetry in Revolt: The Novissimi

In the years following the Second World War, echoes of the Hermetic movement were still reverberating as stylistic traits of a great number of Italian poets. Yet, at the same time, there was evidence of an emerging new trend, which was characterized by a shift towards a representational mode of writing motivated by historical and social issues. The Hermetic position (extremely influential and dominant from the 1930s to the early 1940s), centred around the conception of poetic language as pure and spiritual intuition, made up of sudden illuminations and revelations of truth, was being replaced by a poetic word preoccupied with capturing the atrocities and social devastation of the war. This trend rejected the Hermetic view of writing as an ontological medium capable of giving voice to the transcendental messages of the world in favour of a poetic experience intent on facing the here and now and thereby making sense of the wartime events that had so deeply traumatized the human psyche. Whereas Hermeticism had religious and metaphysical underpinnings that fostered a closed and abstract language, privileging obscure and allusive analogies, the poetry of the immediate post-war period adhered both to history and to a language open to its everyday usage.

This new orientation can be traced to some degree or other in numerous poets, among whom are two important figures: Mario Luzi (*L'inferno e il limbo* [Hell and Limbo], 1949) and Vittorio Sereni (*Diario d'Algeria* [Algerian Diary], 1947, or *Gli strumenti umani* [Human Instruments], 1965; some poems of this latter collection date back to 1945). It subsequently receives clearer expression in the poetry of Salvatore Quasimodo (*Giorno dopo giorno* [Day after Day], 1947; *La vita non è sogno* [Life Is Not a Dream], 1949; *Il falso e vero verde* [True and False

Green], 1956), for whom, in the 1930s and early 1940s, Hermeticism had been that main source of inspiration.

Stylistic shifts and new thematic nuclei are easily uncovered in the post-war production of one of Italy's most representative poets of twentieth century, Eugenio Montale. In Montale's first post-war collection, *La bufera e altro* (The Storm and Other Poems; 1956), a metaphysical gaze on the senselessness of the world and on the limitations of human existence, which was the dominant trait of his work in the 1920s and 1930s, is replaced by a focus on the historical and cultural collapse brought about by Nazism and its horrors. Similarly, the poetry of Sandro Penna, Attilio Bertolucci, and Giorgio Caproni, although retaining some of the lyrical compression typical of Hermeticism, moved towards a linear and narrative style that displays a form of impressionistic realism aimed at capturing the occurrences of everyday life.

The distinct poetic line that emerged as a forceful reaction to Hermeticism was fashioned by poets who believed that an ideologically oriented realism would enable poetry to regain a social and political voice. These poets owed their intellectual formation to Marxist ideology, and to Antonio Gramsci in particular, even though they were constantly in conflict with the Communist Party itself. This trend was to be identified with the journal *Officina* (1955–9). Pier Paolo Pasolini, Roberto Roversi, and Franco Fortini played major roles in the life of this journal, but Pasolini was undoubtedly its driving force. His ideological nonconformity and passionate engagement in political and social debate, often embracing self-contradicting positions, made him one of the dominant literary personalities of the post-war period. However, if we put aside Pasolini's overall cultural impact through his film and journalism, we can see that his poetry is not as innovative as one might expect. His use of a common language, tied to elements of slang and dialect, can be traced back to Cesare Pavese's *Lavorare stanca* (Hard Labour; 1936) and to the general stylistic modes set by neorealism in its filmic and narrative expressions.

Pasolini is dramatically aware of the levelling linguistic and cultural effects of late capitalism – as expressed by the emerging consumer society of the mid-1950s and early 1960s – and he reacts by mythologizing the lumpenproletariat of the working-class Roman neighbourhoods, as he had already done in earlier years with the peasant class of his native Friuli (*La meglio gioventù* [The Best of Youth], 1954). For Pasolini, the marginalized condition of these social classes represented the final and only opposition to the bourgeois homogenization of life. In his view, the authentic and vital drives of these classes constituted a form of resistance to the process of enbourgeoisment that was fostering general decay and alienation in the society at large. Undoubtedly, Pasolini had a lucid perception of the links between the personal, the social, and the political, but his autobiographical confessionalism is still bound to the strains of lament characteristic of the lyrical tradition.

In collections such as *Le ceneri di Gramsci* (Gramsci's Ashes, 1957) and *La religione del mio tempo* (The Religion of My Times, 1961), Pasolini's connected poetic discourse to issues such as the antagonistic force of marginalized groups, political power and control of the body, consumer society and mortification of eros, the oppressive role of the church, and the place of progress within the hegemonic beliefs of late capitalism. In doing so, Pasolini anticipated pivotal questions that were to animate the cultural debate for years to come. Yet these questions are not intrinsically tied to literary preoccupations. In fact, they do not address issues related to the specificity of poetic language, nor do they challenge those hackneyed models of the Italian poetic tradition centred around lyrical intimacy.

In the pages of *Officina* (9–10 [1957]) Pasolini postulates a model of 'neo-sperimentalismo' (neo-experimentalism) but never shows any intention of subverting the literary canon. Here is the central passage taken from an article entitled 'La libertà stilistica' (Stylistic Freedom):

> Il neo-sperimentalismo si definisce ... come una zona franca, in cui neo-realismo e post-ermetismo coesistono fondendo le loro aree linguistiche ... Non abbiamo mai operato alcuna identificazione tra spirito innovatore e sperimentalistico: il neo-sperimentalismo ... tende semmai a essere epigono, non sovversivo, rispetto alla tradizione stilistica novecentesca ... vari neo-sperimentalismi operano per una scelta antecedente a quella stilistica, e, più o meno confusamente, ideologica: un 'impegno sociale,' come si usa dire, o comunque sentimentalmente espanso nei confronti della 'vita di relazione.' (6)

> Neo-experimentalism is defined as a free port in which neorealism and post-Hermeticism coexist by blending their linguistic areas ... We never identified experimentalism with a spirit of innovation ... indeed, neo-experimentalism tends to be an epigone, not subversive vis à vis the stylistic tradition of the 1900s ... the operation of various experimentalisms is based on a choice antecedent that of style, and, in a more or less confusing

fashion, can be termed an ideological choice: a 'social commitment,' as it is usually called, or, at the same time, sentimentally extendable to 'human relations.'

Stylistic freedom is an 'illusory freedom' ('libertà illusoria') according to Pasolini and, thus, in its essence, literature is identified with an ideological hermeneutics of reality. As discussed in the next chapter, this position will create an irreparable conflict between Pasolini and the neoavant-garde.

Another group of poets comprising Luciano Erba (*Il male minore* [The Lesser Evil], 1960), Nelo Risi (*Pensieri elementari* [Elementary Thoughts], 1961), and Giovanni Giudici (*L'intelligenza col nemico* [Intelligence with the Enemy], 1957), like the ideologically oriented realists, conceive poetry as an instrument of social awareness and revolt. In their emphasis on irony and their anti-rhetorical style, they demystify the role of the poet and poetry itself, making impossible the construction of any myth or of any utopian project. These poets, recalling the writing mode of an influential poet of the early 1900s, Guido Gozzano, adopt a subdued and prosaic language seasoned with strong doses of irony that often takes the form of sarcasm or biting satire directed at the superficiality and hypocrisies of contemporary life. Identity and subjectivity are constantly questioned, making it impossible for the poet to claim any privileged position within the alienated existence of mass culture. This poetry can be seen as an expression of a religious and ideological crisis, but it never surrenders to any form of nihilistic resignation. Irony becomes an effective tool of social critique that often tries to displace conventional linguistic modalities. Overall, however, this poetry does not attempt to subvert poetic tradition any more than Pasolini does.

In summary, by the late 1950s, Italian poetry lagged behind music and the visual arts in its embrace of change (consider, for example, experimental music, Abstract Expressionism, and 'informal' art in general). Nor had it witnessed the linguistic turmoil present in writers such as Joyce, Pound, or even Eliot. The revolt of the historical avant-garde was a project interrupted by fascist repression of culture and thus had not been marked by any significant developments.[1]

The turning-point was reached in 1961 with the publication of the anthology *I Novissimi – Poesie per gli anni '60* (*I Novissimi – Poetry for the Sixties*), including the work of Elio Pagliarani, Edoardo Sanguineti, Nanni Balestrini, Antonio Porta, and Alfredo Giuliani (the latter also edited the collection).[2] This provocative and revolutionary anthology shook up the Italian literary scene and opened the way to the formation of Gruppo 63, a group of writers and critics that was soon identified as the Italian *neoavanguardia*.

Collectively, the five poets represented in the anthology rejected both the conservative practices of the literary tradition and the normal linguistic code because, in their view, both had succumbed to forms of reification and commercialization. They championed an alternative language capable of expressing ambiguity, estrangement, and disorder. The Novissimi showed aversion for symmetry and advocated a subversive poetic style dominated by rhythmic dissonances, temporal discontinuities, semantic distortions, and syntactic dislocations. They refused to pursue forms of lyrical effusions centred around the 'I' or to identify poetry with the search of the sublime. For the Novissimi, writing had to become a blasphemous activity, a programmatic laceration and fragmentation of language, and a project aimed at thwarting the reader's habitual horizon of expectations. The new style was to fracture linear discourse and, at the same time, violate worn-out or standard interpretative grammars of reality. In other words, poetry should refuse to court the reader with seductive lyricism and instead should create a distance from the automatism of everyday-language models by becoming the locus of defying and anarchic linguistic constructs.

In his introduction to the anthology, Giuliani conceives of poetry as a provocative linguistic experience. Rejecting any instrumental view of language, he insists that a poet's attention must be devoted to the medium itself. A poet must be preoccupied with words and not with ideologies or 'pre-given truths.' The new poetry must oppose both the stifling effects of literary conventions and the escalating degradation of the word to a commodity as witnessed by the emerging consumer society. Giuliani writes:

La passione di parlare in versi urta, da un lato contro l'odierno avvolgente consumo e sfruttamento commerciale cui la lingua è sottoposta; dall'altro, contro il suo codice letterario, che conserva l'inerzia delle cose, e istituisce *l'abuso di consuetudine* (il fittizio 'è così') nella visione dei rapporti umani. Pertanto, prima di guardare all'astratta ideologia, all'intenzione culturale, noi guardiamo alla semantica concreta della poesia, senza dimenticarci che essa è dopotutto un'arte, una vis mitologica. (*IN*, 18–19)

On the one hand, the passion of 'speaking in verse' jars with today's enveloping consumption and the commercial exploitation to which language is subjected; on the other hand, it jars with its literary code, which maintains the inertia of things, and institutes *the abuse of the habitual* (the fictitious 'that's how it is') in a vision of human relations. Thus, before looking to abstract ideology, to cultural intention, we look to the concrete semantics of poetry, mindful that it is after all an art, a *vis milologica*. (*I Nov*, 23)

Such a poetics generates various corollaries. The major one is the rejection of an *ante poiesim* ideology. Subject and object of its operation, poetry is not seen in an ancillary, servile subordination to reality, and not even as its metaphor. Rather, poetry is conceived as an alternative dimension to our life-world and to everyday linguistic practices. In the preface to the second edition of the anthology, Giuliani effectively states his position:

> Se vivere e già 'rappresentare,' ossia scrivere, incidere biologicamente segni memoriali, fare poesia è un forzare la vita a riscriversi, a scompigliare e rimontare segni memoriali in nessi inediti, spingerla a liberarsi dai feticismi della rappresentazione in visioni che 'traversano,' senza sostare e 'formarsi' né nell'uno né nell'altro, il linguaggio della vita e quello dell'arte.
>
> In altri termini: il primato della struttura, il suo porsi in luogo della rappresentazione, significa che la poesia, anziché offrirsi nel suo insieme come metafora del reale, si costituisce come un altro polo di quel mondo linguistico che tutti scriviamo vivendo. (*IN*, 12)

> If to live is already 'to represent,' i.e., to write, biologically to carve memorial signs, creating poetry means forcing life to rewrite itself, to scramble and reassemble memorial signs in unprecedented connections, to push it to free itself from the fetishes of representations into visions that 'traverse,' without stopping and 'forming' in either one or the other, the language of life and the language of art.
>
> In other words: the primacy of structure, its putting itself in place of representation, means that poetry, rather than offering itself whole as a metaphor of the real, is constituted as another pole of the linguistic world we all write in living. (*I Nov*, 56)

In essence, Giuliani searches for an escape from the tradition of mimesis. He seeks to disengage poetry from obsolete mimetic canons because, without such a separation, its activity will end up being redundant and tautological – merely capturing what is already there or acquired by ordinary experience ('representing is a useless action' ['rappresentare è inutile'], he affirms; *I Nov*, 55; *IN*, 11). Clearly, Giuliani does not claim that the poetry of the Novissimi has no ties with reality. He argues that 'poetry must open up a passage: in mirroring reality it must answer our need to go "through the looking-glass"' (*I Nov*, 20) ('la poesia debba aprirci un varco: nel rispecchiare la realtà rispondere al nostro bisogno di attraversare lo specchio' [*IN*, 16]).

As he underscores in the 1965 edition, a common feature of the poetics of the Novissimi is the conviction that the new poetry must present itself as 'a critical mimesis of universal schizophrenia, a reflection and contestation of a disintegrated social and imaginative state' (*I Nov*, 49) ('mimesi critica della schizofrenia universale, rispecchiamento e contestazione di uno stato sociale immaginativo disgregato' [*IN*, 7]).

Giuliani thus rejects any drab conception of realism based on principles of verisimilitude, factuality, and fidelity in the documentation of social and individual life – in other words, any claim of a Naturalistic representation of reality. He contests any practice of mimetic narration tied to criteria of plausibility, normality, and acceptability – the kind of literature that finds fulfilment in venturing outside its field to take on issues of a social or psychological nature. Poetry cannot be reduced to contents and themes; it does many other things by virtue of its language; its language can become its content and its vision of the world.[3]

Giuliani favours a pragmatic, gestural attitude. By abandoning the constrictions of representational aesthetics, he shifts towards a deliberately arbitrary and deviant poetic structure. Poetry for Giuliani is, first of all, not so much a cognitive medium as a form of contact. As he argues in an essay written in 1962, 'poetry is not a form of knowledge, but a mode of contact. Poetry is made to act ... poetry is a cultivated capacity of contact with the linguistic reality (that is, with the linguistic modality of reality' (la poesia non è una forma di conoscenza, ma un modo di contatto. La poesia è detta per agire ... la poesia è una coltivata capacità di contatto con la realtà linguistica (ossia con la modalità linguistica della realtà' [*Immagini e maniere* (Images and Manners), 146, 148]).

Poetry's content is what it does – how it acts upon the reader, the action it exerts:

Perché ci siamo tanto preoccupati del lessico, della sintassi, del metro e via dicendo? Perché se conveniamo che, in quanto 'contemporanea,' la poesia agisce direttamente sulla vitalità del lettore, allora ciò che conta in primo luogo è la sua efficacia linguistica. Ciò che la poesia *fa* è precisamente il suo 'contenuto' ... nei periodi di crisi il *modo di fare* coincide quasi interamente col *significato*. (*IN*, 17)

Why are we so concerned with diction, syntax, meter, and so on? Because if we grant that, in its 'contemporaneity,' poetry acts directly on the reader's vitality, then what matters most is its linguistic efficacy. What poetry *does* is precisely its 'content' ... in periods of crisis the *modus operandi* coincides almost totally with *meaning*. (*I Nov*, 21)

With a revolutionary formal structure, poetry must constantly put the reader in a state of disquietude. Instead of providing 'relief and comfort' (sollievo), the sort of 'epidermic, ornamental excitement' ('eccitazione epidermica e ornamentale') created by 'declamation' and 'incantation' ('declamazione, canto di scongiuro' [*I Nov*, 43; *IN*, 3]), customarily found in a poetic text or expected from it, poetry for Giuliani – citing Leopardi – must 'increase vitality' ('accrescere la vitalità' (*I Nov*, 19; *IN*, 15]) by radically renewing the reader's encounter with the text.

The deep aversion to literature centred on the production of nicely packaged messages for easy consumption leads Giuliani to focus his attention on the linguistic modes of perceiving reality. Poetry's function is to create a distance from the automatism of dominant and ossified linguistic/literary models by demolishing the syntax and by violently fragmenting semantic articulation. Giuliani speaks of the necessity of adopting the 'discontinuity of the imaginative process, *asyntactism*' ('discontinuità del processo immaginativo, l'*asintattismo*' [*I Nov*, 24; *IN*, 20]), and the 'asemantic assemblage of signs' ('montaggio asemantico dei segni' [*I Nov*, 46; *IN*, 5]).

This operation is aimed at engendering a state of defamiliarization which, in turn, will force the reader to establish a more dynamic and active rapport with the text. The idea is also to foreground the arbitrariness and ambiguity of the sign so that poetry can draw attention to its own artifice, to the way meaning is produced rather than to the meaning of things. Giuliani advocates a form of poetry with an 'open' structure and gives prominence to the role of the reader. He differentiates an 'open' writer from a 'closed' writer and stresses their respective effects on the act of reading. Indeed, Giuliani's views on the openendedness of the text, and the resulting shift towards the importance of the reader's activity, anticipate a critical trend that was to become dominant in the 1960s, 1970s, and beyond. In front of an open text, he claims, the reader's task is not to identify pre-established meanings.

Meanings are deferred. They are essentially created through the collaborative act of reading:

> Lo scrittore 'aperto' trae egli stesso insegnamento dalle cose e non vuole insegnare nulla, non dà l'impressione di possedere una verità ma di cercarla e di contraddirsi oscuramente, non vuole catturare la benevolenza o destare meraviglia, perché inclina a lasciare l'iniziativa al rapporto che si creerà nell'incontro tra due disposizioni semantiche, quella del testo e l'altra, appunto, che appartiene a chi legge ... Una poesia è vitale quando ci spinge oltre i propri inevitabili limiti, quando cioè le cose che hanno ispirato le sue parole ... ci inducono il senso di altre cose e di altre parole, provocando il nostro intervento; si deve poter profittare di una poesia come di un incontro un po' fuori dell'ordinario. (*IN*, 20)

> The 'open' writer learns from things and has no desire to teach; he does not give the impression of possessing a truth but of searching for one, and of dimly contradicting himself. He has no wish to capture the benevolence or rouse admiration, since he tends to leave the initiative to the rapport that will be created in the encounter of two semantic dispositions, that of the text, and that of the reader ... A poem is vital when it forces us beyond its own inevitable limits, that is, when the things that have inspired its words induce in us the sense of other things and other words, prompting our intervention; one ought to profit from a poem as one would from some rather extraordinary encounter. (*I Nov*, 25)

In a period during which poetry seemed to find as its sole destiny the unloading of contents based on the author's sentimental pangs or ethical stands, often combined with nebulous political ambitions, statements of poetics such as these were received by traditional literary circles as a provocation and a threat. Time revealed that they were quite prophetic in foreseeing the course on which the new poetry was to embark. Giuliani insists on the new role of the reader also in the second edition of the anthology:

> Chi scrive una poesia (e dunque anche chi la riscrive leggendola) sperimenta tutta la possibile ambiguità e comprensività del linguaggio. (*IN*, 8)

> Anyone who writes a poem (and thus anyone who, by reading a poem, rewrites it) experiences all of language's possible ambiguity and comprehensiveness. (*I Nov*, 51)

By stressing the need to shatter prevailing linguistic structures and the socialized use of language, Giuliani not only attempts to generate a crisis in the reader's view of the world but also aims at producing other possible dimensions of interaction with reality. Indeed, his poetics cannot be detached from existential motivations. The formal transgression of language conveys the existential urgency to go beyond accepted and mystifying conceptions of reality. The semantic and syntactic disorder advocated by Giuliani coincides with the conception of the poetic structure as a possible window onto the imaginary and the experience of otherness.

In *Immagini e maniere* (the publication of this collection of essays coincides with that of the second edition of *I Novissimi*), Giuliani declares that the poetic structure becomes 'neo-content' ('neo-contenuto' [148]). The emphasis is placed not on what poetry says but on its transgressive structural elements. It is the perturbing effects on the reader caused by the formal ruptures that constitute new messages. The reader is asked to reject the bourgeois model of producer-consumer and to become instead a co-author of the text by constructing its messages.

Giuliani identifies poetry's language of transgression and otherness with a formal organization that he defines as a '"schizomorphic" vision' (*I Nov*, 24) ('visione schizomorfa' [*IN* 19]). For Giuliani, the language of apparent madness constructed by the new poetry, with its chaos, semantic lacerations, and temporal discontinuities, represents the only possibility against silence in a 'schizophrenic age'(*I Nov*, 23) ('età schizofrenica' [*IN*, 18]) such as ours. Giuliani is well aware that the rejection of linear discourse in favour of simultaneity, ambiguity, and montage has an already established tradition initiated by the historical avant-garde – from Futurism to Dada, Surrealism, and Vorticism (cf. *I Nov*, 52; *IN*, 9). He stresses that this tradition 'has not yet died' (*I Nov*, 53) ('non è ancora morta' [*IN*, 9]) and is the only possible point of reference within the social and psychological conditions of our times. Giuliani does not mythologize the experience of the schizophrenic as an alternative model to the alienated and dehumanized subject in the age of late capitalism. He writes:

Intendiamoci: non c'è nulla di più squallido e straziante che la condizione della follia. Il fascino dell'analogia è nondimeno quasi irresistibile per chi sa che le assurde tecniche dell'alienato sono tentativi mal riusciti di congiungersi con la propria ombra e di confondersi nella reciprocità di un'assoluta trasparenza entro un rapporto di vita ... L'affetività turbata dallo sconvolgimento dei termini di relazione, l'intelligenza che registra la dissociazione degli eventi mediante la distorsione semantica, le conseguenti stesure intrecciate del discorso, i giochi linguistici (neologismi, schizofasie), la similarità tra il linguaggio del sogno e l'espressione della psicosi, la giustapposizione degli elementi di logiche diverse, il linguaggio-sfida, il non-finito: tutto ciò coincide con l'attitudine antropologica che precise condizioni storiche hanno esaltato fino alla costituzione di un linguaggio letterario che *fa epoca* e da cui non si può tornare indietro. (*IN*, 7)

Let's keep in mind: nothing could be bleaker or more agonizing than the condition of madness. The lure of the analogy is nevertheless almost irresistible for anyone who knows that the absurd techniques of the mentally ill are unsuccessful attempts to unite with one's own shadow and to merge into the reciprocity of an absolute transparency within life-relations ... The affectivity disturbed by disordering relational terms, the intelligence that registers the dissociation of events through semantic distortion, the resultant interweaving of discourse, the linguistic games (neologisms, schizophasias), the similarity between the language of dreams and the expression of psychosis, the juxtaposition of the elements of different logics, the language-challenge, the non-finite: all this coincides with an anthropological attitude that precise historical conditions have roused to create an *epoch-making* literary language it will now be impossible to turn back from. (*I Nov*, 49–50)

This calculated linguistic derangement is geared to produce both an autonomous formal structure capable of generating its own realities and, at the same time, an *ersatz* aimed at providing a critique of the schizophrenic disintegration that characterizes, according to Giuliani, the society of the late 1950s and early 1960s. His essay is so groundbreaking that the many questions and issues it tackles will remain at the core of literary debate for decades to come.

Giuliani emphasizes the need for a poetry guided by the principle of self-referentiality and self-reflexivity without abandoning the relation of the text to outside reality. As argued above, favouring literariness, Giuliani aims at undoing conventional models of representation but does not advocate the pure poetic self-sufficiency of the text:

Strozzata apparizione, rito demente e schernitore, discorso sapiente, pantomima incorporea, gioco temerario, la nuova poesia si misura con la *degradazione dei significati* e con l'*instabilità fisiognomica* del mondo verbale in cui siamo immersi, ma anche con se stessa, con la sua capacità d'invenzione. (*IN*, 7)

A chocked or muffled apparition, demented, mocking rite, knowing discourse, incorporeal pantomime and reckless game, the new poetry is gauged by the *degradation of meanings* and by the *physiognomic instability* of the verbal world we are immersed in, yet is also to be gauged by itself, by its own inventive capability. (*I Nov*, 50)

The reference to 'pantomime' seems to imply that, just as the gestures and actions of the mime do not reproduce an outside reality (and thus can be seen as a non-referential activity and an artistic expression of anti-mimesis), so poetry is a self-contained activity whose signs are gestural inventions independent of the outside, a performance geared towards the production – not the reproduction – of meanings. However, both in the introduction and in the preface to the second edition, Giuliani persistently draws our attention to the historical context, to the larger cultural map in which the poetry of the Novissimi is to be placed. Poetry must not be doomed to regurgitate a script pre-written and pre-established by the events and experiences of our life-world, but, at the same time, it must not to be (or cannot be) fully disentangled from it. In fact, when Giuliani addresses the modalities of his own poetry, he underscores, on the one hand, that it is not an expansion of the 'already-thought' ('il già pensato') and, on the other, he recognizes that is an objectification of 'life in its moments of crisis: life cleansed of its obviousness, not of its tragic implications' (*I Nov*, 30) ('la vita ... nei suoi momenti di crisi: la vita depurata dall'ovvietà non dalle sue implicazioni tragiche' [*IN*, 25]). Giuliani's key concern is the justification of the specificity of poetic language and its autonomy. He defends literariness as an independent domain and foregrounds the internal organization of the poetic text. Nevertheless, Giuliani's argument in favour of the view of a poem as an intralinguistic construction and a self-focused message avoids situating it within the restricted confines of a narcissistic activity of the sign, absorbed in self-contemplation and without an extralinguistic reality. Giuliani makes a clear effort to maintain a dialectical relation between the principle of autonomy and that of heteronomy – even though there is no doubt that primacy is given to the former. In fact, looking back at the experience of the Novissimi after some years, Giuliani submits that the group shares the 'adventure' lived inside the linguistic signs. He speaks of a 'poetics of the sign' that identifies poetry as an activity in which 'one looks at oneself writing' ('guardarsi scrivere') and, at the same time, 'is looked at by language' ('essere guardati dal linguaggio') ('L'avventura dentro i segni,' *Le droghe di Marsiglia*, [The Adventure inside the Signs, The Drugs of Marseille], 21–2).

Giuliani's position on poetic language is linked to a philosophical orientation whose roots can be traced to phenomenology. His basic assumption is that the historical conditions of our schizophrenic times have created a form of 'existence in which the subjectivity and the objectivity of the world are equally impossible' (*I Nov*, 49) ('esistenza in cui sono altrettanto impossibili la soggetività e l'oggettività del mondo' [*IN*, 17]). In his view – and in that of all the Novissimi – the commodification of the linguistic code, the hackneyed language of dominant literary models, together with the disintegration of the subject as a centred and unifying entity, have created a general state of alienation that can allow neither for the immediacy of experience (or the transparency of true individual sentiments) nor for a personal, unaffected, normal language.

Giuliani identifies the 'reduction of the I' (*I Nov*, 25) ('riduzione dell'io' [*IN* 21]) as an essential feature of the poetry produced by the Novissimi. Following the premises of the phenomenological method, he advocates a return to things as a way to advance a consciousness uncluttered with beliefs and presuppositions. The phenomenological reduction (*epochè*) proposes the suspension of all pre-constituted ideologies (beliefs placed in abeyance as a matter of method) in order to gain access to a pre-conceptual experience of the world (being-in-the-world implies that we experience the world *before* we can come to know it). The phenomenological bracketing of subjectivity does not simply express the rejection of traditional lyrical and sentimental poetry. The 'I' (the empirical self) is bracketed inasmuch as it is considered the result of an alienated subjectivity, divorced from a genuine life of experience. The centrality of the 'I' and of the author is supplanted by the centrality of language and of the other – an assemblage of pre-existing linguistic fragments and voices of characters that speak through that of the poet.

Giuliani derives from phenomenology the idea of constructing a form of poetry that adheres to objects and events as they would appear to consciousness, prior to any reflective process. Poetry should approach the world as an experience which we live before it becomes an object that we know. In other words, poetry should aspire to provide the reader with pre-reflective experiences without conceptualizations or easily consumable ideological constructs. To be sure, Giuliani and the Novissimi as a group do not proclaim the death of the subject or the disappearance of the self. The phenomenological reduction is a strategy generated by the urgency to revisit the world anew and to unfold, through innovative linguistic modes, new possibilities of existence. The task to restore a meaningful and non-alienated relation with oneself and with the world is assigned to a poetic practice guided by an unfettered linguistic imagination. For the Novissimi, this represented the only possibility of confronting linguistic and socio-historical alienation.

Phenomenological and existential psychiatry as conceived by Karl Jaspers and Ludwig Binswanger may have also played a role in Giuliani's articulation of the poetics of the Novissimi. Their research in psychopathology, particularly as manifested in schizophrenia and autism in relation to pathological deformations of language, may have provided Giuliani with clues for his concept of 'schizomorphism.' Within the context of phenomenological psychiatry, psychotic or schizophrenic experiences were explained as different life-worlds which on the surface seem to lack meaning but in fact do not. Such experiences, conceived as different manifestations of existence and as different linguistic modalities, could have a variety of applications in a poetic setting. The radical objectivism of the phenomenological school of psychiatry, its insistence on Husserl's notion of going back to things prior to conceptual constructs, is much in tune with Giuliani's poetic proposal of a necessary reduction of the 'I.'[4]

He seems to have been particularly motivated by Eugène Minkowski's studies on autism and schizophrenia.[5] For Minkowski, life must be understood not in abstract concepts but through the ways in which vital categories, such as time and space, are experienced. In his view, 'syntony' is experiencing life in unison with the external world, whereas schizoidism is a detachment from the external, including social realities (*Lived Time*, 70–6). Autism, in fact, is interpreted as a loss of contact with reality, a breakdown of what Minkowski defines as the 'élan vital,' a primordial force that keeps us in sync with life's becoming. Giuliani was probably inspired in his conception of poetry as a form of 'contact' by Minkowski's notion of 'lived synchronism' as a way to regain contact with reality (64).

Adopting Husserl's principle of 'intentionality' (consciousness is always directed towards an object, it is always something other that itself), Minkowski advocates a return to the concreteness of the world through which the 'I' is incessantly transcended by the presence of 'ambient becoming' (48). By turning away from the 'I,' Minkowski maintains, 'we no longer find ourselves in the presence of a void or in the presence of chaos, but we discover a new phenomenon before us – *vital contact with reality*' (64). Giuliani's concerns with the condition of alienation, with the language of pathology, and with poetry as a medium of contact with reality doubtlessly present significant correlations with phenomenological psychiatry and with Minkowski's research in particular.

The tenets of phenomenology do not constitute the exclusive backdrop to this central aspect of the Novissimi's poetics. In their 1912 manifesto, the Futurists had already stressed the need 'to destroy the "I" in literature' ('distruggere nella letteratura l'"io"') by shifting to the 'obsession of matter' ('l'ossessione ... della materia').[6] For the Italian Futurists, the lyrical tradition of Romanticism and Symbolism, centred upon the filtering of the world trough the subjective and emotive reactions of the poet's 'I,' was to be demolished by promoting a form of objectivism that adhered to the immediate physical reality.

A similar correlation can be drawn with Ezra Pound and Imagism. This latter poetic movement also highlighted the concentration on the object and thus the necessity of showing the external world rather than just talking about it. Against emotional diffusiveness, Imagism insisted on the concreteness of detail as a way of encountering the phenomenal world. Indeed, Pound constantly asserted that poetry must adopt as its fundamental principle the 'direct treatment of the thing' and utilize the 'natural object' as its only source of symbols.[7] This poetic orientation is relevant also in another American poet, William Carlos Williams, who summarizes his position in the dictum 'no ideas but in things.'

Ties can also be established with Eliot's principle of the 'objective correlative' as expressed in *The Sacred Wood*, translated into Italian by Luciano Anceschi (*Il bosco sacro*, 1946). Anceschi, editor of *Il Verri*, the journal through which the Novissimi articulated their aesthetic and intellectual program, pioneered in Italy studies on the American new poetics (*Poetica americana*, 1953) and championed a poetry focused on objects. His influence on the young Novissimi cannot be underestimated.[8]

Giuliani makes direct references to Pound in a statement of poetics included in the closing section of the anthology, entitled 'Dietro la poesia' (Behind the Poetry). He discusses Pound's metrical experimentation and suggests that, in general, 'metrical restlessness is a symptom revealing the poet's anxiety about reality' (*I Nov*, 407) ('L'inquietudine metrica è un sintomo per cui si manifesta nel poeta l'angoscia della realtà' [IN, 217]). Giuliani pays particular attention to one of the most representative figures of the American postwar avant-garde, Charles Olson, and specifically cites Olson's most influential essay, 'Projective Verse.'[9] Giuliani remarks:

> Così non abbiamo nessuna difficoltà a comprendere, *in questo momento,* e inserire tra i nostri arnesi anche il tipo americano (di cui parla Charles Olson) di quel verso 'dinamico' o 'aperto' o 'atonale' che abbiamo già sperimentato negli ultimi anni ... È importante più che non sembri, l'osservazione semplificatrice di Olson che il verso nuovo va scritto nella misura del respiro, e non per l'occhio ma secondo l'orecchio. (*IN* 220, 221)

> Thus *at the present moment* we have no trouble understanding and adding among our tools the American type (as Charles Olson presents it) of 'dynamic' or 'open' or 'atonal' verse we have already experimented with over the last few years ... Important here – more than it would seem – is Olson's helpful observation ... that the new verse is written in the meter of breath, and not for the eye but according to the ear. (*I Nov*, 411, 413)

Points of convergence between the poetics of the Novissimi and that of Olson go beyond metrical preoccupations. Olson's 'composition by field' and 'objectism' is directly related to the reduction of the 'I.' Here is, in the second part of 'Projective Verse,' Olson's view on the necessity of demoting the ego from its traditional centrality:

> Objectism is the getting rid of the lyrical interference of the individual as ego, of the 'subject' and his soul, that peculiar presumption by which western man has interposed himself between what he is as a creature of nature (with certain instructions to carry out) and those other creations of nature which we may, with no derogation, call objects. For a man is himself an object, whatever he may take to be his advantages, the more likely to recognize himself as such the greater his advantages, particularly at that moment that he achieves an humilitas sufficient to make him of use. (*Selected Writings of Charles Olson,* 24–5)

Like the Novissimi, Olson too is guided by the principle that objects and occurrences constituting a poem must not be subjected to any interference from the 'I' (the poet is an object among many others) or from preconceived ideas:

The objects which occur at every given moment of composition (of recognition, we can call it) are, can be, must be treated exactly as they do occur therein and not by any ideas or preconceptions from outside the poem, must be handled as a series of objects in field in such a way that a series of tensions (which they also are) are made to *hold*, and to hold exactly inside the content and the context of the poem which has forced itself, through the poet and them, into being. (*Selected Writings*, 20)

The notion of a direct perception of the object without any mediation by the 'I,' then, shows a close connection between Olson's poetics and that of the Novissimi. The results, for both, are a series of ramifications which include the adoption of a fragmented mode of writing (a non-hierarchic or non-linear sequences of materials), with its apparent effects on traditional syntax and temporal progression ('against tenses, in fact against syntax, in fact against grammar generally, that is, as we have inherited it,' Olson writes in the same essay, 21).

Revolting against the language of Symbolism and its aspiration to transcend phenomenical reality in search of the essences concealed behind the object, both Giuliani's introduction and Olson's essay reject the abstractions of discourse, metaphoric and analogic practices, or descriptive effusions, and subscribe to a poetics that endeavours to anchor to the page our experience of reality ('to hew to experience as it is,' as Olson writes in his essay 'Human Universe,' *Selected Writings*, 56). A passage from this latter essay addresses directly the issue in question:

Right here is the trouble, that each thing is not so much like or different from another thing (these likenesses and differences are apparent) but that such an analysis only accomplishes a *description*, does not come to grips with what really matters: that the thing, any thing, impinges on us by a more important fact, its self-existence, without reference to any other thing, in short, the very character of it which calls our attention to it, which wants us to know more about it, its particularity. This is what we are confronted by, not the thing's 'class,' any hierarchy, of quality or quantity, but the thing itself, and its *relevance* to ourselves who are the experience of it. (56)

Furthermore, Giuliani's notion of poetry as a way of increasing the reader's 'vitality' finds a correspondence in Olson's notion of poetry as a means of energy transfer. 'A poem,' Olson writes, 'is energy transferred from where the poet got it ... by way of the poem itself to, all the way over to, the reader' ('Projective Verse,' 16). Finally, like Giuliani, Olson radically questions traditional canons of mimesis. As he declares in 'Human Universe,' 'art is the only twin life has – its only valid metaphysic. Art does not seek to describe but to enact' (61). Poetry's function is not to duplicate life but to invent it.[10]

Although Giuliani and the Novissimi recognize the historical avant-garde and Pound and Olson's poetics as points of reference, they also look outside literature to find shared objectives and concerns. In his preface, not surprisingly, Giuliani mentions the name of John Cage in relation to the structural 'disorganization' of a poetic text (*I Nov*, 54; *IN*, 10). Cage was in fact associated with the group of artists that in the early 1950s represented the emerging post-war American avant-garde cantred mainly around Black Mountain College, in North Carolina, where Olson became the rector. Cage had travelled in Italy in the second half of the 1950s and Giuliani was by then familiar with his work (Sanguineti, who – as will be highlighted – makes musical practices a central point of contact for his poetry, must also have been exposed to the work of the American composer). For Cage (as for Olson and the Novissimi), art – music in his case – is an experiential process that demands the creative role of the listener. But more important, Cage's experimental music is an assemblage (often dictated by mere chance) of sounds, such as fragments of existing musical compositions, screams, passing conversations, and noises such as a creaking door, rushing water, or a car collision. The avant-garde solutions of chance and assemblage play in Cage a role very much in tune with the reduction of the 'I' that Giuliani presents as a central feature of the Novissimi's poetics. Cage's experimental music can be defined as sounds in motion that are intended to bypass his own self. Sounds establish free relations among themselves; they are not controlled by harmony, tonality, or any other methodological stricture. Unhampered by any logic of progression, music becomes a succession of sounds flowing freely, independent of the composer's direct control.

For the Novissimi, Cage does not represent a single point of reference as far as the musical context is concerned. The 'atonal' verse of the Novissimi, their tendency to experiment with dissonances, together with their adoption of plurilinguism, can undoubtedly be situated within the perspectives that have constituted the most radical innovations of twentieth-century music. A few examples will suffice. The Futurists, as the Manifesto of 1913 attests, had already expanded the music environment to include non-instrumental sounds, and so-called *bruitism* (a sort of musical equivalent to plurilinguism) advocated the breakdown of tonal movement and relations.[11]

Serial dodecaphony, as practised by Schönberg (Cage's teacher) and Webern, discloses numerous correlations with the iconoclastic language of the Novissimi. Like dodecaphonic music, which completely rejects consonances, conventional harmonies, and contrapuntal constructions, the Novissimi aim at subveting the order and lyrical symmetries of traditional literary language. Just as in dodecaphony, particularly in its practice of a-thematic serialism, there exists no central sound around which the others are hierarchically coordinated, so in the Novissimi's poetry there is no linear discourse but an accumulation of materials which rigorously excludes all congruity and continuity.

Looking back at his first poetic collection, *Laborintus*, Sanguineti stated in an interview:

> Il mio modello era una poesia che fosse dicibile come lo *Sprechgesang* del *Pierrot lunaire* di Schönberg. Ciò significava tornare indietro nel tempo, ma quella era l'unica strada per adeguarmi a quelle che sentivo come le necessità della contemporareità.[12]

> My model was a type of poetry expressible like the *Sprechgensang* of Schönberg's *Pierrot Lunaire*. This meant to go back in time, but it represented the only way to be in tune with those necessities which I considered part of our contemporariness.

Clearly, the poetic project of the Novissimi was informed by the awareness that there was a wide gap between experimentations in music – and, as will be discussed, in the visual arts – and the literary production of those years. Indeed, one of the Novissimi's main goals was to bring poetic experimentation to the level of that accomplished in a field such as music. The tensions and ruptures created by music had to be put to the test within the language of poetry.

Analogies can also be drawn with concrete music. As in the case of Stockhausen, one of its most prominent representatives, concrete music presents a juxtaposition of musical fragments (the order of which is left exclusively to the initiative of the performer) that closely resemble the montage of unrelated linguistic sequences adopted by the Novissimi. Furthermore, the Novissimi did not have to search outside Italy to familiarize themselves with daring musical experiments. In fact, in 1955 the RAI (the Italian public radio and television network) founded in Milan the Studio di Fonologia where composers, such as Luciano Berio, Bruno Maderna, and Luigi Nono, pursued post-Webernian musical experimentation. The first two composers were Italy's most radical proponents of electronic music, embracing abstract *pointillisme* and leaving behind the expressionism tied to Schönbergian music. Sanguineti, with the collaboration of Berio, wrote the libretto for *Passaggio* (Passage; 1961–2), *Esposizione* (Exposition; 1963), and *Laborintus II* (1965). In the 1950s Giuliani established a close friendship with the composer Franco Evangelisti, a proponent of aleatory music and collective improvization.

As for the relation to the visual arts, in his conclusion to the 1965 preface, Giuliani rightly remarks that the poetic experimentation of the Novissimi has brought them 'organically closer to the language of music and painting' (*I Nov*, 57) ('ci ha avvicinati più organicamente al linguaggio della musica e della pittura' [*IN*, 12]). Sanguineti, in particular, draws specific attention to the visual arts. In his essay 'Poesia informale?' (Action Poetry?), included in the anthology's section 'Behind the Poetry,' he claims that the formal structure of *Laborintus* presents more affinities with music and the visual arts than with literary forms. More specifically, he makes references to Abstract Expressionism and Action Painting, stressing that he finds 'comfort' ('conforto') in them since they alleviate the sense of 'solitude' ('solitudine') (*I Nov*, 388; *IN*, 202) that he experiences while cultivating a poetic language profoundly different from the dominant literary models. Undoubtedly, Sanguineti must have been attracted by images based on the expressive function of matter, disorder, formlessness, and rhythmic tension displayed in works by painters such as Fautrier, Gorky, Pollock, Rothko, and De Kooning. The dramatic spattering and dripping of the paint, the free-flowing gestures, the chance effects, and the energy in motion evident in these works are all elements that find correspondence in the linguistic agitation, nervousness, and chaos of Sanguineti's first poetic collection. It is no coincidence that in the 1950s he established a close friendship with Enrico Baj, a painter fully focused on the material reality of his medium and a proponent of the so-called *pittura materica*.

In the years preceding the publications of *I Novissimi*, *Il Verri* promoted Abstract Expressionism, and abstract painting in general, particularly through the contributions of Renato Barilli, the journal's official art critic.[13] It paid attention not only to the painters mentioned above but also to Wols, Mathieu, Tobey, Burri, Fontana, and Dubuffet. Dubuffet in particular must have captured the attention of Giuliani and Sanguineti because he was pursuing an art form based not merely on the expressive possibilities of matter but on psychotic disclosures as well.[14]

The visual arts exposed the Novissimi to other influences. Unquestionably, all the Novissimi appreciated the resourcefulness of the collage technique (Balestrini adopted it extensively) and the disassembling of found materials pioneered by the Futurists and Dadaists, which some artists (Tapies, Burri) were re-exploring with renewed interest. Moreover, Giuliani had close contact with a group of Roman painters, such as Gastone Novelli and Achille Perilli, who were investigating the visual possibilities offered by alphabetical structures depicted as enigmatic signifiers cut off from any definitive signification – a feature found also in his poetry. On the other hand, Porta displayed some affinities with the Expressionistic tendencies of painters such as Beckmann and Bacon; the fragmentation of narrative, the disfiguration and the dismemberment of figures, the horror and violence of the modern world are some of the elements shared by Porta's poetry and works by these painters. Yet it should also be clear that, although the Novissimi have in common a subversive attitude towards the traditional poetic forms of communication and all five call for a deep renewal of poetry's functions and objectives, each one of them pursues a personal poetics and language. In fact, the statements of poetics written by all five poets and included in 'Behind the Poetry' testify to the necessity of giving voice to individual poetics.

For Sanguineti, dodecaphonic music and Action Painting were points of reference for developing a poetics that would be based on an understanding of the general crisis afflicting contemporary language. Rebutting observations made by the poet Andrea Zanzotto, who had claimed that his *Laborintus* was the result of a personal 'nervous breakdown,' Sanguineti states that the breakdown is real but it has its origins in an 'objective historical' predicament (*I Nov*, 388) ('oggettivo esaurimento storico' [*IN*, 202]). He explains:

Perché quando nel *Laborintus* si parla, con preciso rigore, di 'alienazione,' si sommano insieme l'ovvio significato clinico (che è l''esaurimento' appunto, ad arte esasperato e provocatamente sottolineato), e quello, diversamente tecnico, di 'Verfremdung,' comprendente a sua volta sia il valore sociologicamente diagnostico del concetto marxista ('Veräusserung'), sia quello estetico ('straniamento') di marca brechtiana ... Una poesia *autre* doveva documentare e rispecchiare, presendandosi, nella cronaca polemica, come un diverso dalla poesia assolutamente intesa, lo straniamento posto *in re, a parte subjecti*, e *a parte objecti*, nella dialettica storica. Quegli effetti sovrastrutturali che la crisi di un linguaggio dato dimostrava nelle altre arti, sotto la specie di una crisi *del* linguaggio, erano per me da ritrovarsi nei confronti di *un* linguaggio poetico (o meglio di una pluralità di linguaggi storicamente offerti), nella speranza, come mi avvenne di dichiarare una volta, di 'fare dell'avanguardia un'arte da museo': con un'espressione, devo concederlo, assai più suggestiva che perspicua. (*IN*, 202–3)

Because when there is talk in *Laborintus* of 'alienation,' in the strict sense, both the obvious clinical meaning (the 'breakdown,' deliberately aggravated and provocatively emphasized) and the otherwise also technical meaning of 'Verfremdung,' comprising in turn both the sociologically diagnostic sense of the Marxian concept ('Veräusserung'), and the derivatively aesthetical one ('estrangement'), of Brechtian provenance ... In presenting itself polemically as dissenting from poetry understood in absolute terms, this other poetry documents and reflects the estrangement posited *in re, a parte subjecti*, and *a parte objecti*, in the historical dialectic. These superstructural effects which the crisis of *one particular* given language has demonstrated in the other arts, as a sort of crisis of language, were for me to be found in comparing *one particular* poetical language (or better, a plurality of historically available languages), in the hope, as I stated of another occasion, of 'turning the avant-garde into a museum art': an expression, I must admit, somewhat more evocative than clear. (*I Nov*, 389–90)

Sanguineti's poetics registers the exhaustion of conventional literary language and the impossibility of communicating through it the alienating and pathological condition of the social realities of the times. This poetics aspires to stretch to extreme limits the linguistic fragmentation and disorder inaugurated by the historical avant-garde, with a double intention. On the one hand, pathological language conveys an objective historical reality and, on the other, through the structural organization of the texts, motivated by the *Verfremdungseffekt*, it puts in motion in the reader a critical perspective on language and on the world. In doing so, it offers the only possible dialectical antithesis to the prevailing linguistic and social situation.

Sanguineti clarifies his position as follows:

Si trattava per me di superare il formalismo e l'irrazionalismo dell'avanguardia (e infine la stessa avanguardia, nelle sue implicazioni ideologiche), non per mezzo di una rimozione, ma a partire dal formalismo e
dall'irrazionalismo stesso, esasperandone le contraddizioni sino a un
limite praticamente insuperabile, rovesciandone il senso, agendo sopra
gli stessi postulati di tipo anarchico, ma portandoli a un grado di storica
coscienza eversiva ... Fare dell'avanguardia un'arte da museo voleva dire
invece (allo stato, s'intende, di poetica intenzionale, ché qui di questo si
parla, come si deve), riconoscere l'errore della regressione, significava
gettare se stessi, subito, e a testa prima, nel labirinto del formalismo e
dell'irrazionalismo, nella Palus Putredinis, precisamente, dell'anarchismo
e dell'alienazione, con la speranza, che mi ostino a non ritenere illusoria,
di uscirne poi veramente, attraversato il tutto, con le mani sporche, ma
con il fango, anche, lasciato davvero alle spalle.
   Per questo la poetica stretta dell'informale era naturalmente destinata
ad essere tradita, al di là del *Laborintus*, ma sulle mani sporche per-
mangono, e certo permarranno, le buone macchie di melma. (*IN*, 203, 204)

For me this was a matter of superseding the avant-garde formalism and
irrationalism (and finally the avant-garde itself, in its ideological implications), not by a repression, but by formalism and irrationalism itself,
heightening their contradictions to a practically unprecedented degree,
turning their meanings around, working on their very own anarchist postulates, but carrying them to a degree of subversive historical consciousness ... To turn the avant-garde into museum art meant (on a level, of
course, of intentional poetics, since this is what we are necessarily talking
about), recognizing the error of regression; it meant suddenly throwing
oneself head first into the labyrinth of formalism and irrationalism, the
Palus Putredinis of anarchism and alienation, with the hope I refuse to
consider illusory of eventually getting out of it once and for all, if with
sullied hands, yet ultimately with even the mire truly left behind. To this
end the strict poetics of *action poetry* was destined to be abandoned,
beyond *Laborintus*, while the fine mud stains remain – and no doubt will
remain – on our sullied hands. (*I Nov*, 390, 391)

These statements of poetics exhibit a view of poetry, and of literature
in general, as an activity closely tied to ideological and political objectives. Poetry is assigned a role of subversion and becomes a revolution-

ary force aimed at opening the way to new worlds. Sanguineti seems to merge Marxist dialectics (poetry functions as a pole of opposition), utopian thought (non-alienation as a vision for the future), and Dantean itineraries (the descent into the historical hell of alienation as a necessary stage towards liberation). Sanguineti's Marxist stand is further clarified in a second essay, included in the same section of the anthology, entitled 'Poesia e mitologia' (Poetry and Mythology).

In his view, literary production and fruition are inextricably bound to the economic base, social structures, and the 'general system of ideological superstructures' (*I Nov*, 398) ('sistema generale di sovrastrutture ideologiche' [*IN*, 210]). In other words, Sanguineti does not see any validity in the view of literature as an autonomous activity and insists that the ideological perspective is inseparable from any superstructure – literature included. In this essay, Sanguineti addresses issues that, as will be discussed in chapter 2, are central to the debates initiated by Gruppo 63. He summarizes his position as follows:

> Una volta infatti che si sia avvertito, in una concezione maturamente dialettica, il carattere ideologicamente attivo (pratico) che spetta ad ogni prodotto sovrastrutturale, e non meno a qualsivoglia altro ad ogni prodotto di mistificazione mitica, occorre affermare che il giudizio estetico si definisce esclusivamente *in relazione alla* prassi, ossia, nel senso in cui la prassi è misura esclusiva dell'ideologia, direttamente *nella* prassi. (*IN*, 212)

> Once one has realized, in a maturely dialectical conception, the ideologically active (practical) character implicit in every superstructural product, and equally in any other product of mythical mystification, one must affirm that the aesthetic judgment is defined exclusively *in relation to* praxis, or rather in the sense in which praxis is the sole measure of ideology, directly *in* praxis. (*I Nov*, 401)

A similar political orientation is revealed in Balestrini's essay 'Linguaggio e opposizione' (Language and Opposition). It, too, underscores the vision of poetry as a subversive activity. For Balestrini, poetry is essentially an exploration of language and an attempt to liberate the linguistic code from the state of 'inertia' ('inerzia') produced by the 'continual sedimentation' ('continua sedimentazione') to which it is subjected (*I Nov*, 383; *IN*, 197). He adopts a materialist approach (shared by all the Novissimi), shifting the creative process from pre-given signifieds (that is, a signification already present in one's consciousness) to signifiers as producers of meaning. Indeed, Balestrini maintains that 'ultimately what gets transmitted by language will no longer be thought and emotion, which have been the germ of the poetical operation, but language itself generating new, unrepeatable meaning' ('da ultimo non saranno più il pensiero e l'emozione, che sono stati il germe dell'operazione poetica, a venire trasmessi per mezzo del linguaggio, ma sarà il linguaggio stesso a generare un significato nuovo e irrepetibile' [*I Nov*, 382–3; *IN*, 196–197]).

As a metalinguistic process, poetry can exhibit its own specific tools for producing meaning, independently of other human activities related to communication. These tools, Balestrini argues, are to be employed in opposition to the linguistic automatism in which we are immersed in our everyday verbal exchanges. The social context of the times helps to explain Balestrini's concerns. From the mid 1950s to the early 1960s, Italy, until then a predominantly agricultural society, rapidly evolved into an urban, highly industrialized nation. The so-called economic miracle of these years led to the advent of a consumer society dominated by powerful media forces, mass culture, and a linguistic conformity that tended to flatten language and reduce it to banalities and stereotypes. As an act of revolt against these paralysing trends, according to Balestrini, poetry must violate all norms in order to restore in the reader a healthy linguistic and cognitive tension. This is how Balestrini describes the main function of poetry as opposition:

> Un atteggiamento fondamentale del fare poesia diviene dunque lo 'stuzzicare' le parole, il tendere loro un agguato mentre si allacciano in periodi, l'imporre violenza alle strutture del linguaggio, lo spingere a limiti di rottura tutte le sue proprietà. Si tratta di un atteggiamento volto a sollecitare questa proprietà, le cariche intrinseche e estrinseche del linguaggio, e a provocare quei nodi e quegli incontri inediti e sconcertanti che possono fare della poesia una vera frusta per il cervello del lettore, che quotidianamente annaspa immerso fino alla fronte nel luogo comune e nella ripetizione. (*IN*, 197)

The fundamental attitude thus becomes one of getting poetry to 'prod' words, to lay an ambush for them at the very moment they are bound up in sentences, to do violence to the structures of language, pushing all its properties to the breaking point. Such an attitude is meant to stimulate these properties, the intrinsic and extrinsic charges of language, and to provoke the unprecedented, baffling cruxes and encounters that can

make poetry a true whip to the reader's brain, a brain that gropes through
daily life immersed in commonplaces and repetition. (*I Nov*, 383)

For Pagliarani (his essay is entitled 'La sintassi e i generi' [Syntax and
Genres]), the opposition to traditional linguistic modes and content
must start from the search for a new poetic genre. In his view, the creation of a new genre must make its initial moves by expanding the lexicon (for example, commercial jargon, everyday spoken language)
which, in turn, affects the syntactic structure of poetry. As a consequence, innovative syntactic organization and patterns 'impress speech
with different tension, duration, rhythm' ('imprimono al discorso ten-
sione durata ritmo diversi [*I Nov*, 385; *IN*, 199]).

Pagliarani maintains that lexical and syntactic innovations are necessary tools in contesting the lyric genre, with its outmoded conventions,
and in promoting a theatrical poetic language capable of expressing
plurilinguistic social realities. Pagliarani defines his genre as 'verse
drama' ('dramma in versi') ([*I Nov*, 386; *IN*, 200]), which seems to
recall, on the one hand, T.S. Eliot's verse plays and, on the other, Majakovskij's call for a poetry that incorporated the language of newspapers and everyday life.[15]

Unquestionably, Pagliarani's poetics, with its stress on plurilinguism and theatrical language, expresses the Novissimi's commitment
to the reduction of the 'I' and linguistic experimentation. Nonetheless,
as will be underlined in the chapter devoted to his poetry, his views
cannot be completely disengaged from the canons of Realism and his
own connections to Pasolini and the *Officina* group.

The essay by Porta, 'Poesia e poetica' (Poetry and Poetics), denounces
both the literary canons of neorealism and any kind of poetry that places
the individual 'I' of the poet at the centre of attention. For Porta, the neorealistic movement represents total 'bankruptcy' ('bilancio fallimen-
tare'). Focused exclusively on socio-political issues, it has contributed,
in Porta's view, to a 'general distrust of literature' ('una sfiducia generale nella letteratura' [*I Nov*, 378; *IN*, 193]). At the same time, he
expresses a deep antagonism towards the narcissistic assumptions of
the '*I-poet*' ('*poeta-io*'). (Ironically, Porta comments that this poet's main
principle is that his life story, 'insofar as it happens to him,' must be
'extremely interesting.') A new poetry must be guided, Porta states, by
the '*poetics of objects*' ('*poetica degli oggetti*') and '*external events*' ('*evento
esterno*'). Sharing the phenomenological belief in the need to return to
things (Husserl's principle of *Lebenswelt* is an example), he advocates a

poetic gaze focused on the outside world as a medium of cognition. Poetry's task is to use its specific tools to penetrate into reality and to capture some of its true expressions. Porta writes:

Si è avvertita, insomma, l'importanza dell'*evento esterno*, da cui sentiamo colpita la comunità e non più, soltanto, la persona del poeta isolato: è lì ci si misura, noi, uomini ... In questo senso si è interpretata la *poetica degli oggetti*, la poesia *in re*, non *ante rem*. Gli oggetti e gli eventi rilevati e composti in un *unicum* ritmico, riescono a calarci nella realtà ... Direttamente alla *poetica* degli oggetti si riallaccia il problema del *vero* e della *verità*, in simbiosi con la ricerca delle immagini e il bisogno di penetrazione. Qualcosa si vuol trovare, alla fine. Le cose che manovriamo o che ci manovrano, i fatti che determiniamo o che ci determinano, sono certamente in relazione con la verità: proprio per avvicinarla ci serviamo del *vero*, cercandolo negli oggetti e negli eventi. (*IN*, 194)

One is, in short, made aware of the importance of the *external event*, which we feel affects the community and no longer only the figure of the isolated poet: it is there we are measured as human beings ... This is how the *poetics of objects*, poetry *in re*, not *ante rem*, has been interpreted. The objects and events selected and composed into one rhythmic *unicum* – these do manage to plunge us into reality ... The *poetics* of objects must be directly linked with the problem of *the true* or of *truth*, in symbiosis with the quest for images and the need for penetration. Ultimately one wants to find something. The things we plot and maneuvre, or that plot and maneuvre us, certainly bear relation to the truth: and precisely to approach the truth we make use of *the true*, which we perceive in objects and events. (*I Nov*, 379–80)

The suggestion here is not that poetry pursue metaphysical or transcendental truths. Rather, Porta's poetic pogram is rooted in a secular view of the world and is submitted to a constant process of revision by throwing into question all certainties. Being-in-the-world entails the impossibility of achieving absolute and totalizing truths. Existence is not perceived as bound within definitive and reassuring forms of knowledge; instead, it is inevitably forced to strive for ulterior experiences and projects. In Porta's view, the poetics of the object succumbs neither to a cognitive stasis nor to a dangerous lack of distinction between the subject and external reality. He concludes that such poetics does not represent 'some naive, needlessly feared dive into the sea of objectivity, but an articulation of knowledge, in our own *present moment*' ('non il tuffo ingenuo, inutilmente temuto, nel mare dell'oggettivita, ma l'articolarsi del conoscere, nel nostro *ora*' [*I Nov*, 381; *IN*, 195]).

This last statement is an explicit rebuttal to an essay by Italo Calvino, 'Il mare dell'oggetività' (The Sea of Objectivity), which appeared around the same time.[16] For Calvino, the poetics of the object, as practised in those years by the *école du regard*, drowns the 'I' in a sea of objects and thus annihilates human consciousness. The loss of the 'I' has as its immediate result not only the eradication of human subjectivity but the 'end of history' ('la fine ... della storia'), inasmuch as there is no longer a subject to guide the course of events' (*Una pietra sopra: discorsi di letteratura e società* [Put It to Rest: Discourses on Literature and Society, 44]).

Porta's intent to capture the object, as it manifests itself physically to the gaze, seems to share with Robbe-Grillet and the *école du regard* the tendency towards a neutral, impersonal form of writing, a 'writing degree zero,' as defined by Roland Barthes.[17] However, Porta's poetics is decisively different from that of the French movement, even though he is well acquainted with it, as were all the members of the *Il Verri* group. Unlike the *école du regard*, Porta does not abandon the goal of transcending the object and scrutinizing it in search of hidden meanings. His poetics, rather, is charged with a sense of restlessness and a cognitive tension that unfolds objectives substantially distinct from those of the French school.[18]

Here is how Porta clarifies the relation between a poetics of objects and poetic language or method:

> Gli eventi, gli oggetti, gli emblemi del vero, sono poi materia da lavorare in modo quasi artigianale: quasi, perché entrando direttamente nei problemi d'espressione, nelle ricerche di linguaggio, si vuole sottolineare il fatto che, assumendo senza riserve la metrica accentuativa, non si dà a questi problemi soltanto il valore dell'ordine e della 'misura.' La metrica accentuativa è soprattutto un metodo di penetrazione. (*IN*, 194–5)

> The events, objects, emblems of the true are, then, material to be worked in an almost artisanal fashion: almost, because in entering directly into the problems of expression, into linguistic investigations, one should emphasize the fact that, by unconditionally assuming accentual metrics, one does not confer on these problems the value merely of order or 'measure.' Accentual metrics are primarily a method of penetration. (*I Nov*, 380)

For Porta, as for the Novissimi in general, poetry must become a language of interrogation, a questioning of language and, at the same time, of the world. Porta's definition of the poet as an artisan may be applied to the Novissimi in general. They all approach language as artisans, working in linguistic laboratories and equipped with a method of production. They take poetry back to its etymological roots, the Greek *poiesis*, from *poiein*, meaning to make, to produce. For the Novissimi, through its exploration of language and the critique of hegemonic modes of communication, poetry points toward an otherness that can be a harbinger of new perceptions of the world and of our relations with it. Their impact on the Italian poetic landscape was radical and deeply significant, for it was through their work that the Italian neoavant-garde was born.

2 The *Neoavanguardia* and the Theoretical Debate

The publication of *I Novissimi*, combined with the aesthetic and cultural innovations promoted by *Il Verri*, prompted a series of reactions within Italian intellectual circles. Of particular note were the views of one of the most influential journals of the time, *Il Menabò*, edited by Elio Vittorini and Italo Calvino.

During these years, *Il Verri* periodically published special issues on topics such as the *nouveau roman*, 'informal' art (from Action Painting to *tachisme* and *art brut*), phenomenology, and new poetic experimentation in Europe and North America,[1] and the group of regular contributors gradually expanded to include not only the five Novissimi but also young intellectuals like Renato Barilli, Angelo Guglielmi, Alberto Arbasino, Fausto Curi, and Umberto Eco. It was Eco who in 1962, one year after the publication of *I Novissimi*, provided a general aesthetic framework in which to locate the poetic experience of the five defiant poets. In fact, one of the central objectives of Eco's first major publication on contemporary art, *Opera aperta* (Open Work), was not only to elucidate the significant shifts that art was experiencing in the postwar period but to provide support to the poetic strategies that were being pursued by the young poets with whom, through *Il Verri*, he had established contact.[2]

At the University of Turin, studying under Luigi Pareyson, Eco was exposed to aesthetic principles that radically questioned the dominant positions embodying the idealist legacy of Benedetto Croce. Against the Crocean view of art as lyrical intuition, an interior process detached from any material reality and aimed at capturing transhistorical truths, Pareyson proposed the concept of 'formativity' ('formatività').[3] Art, like all other human activities, is understood as a production of forms, an action conducted under specific historical conditions. Style is seen as the result of a dialectics between the intrinsic potentiality of matter and human creativity – the latter identified totally with forms. Indeed, style is perceived as inseparable from all spiritual contents. The artist's personality brings to completion the potential of matter and exposes it to an infinite number of other personalities. It thus follows that the work of art is open to an infinite number of possible interpretations. From the aesthetic investigation conducted by Pareyson, Eco derives pivotal concepts that revolve around the primacy of formal structures and the openness of the art work.

Furthermore, *Opera aperta* is grounded in the new aesthetic directions of experimental music. In the late 1950s, in fact, while working in Milan for RAI, Eco came into contact with Luciano Berio and, through him, with musicians such as Pierre Boulez and Henri Pousseur. The introductory chapter of *Opera aperta* centres completely around the poetics of experimental, post-Weberian music which, according to Eco, features the rejection of 'definiteness' and adopts a deliberate openness that exposes the performer to the freedom of infinite acts of reception and execution.[4]

Eco applies the concept of openness to literary texts (from Verlaine to Mallarmé, to Valéry, Kafka, and Joyce) and draws inspiring correlations between aesthetics and epistemology and politics. With reference to Kafka, Eco writes:

In effetti l'opera rimane inesauribile ed aperta in quanto 'ambigua,' poiché ad un mondo ordinato secondo leggi universalmente riconosciute si è sostituito un mondo fondato sull'ambiguità, sia nel senso negativo di una mancanza di centri di orientamento, sia nel senso positivo di una continua rivedibilità dei valori e delle certezze. (*OA*, 33–4)

The work remains inexhaustible insofar as it is 'open,' because in it an ordered world based on universally acknowledged laws is being replaced by a world based on ambiguity, both in the negative sense that directional centres are missing and in a positive sense, because values and dogmas are constantly being placed in question. (*OW*, 9)

Discussing Brecht, in particular his play *Galileo*, Eco concludes that in this case the poetics of openness becomes 'an instrument of revolutionary pedagogics' (*OW*, 11) ('strumento di pedagogia rivoluzionaria' [*OA*, 37]). Undoubtedly, Eco's notion of openness (the emphasis on the collaborative relationship between composer, performer, and listener, or between author and reader) and the cultural orientation it displays are very much aligned with the poetics of the Novissimi, particularly as defined by Giuliani in his introduction to the anthology. As has been illustrated, the concept of openness is present also in Giuliani, as is that of the autonomy of the work of art, together with the rejection of any form of representational realism. For Eco, in fact, although the work of art can be seen as 'epistemological metaphor' ('*metafora epistemologica*' [*OA*, 42]) – in the sense that the structure of its forms 'reflects the way in which science and contemporary culture view reality' (*OW*, 13) ('riflette ... il modo in cui la scienza o comunque la cultura dell'epoca vedono la realtà [*OA*, 42]) – it '*produces* complements of the world, autonomous forms that are added to the existing ones' (*produce* dei complementi del mondo, delle forme autonome che s'aggiungono a quelle esistenti' [*OA*, 42]). All the attributes assigned to the open work (ambiguity, indeterminacy, discontinuity, polyvalence), and particularly disorder (which Eco, with great ability, connects to the principle of entropy derived from thermodynamics and information theory),[5] make up the essential fabric of the poetry championed by the Novissimi. Their pursuit of a poetic language closer to the developments occurring in other arts resembles Eco's interdisciplinary approach. Indeed, his aesthetic theory combines serial/aleatory music, 'informal' art, Calder's mobiles, quantum physics, phenomenology, and information theory, establishing correspondences that are defined as '*structural homologies*' (*OW*, 18) ('*analogie di struttura*' [*OA*, 48]).

In the section 'L'opera aperta nelle arti visive' (The Open Work in the Visual Art), Eco makes direct reference to the relation between the 'poesia novissima' (*OA*, 146) and 'informal' art (this chapter, in fact, first appeared in *Il Verri*'s special issue devoted to that movement). Here Eco, like the Novissimi, claims that contemporary art strives 'to break with the conventions of accepted language and the usual ways of linking thoughts together' (*OW*, 95) ('rompere le convenzioni del linguaggio accettato e i consueti moduli di concatenamento delle idee acquisite' [*OA*, 161]). As well, Eco's assertion that 'informal' art does not intend to destroy form but to conceive '*form as a field of possibilities*' (*OW*, 103) '*la forma come campo di possibilità*' [*OA*, 174]), is directly applicable to the poetic project of the Novissimi.

The closing chapter of *Opera aperta* in the Italian edition, 'Del modo di formare come impegno sulla realtà' (Form as Social Commitment), was first published in *Il Menabò* (5, 1962) in response to a discussion initiated by Vittorini, in the preceding issue of the same review, on the relationship between literature, the arts, and industrial society.[6] The question of an ordered and rational literary language, versus the seemingly irrational disorder of avant-garde movements and the changes brought about by industrialization, was central for Vittorini in those years. Even though he kept a critical distance from the Novissimi and the literature promoted by *Il Verri*, Vittorini fully understood that forms espoused by movements such as *neorealismo* no longer fitted the new realities. He, too, saw the urgent need for renewal and thus was open to new perspectives like the one championed by the Novissimi. In fact, under his editorship, *Il Menabò* published poetic texts written by Sanguineti, Porta, and Pagliarani. Eco's essay appeared too, together with Calvino's 'La sfida al labirinto' (Defying the Labyrinth), and it unequivocally demonstrated the wide aesthetic gap separating *Il Verri*'s positions from those of *Il Menabò*.

Eco begins his essay by analysing a concept that defines the condition of modernity, namely, the Hegelian principle of alienation, together with the distinction between objectification and alienation as it emerges in Marx in his critique of Hegel's thought. Eco distinguishes alienation as a result of social conditions from alienation as objectification, that is, as a structure of existence present every time a human being externalizes him/herself or, in his words, 'objectifies himself in the works he has created, and in the nature he has modified'(*OW*, 126) ('si oggetiva nel mondo delle opere che ha creato, della natura che ha modificato' [*OA*, 233]). Eco points to the implication in Hegel's dialectics that tension between subject and object is present in all human activity. He comments:

> Si crea una sorta di tensione ineliminabile i cui poli sono, da un lato, il dominio *dell'*oggetto e *sull'*oggetto, dall'altro la perdita totale *nell'*oggetto, la resa ad esso, in un equilibrio che può solo essere dialettico, e cioè fatto di una lotta continua, di una negazione di ciò che si afferma e una affermazione di ciò che si nega. Si profilano così le analisi del rapporto di alienazione visto come costitutivo di ogni mia relazione con gli Altri e con le cose, nell'amore, nella convivenza sociale, nella struttura industriale. (*OA*, 233)

The two poles of such a tension are, on the one hand, his domination of the object, and, on the other, his total dissolution in the object, his total surrender to it. This is a dialectic balance that is based on a constant struggle between the negation of what is asserted and the assertion of what is denied. Thus, alienation would seem to be an integral part of every relationship one establishes with others and with things, whether this be in love, in society, or within an industrial structure. (*OW*, 126)

In his reading of Hegel's *Phenomenology of Spirit*, Eco argues that if rejection of the object resulted in the contemplation of a feeling of emptiness (the 'beautiful soul,' as the German philosopher defines it), integration with the object led to the annihilation of the self – the abdication of the subject. The impossibility of achieving a total unity of subject and object ends up in an irresolvable contradiction inasmuch as the antinomy cannot be surmounted. This failure to achieve unity (oneness) means that alienation cannot be transcended. At best, Eco contends, we can live with alienation, all the while attempting to make it 'transparent,' demystify it, and 'denounce its paralysing aspects' ('vederli in trasparenza, di denuciarne le possibilità paralizzanti' [*OA*, 250]).

Accordingly, Eco proposes not to accept passively the state of alienation but to develop inventive strategies to allow one to function within it. He writes:

L'alienazione costituisce per l'uomo moderno una condizione come la mancanza di gravità per il pilota spaziale: una condizione in cui imparare a muoversi e a individuare le nuove possibilità di autonomia, le direzioni di libertà possibile. (*OA*, 250)

To modern man, alienation is as much a given as weightlessness is to an astronaut: it is a situation in which we have to learn how to move, how to acquire new autonomy, and how to devise new ways of being free. (*OW*, 136)]

Eco sets Marx aside and returns to Hegel by identifying alienation with objectification. In his view, the knowledge of the object and the ensuing construction of self-consciousness does not lead, as Marx had envisioned, to the overcoming of alienation to the object or to its negation.

Having established these principles, Eco has set the ground for an analysis of alienation within the realm of art forms. In all systems of forms, Eco maintains, can be detected an analogous condition of alienation. In formal systems as well, it is possible to uncover a tension between 'invention and manner,' between 'freedom and restrictions dictated by conventions' (*OW*, 137) ('invenzione e maniera ... libertà e necessità delle regole formative' [*OA*, 251]). A case in point is the system of rhyme. Eco writes:

> Dal momento che è posta, la convenzione ci aliena ad essa ... Più la pratica si afferma, più mi propone esempi di alta libertà creativa, più mi imprigiona; la consuetudine della rima genera il rimario, che dapprima è repertorio del rimabile ma via via diviene repertorio del rimato. (*OA*, 252)

> As soon as we accept a convention we find ourselves alienated in it ... The more a certain practice asserts itself, and the more it pushes us to contemplate creative alternatives, the more it imprisons us. The use of rhyme will result in a dictionary of rhymes, which will start as a compendium of possible rhymes and end up as a catalogue of common rhymes. (*OW*, 137–8)

Conventions and manner generate obsolescence, exhausted and stale forms, stereotypes drained of any communicative force, and become alienated constructs within the linguistic system. Obviously, dried-out forms are expressions of alienation not only for the artist but for the public as well, inasmuch as they can command only standardized acts of reception. The investigation of both social and artistic alienation leads Eco to arrive at a lucid defence of avant-garde practices. In his view, the avant-garde artist is engaged in dislodging and rupturing conventional language inasmuch as it refuses to express through that language a false sense of order that no longer corresponds to the state of alienation; as Eco says, the 'order of words no longer corresponds to the order of things' (*OW*, 141) ('all'ordine delle parole non corrisponde più un ordine delle cose' [*OA*, 257]).

Eco illustrates his position by making reference to the field of music:

> Il musicista si rifiuta di accettare il sistema tonale perché in esso si sente alienato soltanto ad una struttura convenzionale; si sente alienato a tutta una morale, una etica sociale, una visione teorica del mondo che in quel sistema si è espresso ... In questo senso l'artista che protesta sulle forme ha compiuto una duplice operazione: ha rifiutato un sistema di forme, e tuttavia non lo ha annullato nel suo rifiuto, ma ha agito al di dentro di esso (ne ha seguito alcune tendenze alla disgregazione che già si andavano profilando come inevitabili), e quindi per sottrarsi a questo sistema e modificarlo ha tuttavia accettato di alienarsi parzialmente in esso, di accettarne le tendenze interne; d'altro canto, adottando una nuova gram-

matica fatta non tanto di moduli d'ordine quanto di un progetto permanente di disordine, ha accettato proprio il mondo in cui vive nei termini di
crisi in cui esso si trova. Quindi di nuovo egli si è *compromesso*, col mondo
in cui vive, parlando un linguaggio che egli artista crede di aver inventato
ma che invece gli è stato suggerito dalla situazione in cui si trova; e tutta-
via questa era la sola scelta che gli rimaneva, poiché una delle tendenze
negative della situazione in cui si trova è proprio quella di ignorare che la
crisi esiste e tentare continuamente di ridefinirla secondo quei moduli
d'ordine dalla consunzione dei quali la crisi è nata. (*OA*, 255, 257–8)

The avant-garde musician rejects the tonal system not only because it
alienates him to a conventional system of musical laws, but also because it
alienates him to a social ethics and to a given vision of the world ... The
artist who protests through form acts on two levels. On one, he rejects a
formal system but does not obliterate it; he transforms it from within by
alienating himself in it and by exploiting its self-destructive tendencies.
On the other, he shows his acceptance of the world as is, in full crisis, by
formulating a new grammar that rests not on a system of organization but
on an assumption of disorder. And this is one way in which he implicates
himself in the world in which he lives, for the new language he thinks he
has invented has instead been suggested to him by his very existential situation. He has no choice, since his only alternative would be to ignore the
existence of crisis, to deny it by continuing to rely on the very systems of
order that have caused it. (*OW*, 140–1)

In other words, the avant-garde solution develops as a result of a
dialectics that still reflects the historical condition that engendered it.
The avant-garde artist is compelled to opt for a total immersion in the
alienated language because it is the only way of objectifying in a form
the state of alienation and, thus, to some extent, arriving at some clarification (the awareness of alienation does not produce its elimination).[7]
Eco argues that although avant-garde artists, with their attention to
formal structures, seem to be concerned only with abstractions and not
with the real human condition, in fact they are the only ones 'capable
of establishing a meaningful relationship with the world in which they
live' (*OW*, 142) ('l'avanguardia artistica è l'unica a intrattenere un rapporto di significazione col mondo in cui vive' [*OA*, 258]). Their forms
represent their discourse on the world, their cultural project, and their
social commitment.

   In his closing remarks, Eco addresses some of the poetic issues raised by the Novissimi and by Sanguineti in particular (reference is made to his essay 'Poesia informale?' (Action Poetry?). For Eco the language of crisis assumed by Sanguineti, and by the Novissimi at large, exposes itself to the risk of becoming manneristic as soon as another poet embraces it without fully understanding its project. And there is another risk, too, namely, of being co-opted by the same system which the language of crisis tries to oppose and in which lie the roots of the very historical conditions that the poet is protesting against. However, Eco concludes, even in the face of these risks, there is no artistic possibility outside the work of the avant-garde. Defending the avant-garde against recurrent accusations of irrationality, Eco states:

> L'operazione dell'arte che tenta di conferire una forma a ciò che può apparire disordine, informe, dissociazione, mancanza di ogni rapporto, è ancora l'esercizio di una ragione che tenta di ridurre a chiarezza discorsiva le cose; e quando il suo discorso pare oscuro è perché le cose stesse, e il nostro rapporto con esse, è ancora molto oscuro. Così che sarebbe azzardato pretendere di definirle dal podio incontaminato dell'oratoria: questo diventerebbe un modo di eludere la realtà, per lasciarla stare così come è. Non sarebbe questa l'ultima e più compiuta figura dell'alienazione? (*OA*, 283–4)

> The artistic process that tries to give form to disorder, amorphousness, and dissociation is nothing but the effort of a reason that wants to lend a discursive clarity to things. When its discourse is unclear, it is because things themselves, and our relationship to them, are still very unclear – indeed, so unclear that it would be ridiculous to pretend to define them from the uncontaminated podium of rhetoric. It would be only another way of escaping reality and leaving it exactly as it is. And wouldn't this be the ultimate and most successful figure of alienation? (*OW*, 157)

At the outset, Calvino's essay seems to take the same direction. He, too, identifies the state of alienation as a dominant trait of industrial society and underlines the effects of automation and reification. Yet his essay deals with alienation essentially in relation to the social developments of capitalism and does not place much weight on aesthetic forms. Calvino writes:

> Dalla rivoluzione industriale, filosofia letteratura arte hanno avuto un trauma dal quale non si sono ancora riavute. Dopo secoli passati a stabi-

lire le relazioni dell'uomo con se stesso, le cose, i luoghi, il tempo, ecco
che tutte le ralazioni cambiano: non più cose ma merci, prodotti in serie,
le macchine prendono il posto degli animali, la città è un dormitorio
annesso all'officina, il tempo è orario, l'uomo un ingranaggio ... Ora siamo entrati nella fase dell'industrializzazione totale e dell'automazione ...
le cose comandano le coscienze.[8]

Since the industrial revolution, philosophy, literature, and art have experienced a trauma from which they have not yet recovered. After centuries
spent by man in establishing a relation with himself, things, places, time,
all relations are now changing: there are no longer things but mass-pro-
duced commodities, machines take the place of animals, the city has
become a dormitory attached to the factory, time is a schedule, man the
peg of a mechanism ... We have now entered a total phase of industrialization and automation ... things give orders to the conscience.

For Calvino, culture represents the resourceful ways in which human
beings have faced constantly shifting realities. In his view (one that
would undoubtedly be shared by Eco and the Novissimi), both science
and literature partake in the same human endeavour: to guide, in an
imaginative manner, our actions and activities. 'The scientific and
poetic attitudes,' Calvino declares, 'coincide: both are attitudes of
inquiry and project-making, discovery and invention' ('l'atteggiamento
scientifico e quello poetico coincidono: entrambi sono atteggiamenti
insieme di ricerca e di progettazione, di scoperta e di invenzione' [SL,
84]).
    Like Vittorini, Calvino acknowledges that Naturalism or social real-
ism have become inadequate tools to represent the complexities of the
industrial age. The crisis of Naturalism is evident according to Calvino,
in Cézanne's paintings, Cubism, and Futurism, as well in movements
such as Constructivism and Bauhaus in the area of architecture. For
Calvino, these movements embody the 'rationalist trend' ('linea razi-
onalista' [SL, 88]) of the avant-garde which aspires to discover redeeming aesthetic and moral qualities within the mechanized world. In
Calvino's view, this tendency is characterized by a 'historicist opti-
mism' ('ottimismo storicista' [88]) that is opposed by a far less optimis-
tic avant-garde trend that he defines as 'visceral' ('viscerale' [89]). In
this latter classification, Calvino places Expressionism, Céline, Artaud,
in part Joyce, certain aspects of Surrealism, and other writers such as
Henry Miller. Although Calvino acknowledges that this current exem-

plifies formal solutions that possess a certain degree of validity within the time frame in which they have appeared, he rejects them on the ground that they espouse an 'existential and religious thrust' ('spinta ... esistenzial-religiosa' [89]) that does not coincide with his idea of a writer guided by the project of Enlightenment. Calvino shifts his discourse to the area of personal alternatives and falls short of investigating the historical, linguistic, and literary conditions that made those formal options necessary. He settles for a conventional style and shows high esteem for Hemingway's dry and linear language, asserting:

> Il problema espressivo e critico per me resta uno: la mia prima scelta formal-morale è stata per soluzioni di stilizzazione riduttiva, e per quanto tutta la mia esperienza più recente mi porti a orientarmi invece sulla necessità di un discorso il più possibile inglobante e articolato, che incarni la molteplicità conoscitiva e strumentale del mondo in cui viviamo, continuo a credere che non ci siano soluzioni valide esteticamente e moralmente e storicamente se non si attuano nella *fondazione di uno stile*. (*SL*, 89)

> For me both the expressive and critical problem remains one: my first formal and moral priority has been dictated by solutions of reduced stylization, and even though, on the contrary, my most recent experience orients me towards the necessity of an inclusive and articulated discourse that embodies the cognitive and instrumental multiplicity of the world in which we live, I continue believing there are no aesthetically, morally, and historically valid solutions if they are not carried out in the *foundation of a style*.

Calvino does not share Eco's conviction about the revitalizing possibilities offered by the forms of the open work.[9] For him, the developments of the 'visceral' current of the avant-garde (from Beckett to 'informal' painting, Burri, beat generation, and experimental music) have totally abandoned the dialectical tension between subject and object and, as he had already claimed in his essay 'Il mare dell'oggettività' (*Il Menabò*, 2, 1960), they represent the death of the self, absorbed by the world of objects. This predicament is embodied, according to Calvino, in the figure of the labyrinth that under various guises dominates the literature of these years – the spatial labyrinth and absence of human beings in Robbe-Grillet, the labyrinth of cognition in Butor, the cosmic one in Borges, or that of the linguistic entanglements in Gadda (for the latter, Calvino speaks of a 'neo-Rabelaisian, babelic, gothic baroque' trend ('filone neorabelaisiano-babelico-goticobarocco' [95]), which can be discerned as well in writers such as Queneau, Nabokov, and Günter Grass). Even though Calvino does not assign to literature the responsibility of finding a way out of the historical labyrinth, he concludes that these writers simply surrender to it, without showing any resistance. He writes:

> È la *sfida al labirinto* che vogliamo salvare, è una letteratura della *sfida al labirinto* che vogliamo enucleare e distinguere dalla letteratura della *resa al labirinto*. (*SL*, 96)

> It is the *defiance of the labyrinth* we want to safeguard, it is a literature that *defies the labyrinth* we want to lay open and distinguish it from the literature that *surrenders to the labyrinth*.

The distance that separates Calvino from the positions of the Novissimi and *Il Verri*'s contributors is readily apparent. Calvino remains essentially tied to canons of Naturalism and conventional language, even when he adopts the genre of the fantastic. Indeed, to use Barilli's expression, he does not break through (at least in that period) the 'barrier of Naturalism' and remains attached to a literary tradition that is sustained by imposing on the complexities of reality a seemingly rational grid that does not dare to surmount an accepted representation and vision of the world.[10] In contrast, *Il Verri* (through the contributions of Barilli and Angelo Guglielmi in particular) favours the writers of the *nouveau roman* or Gadda.[11]

Although Barilli admires Vittorini's receptiveness to new ideas and his ability to promote cultural dialogues, he condemn sharply the literary outlook exemplified by *Il Menabò* and by the supporters of, what he calls, a 'generic humanism' ('umanesimo generico' [*BN*, 304]). In his view, most post-war intellectuals and writers still subscribe to a content-oriented model of literature that is trapped in moral, economic, and political issues essentially extraneous to the specific properties of a literary landscape. Essentially, for Barilli, the majority of post-war Italian intellectuals and writers are unable to 'surmount the blocks imposed by "common sense" and to attempt non-conformist projects' ('superare gli sbarramenti del "senso comune," di tentare imprese non conformiste' [*BN*, 322]). According to him, the intellectual and artistic history of post-war Italy is marked by a pervasive inability to relinquish old cultural and literary schemes. Notwithstanding the degree of cultural openness exhibited by *Il Menabò* (in Barilli's view, the general situation is much more grievous), the journal remains substantially traditional and, at best, shows, *vis à vis* the fundamental literary problems of the times, a 'cautious reformism' or 'enlightened conservatism' ('cauto riformismo; conservatorismo illuminato' [*BN*, 316]). Barilli is critical of Calvino's negative appraisal of the new artistic forms, like 'informal' art, *nouveau roman*, or the 'visceral' trend of the avant-garde.

For Calvino, in these artistic forms, the self is dissolved in an undifferentiated world of objects (in his words, 'the rationalizing and differentiating conscience feels absorbed just like a fly on the petals of a carnivorous plant' ['la coscienza razionalizzatrice e discriminante si sente assorbire come una mosca sui petali di una pianta carnivora']).[12] Barilli objects to Calvino's atemporal categories of 'reason' and 'conscience.' In his view, they are historical constructs, and he defines Calvino's interpretation of conscience as 'an empty simulacrum' ('vuoto simulacro' [*BN*, 305]). He advocates the phenomenological approach tied to Husserl's and Sartre's concept of intentionality, namely, the relation with things as they manifest themselves to the conscience and not as entities that can be known in themselves. (Basically, for phenomenology, only the intentional object of a mental state can be described; the object as an entity in itself does not exist.) For Barilli, Calvino and other conventional writers are unable to let go of the so-called 'rational' schemes that act as diaphragms between the subject and the object. In contrast, writers ready to break with stale conventions are inclined to explore the 'opacity' and the 'materiality' ('opacità, materialità' [*BN*, 307]) of the world without predetermined constructs that serve only to mask the objects. Conventional writers, Barilli concludes, reveal no interests in exploring new territories. They are guided by a 'foolish moralistic ambition ... an emotional choice made for keeping the conscience at peace' ('velleitarismo moralistico ... una scelta emotiva fatta per mettere la coscienza a posto' [*BN*, 308]).

Another critic who offered, in a subsequent issue of *Il Menabò*, an explicit and incisive critique of Calvino was Guglielmi. He contested first of all Calvino's classification of a 'rationalist' avant-garde.[13] For Guglielmi, most of the writers included by Calvino in this current are representatives of the outdated discourse to which humanistic culture is attracted, specifically, 'the search for the soul of things, for an order and a precept in which the diversity of the world discovers its configuration, together with its perspective' ('ricerca dell'anima delle cose, di un ordine e regola nella quale la varietà del mondo trova la sua composizione e, insieme, la sua prospettiva' [*AS*, 63]). This culture is deeply imbued with the axiom that *essence* is inseparable from things and from life in general. In Guglielmi's view, humanistic culture, faced by the commodification of things and the reification of man in the industrial era, interprets such changes as a decay of the relationship between things and their presumed essence, that is the 'values and norms in which traditional culture has accustomed us to search for the meaning and mechanism of existence' ('valori e norme in cui la cultura tradizionale ci ha abituati a ricercare il significato e il meccanismo dell'esistenza' [*AS*, 64]). What Calvino defines as a 'rationalist' avant-garde is seen by Guglielmi as a 'retro-guard' ('retroguardia' [*AS*, 65]) that obstinately defends a front already heavily penetrated by enemy forces. This front, Guglielmi explains, is represented by a humanistic culture 'centred around a concept of History as a field of action in which man is engaged in achieving a divine plan or, being essentially the same, a human project' ('incentrata su un concetto di Storia quale campo di azione dell'uomo impegnato nella realizzazione di un piano divino o, non è molto diverso, di un progetto umano' [*AS*, 65]). Guglielmi accuses humanistic culture of being grounded in metaphysical belief – belief in which the inclusion of Marxism can be open to debate – which in turn, stems from an 'anthropological conception of History' ('concezione antropologica della Storia') geared to producing an atemporal image of man as 'judge and interpreter of reality, which exists and lives only in his interpretation' ('giustiziere e interprete della realtà, la quale, solo nella sua interpretazione, esiste e vive' [*AS*, 66]).

According to Guglielmi, the rationalist current, as interpreted by Calvino, continues to base its convictions merely on the appearance of things, ignores the disintegration of traditional ideologies (moral, social, religious, aesthetic), and thus is unable to create a new cultural front. For Guglielmi, the spatial disintegration expressed by an artist like Cézanne (included by Calvino, as has been pointed out, in the rationalist current) does not capture the new 'morality' ('moralità') or the new 'beauty' ('bellezza') of the industrial age. It expresses a 'drama' ('dramma') and a 'difficulty' ('difficoltà') that are entrusted to a stylistic mode that communicates both the destruction of appearances ('apparenze') of things and the 'non significance of the forms given to things' ('la non significanza delle forme delle cose' [*AS*, 65]).

To the question whether a new culture has been created to displace the humanistic paradigm, Gaglielmi's answers in the negative. For him, the 'visceral' avant-garde, as proposed by Calvino, does not represent a 'cognitive alterative' ('alternativa gnoseologica' [*AS*, 67]) to traditional culture. In his judgment, the visceral avant-garde 'refuses to express any idea on the world' ('rifiutarsi a esprimere una qualsiasi idea sul mondo' [*AS*, 67]) and does not propose any method of understanding existence. Indeed, Guglielmi argues, this avant-garde declares the impossibility of History because the world is seen as an 'invincible centre of disorder' ('centro invincibile di disordine' [*AS* 67]) governed totally by chaos.

From this viewpoint, dialectics is no longer possible inasmuch as assertions, negations, and therefore conflicts and syntheses are features of a past long gone. Guglielmi writes:

> Il polo positivo è sparito, determinando l'impossibilita di ogni giuoco dialettico, quindi l'impossibilità della Storia. (Mai l'uomo si è sentito maggiormente senza futuro come oggi quando la possibilità del futuro, grazie al meraviglioso progresso della scienza, paiono tanto prossime e suggestive.) Al posto della Storia è subentrato uno spazio in cui tutto ciò che accade diventa insensato e viene falsificato. (*AS*, 67–8)

> The positive pole has disappeared, determining the impossibility of any dialectical confrontation, and hence the impossibility of History. (Never has man had the strong sensation of the lack of a future as today, when the possibilities of a future, thanks to the marvellous progress of science, seem so near and attractive.) The place of History has been overtaken by a space in which everything that happens becomes senseless and is falsified.

The visceral avant-garde (including artists and writers such as Pollock, Fautrier, Gadda, Céline, Robbe-Grillet, and in part Joyce) degrades all values and thus practises 'the interchangeability of viewpoints' ('l'intercambiabilità ... dei punti di vista' [*AS*, 68]) and ideologies. Within this perspective, literature has espoused the form of 'pastiche' ('pastiche' [*AS*, 68]), a stylistic approach that reveals a demystifying function inasmuch as it assembles its materials randomly and in an indiscriminate fashion.

Guglielmi radicalizes the position, expressed by Roland Barthes in *Le degré zero de l'écriture* (*Writing Degree Zero*; Paris: Seuil, 1953), that favours an avant-garde able to disclose the collapse of the humanistic anthropocentrism and anthropomorphism by embracing a neutral writing at the 'zero degree.' If Barthes envisages a writing at zero degree as a commitment to make transparent the disintegration of bourgeois consciousness, Guglielmi sees it as a form of writing that does not advance an interpretation of the world but rather presents things as being pure matter, neutral 'samples' of reality (or, better said, samples of the appearances of reality). He writes:

La linea viscerale della cultura contemporanea è aideologica, disimpegnata, astorica; non contiene messaggi, né produce significati di carattere generale. (*AS*, 69)

The visceral current of contemporary culture is a-ideological, dis-engaged, a-historical; it does not involve messages, and neither it produces meanings of a general character.

Against Calvino's claim that literature is an activity committed to putting into effect the cognitive achievements offered by historical development, Guglielmi insists that there are no new methods of cognition but only 'a more dramatic awareness' of the 'exhaustion of the traditional historical picture' ('più drammatiche consapevolezze ... esaurimento [del] quadro storico tradizionale' [*AS*, 71]).

Calvino's theoretical exhortation to strive for a literature capable of challenging the labyrinth – however noble in its intent – is seen as a pointless project insofar as it cannot be situated on any cognitive ground. For Guglielmi, Calvino commits the error of thinking that there are responsible alternatives to a visceral avant-garde. In a world in which access to an independent reality is deemed an illusion and the guiding principles of the old humanistic culture have not been replaced by contemporary ones, it is impossible to ask literature to draw a map capable of showing us the way out of the labyrinth.

In response to the contentious subjects raised by the debate in *Il Menabò*, *Il Verri* published in June 1963 a special issue entitled 'Avanguardia e impegno' (Avant-garde and Commitment).[14] By then, it must have been clear to *Il Verri*'s regular contributors that the possibility of forming an avant-garde group, as a force opposed to conventional literary modes, could become a reality. Indeed, a few months later, spearheaded by *Il Verri*'s contributors (Balestrini's organizational skills were instrumental) a group of writers, artists, and critics gathered in Palermo for six days (3–8 October) and were immediately termed the neoavant-garde movement.[15]

The gathering, the accompanying proceedings, and the publications related to Gruppo 63 sparked the most daring and iconoclastic literary debate witnessed by Italy in the second half of twentieth century. It would hardly be an overstatement to maintain that many of the issues addressed by Gruppo 63 (avant-garde and social commitment, literary language and ideology/political responsibilities, autonomy and heteronomy of literary production, the new avant-garde and late capitalism, literature and the new role of the reader, literature and the human sciences, literature and the other arts, literature and the end of dialectics, the end of the avant-garde and the death of art – to name just a few) anticipated a vast number of concerns that would be the focus of research and discussions, at an international level, long after the group itself had ceased to exist. Twenty years later, Calvino fittingly remarked that Gruppo 63 represented the 'last attempt to draw a general map of literature' ('l'ultimo tentativo di disegnare una mappa generale della letteraura').[16] In fact, as will be emphasized, most of the issues that were to become central to the theoretical exploration – conducted in the 1970s, both in Europe and North America – of the conflict between modernism and postmodernism were raised by Gruppo 63, even though the latter did not employ the term postmodernism.[17]

Gruppo 63 did not aim to reach a consensus. At its various gatherings, theoretical differences were quite pronounced and the creative texts read by the participating authors were regularly submitted to fierce criticism. Indeed, a couple of years after its foundation, Eco defined the group as 'the gathering place for people with whom I consider worthwhile to argue' ('il luogo d'incontro con coloro con cui giudico proficuo litigare'). And Giuliani, in a recollection twenty years later, wrote, without irony, that 'the Gruppo 63 never existed ... it was a ghost ... that spread a little bit of fear' ('il Gruppo 63 non è mai esistito ... era un fantasma ... che mise in giro un po' di paura').[18]

Contrary to the practice, inaugurated by the historical avant-garde, of publishing manifestos as evidence of a unified literary or artistic project, Gruppo 63 always presented its theoretical stands in the form of a debate. Consequently, it seems inappropriate to apply the term movement to the group. On the other hand, its theoretical dissensions were somewhat tempered by its common project of cultural renewal and by its shared sense of rebellion against established literary canons.

In general terms, it can be stated that the Italian neoavant-garde was split into two major camps. The first, still loyal to the project of modernity, assigned to literature and to the arts a role of emancipation and social antagonism by adopting an iconoclastic language as the expression of a subversive ideology. This bloc, guided mainly by neo-Marxist theory and utopian thought, held that literature can strip the world of its mythologies and disguises and is capable of envisaging a political, social, and psychological revolution. The second, anticipating a postmodern aesthetics, saw literature as completely impotent when confronted by sociopolitical realities.[19] For this faction, literature shows the arbitrariness and fictive nature of all artistic expressions. Inasmuch as any system of meaning has a gratuitous structure and all forms of writing are reduced to a language game, there is no access to the essence of reality. Poetry can at best provide a critical *ersatz* of the chaotic and 'schizomorphic' nature of the world by practising techniques of quotationism, montage, and pastiche totally indifferent to traditional concepts of social and political commitment.

To put it differently, the postmodern camp saw poetry and literature strictly as an exploration of language, which in turn entailed the abolition of its mediating function. Language can speak only of itself, concurrently subject and object of its own operation. The modernists, on the other hand, perceived language as a constant projection of something other than itself on the ground of the dialectical relationship it establishes with social, political, and any other extraliterary aspect of life. For both groups, however, literature is conceived as a linguistic activity and the question of the specificity of literariness is a central preoccupation.

At the first gathering in Palermo, Giuliani starts the debate by focusing on avant-garde literature and the problematics of language. He emphasizes that traditional literature erroneously adopts the prevailing 'elevated language' ('lingua colta') as a form of 'warranty' ('garanzia' [373]).[20] In essence, he claims, such a language is simply a historical construct and not necessarily bound to rational structures. The classic language of literature is seen as a 'bourgeois product' ('prodotto ... borghese' [373]) and the everyday language, spoken within mass culture (a sort of homogenized 'television Esperanto'[l'esperanto televisivo]), has become a 'pathological phenomenon' ('fenomeno patologico' [374]). Even though, for Giuliani the term 'avant-garde' has become worn out by the different uses to which it is put, he declares that the works associated with it represent the only 'good literature' ('la buona letteratura' [375]) of the past one hundred years. In his view, avant-garde literature is the result of a different awareness of language. Conventional literature accepts language as an assured medium of representation, whereas the avant-garde regards it as a code which cannot provide any sure access to brute reality. He declares:

Si ha letteratura d'avanguardia là dove la delucidazione del linguaggio si presenta come enigma e interrogazione oltre la mistificazione dei falsi enigmi, cioè senza prendere per buona fino in fondo né l'apparenza reale né la letteratura in quanto tale. (375)

One produces avant-garde literature when the elucidation of language is seen as an enigma and an interrogation, reaching beyond the mystifica- tion of the false enigmas, that is without considering completely depend- able neither the appearance of the real, nor literature as such.

Avant-garde literature, Giuliani concludes, exhibits 'an arbitrary and maniacal structure' ('una struttura arbitraria e maniaca' [374]) inas- much as it negates ordinary perceptions of reality and favours what he calls 'a realism of inventiveness' ('realismo dell'invenzione' [376]), identifiable with the force of language and imagination.

Giuliani displays some oscillations between paradigms of modern- ism and those of postmodernism, but he definitively leans to a much greater extent towards the latter. On the one hand, he maintains a criti- cal distance from accepted versions of reality (making conceivable the identification of mere appearances or of the unauthentic within the horizons of a culture of opposition) but, on the other, he finds it impos- sible to foster a literary project aimed at reintegrating art in the life- world.[21]

The visionary slant of his address does not translate into a new cog- nitive map that transcends the alienating structure of the current sys- tem. Nor does his critical perspective on the world generate the possibility of exposing new truths. Instead, Giuliani's postmodernism resides not only in the emphasis given to the crisis of representation but in the conception of reality as a constant eruption of simulacra – appearances that escape both a definitive metanarrative and a political redemption. The reference to the 'maniacal' construction of the avant- garde's linguistic modalities expresses a position close to the Dadaist program for absurdity and the destruction of all meaning, a posture much in line with the so-called postmodern condition.

It was Angelo Guglielmi's contribution to the debate that most elo- quently exemplified the position of the postmodern camp. Guglielmi draws the core issues of his statements from the essay he published in *Il Menabò* as a rebuttal to Calvino. The basis of his position is the reduc- tion of ideology to the zero degree and the catastrophe of History. His assumption is that the primary function of avant-garde literature is that of reproducing the contradictions and ruins of contemporary real- ity and thus 'refusing to express any idea at all on the world' ('rifiutarsi

di esprimere una qualsiasi idea sul mondo' [376]). Reality's disclosures
must be totally severed from old hermeneutic schemes and presented
in a 'neutral space' ('spazio neutro') where things appear 'real and
immobile, without any expectation' ('reali e immobili, nemmeno in
attesa' [379]). He explains:

> Né d'altra parte l'avanguardia è cosi ingenua e cieca da credere al sofisma
> che una non visione del mondo possa essere a sua volta una nuova
> visione, il caos una nuova forma di ordine, il caso un nuovo modo di
> atteggiarsi della legge, l'imposibilità della Storia il nuovo procedere
> dell'umanità. (376)

> On the other hand, the avant-garde is not so naive and blind to believe in
> the sophism that the absence of a world-view may be seen as a new world-
> view, or chaos as a new model of order, chance as a new way to formulate
> a law, the impossibility of History as a new course for humanity.

Guglielmi's position seems to eradicate the revolutionary ethos of
early-twenty-century avant-gardism, with its ambition to bridge art
and life. For Guglielmi, literature's task is not that of proposing a system to replace the existing one. Such a perception of the role of literature is deemed to be a mystification derived from mythologizing a
system of thought. For this reason, Guglielmi declares the groundlessness of all meaning, of being, and of History. The historical processes
have simply led to the exhaustion of History itself.

In Guglielmi's outlook, the 'death of ideologies' ('morte delle ideologie') must be at the base of the new avant-garde's literary strategy
insofar as ideologies are negated as epistemological grids. An 'a-ideological' and 'visceral' avant-garde assumes the world to be a space of
chaos and disorder. Chance and 'the interchangeability of meanings
and viewpoints' ('l'interscambiabilità dei significati e dei punti di
vista' [377]) become the last resources for resisting silence or fabrica-
tions of reality. Faced by the death of ideology and the crisis of cognition, the new avant-garde literature must undertake the function of
demystifying the alienated representations of the world through the
use of pastiche (a conflation of a multiplicity of styles and viewpoints
reached through intertextual quotationism and the use of conflicting
levels of language). Guglielmi declares:

> A questa funzione demistificante provvede la formula del *pastiche*, che,

nella misura in cui intreccia in tutta disinvoltura piani conoscitivi con-
trastanti, decreta la morte delle ideologie, rifiutandole, appunto, quali
piani di conoscenza. Il *pastiche* ha, per proprie virtù fisiologiche, una forte
carica svalorizzante (nei riguardi degli ingredienti cui si alimenta) che, in
questo caso diventa una carica demistificante in quanto impegnata a sval-
orizzare significati che oggi si presentano come falsi significati. (378)

This demystifying function is provided by the formula of *pastiche*, which,
inasmuch as it weaves very nonchalantly contrasting cognitive levels, it
decrees the death of ideologies, refusing them, in fact, as grounds for cognition. On the account of its physiological qualities, *pastiche* possesses a
strong devaluing drive (*vis à vis* the ingredients it uses to sustain itself)
that, in this case, becomes a demystifying drive inasmuch as it is engaged
in devaluing meanings that today are considered false.

Discontinuity, heterogeneity, and fragmentation engendered by the
technique of pastiche establish a homological relationship with the
new version of the self interpreted as a decentred and shifting 'non-
entity,' caught in a web of incessant instability. Indeed, pastiche is the
linguistic equivalent of the reduction of the 'I.' For Guglielmi, the self,
subjectivity, the inner realities should not be of interest to the literature
of the new avant-garde. Its purpose should rather be to capture objects
in their most elementary state. However, it is relevant to ask this question? In what ways does the process of demystification that writing
should engender affect an author's 'I' or that of the reader? Of course,
given the postulate that the deep structures of reality are unknowable
(past approaches adopted by literature, the other arts, or social sciences are deemed no longer credible), it follows that the authentic/
unauthentic opposition which sustained modernist conceptions of the
subject is dissolved.

Guglielmi's depoliticized version of the new avant-garde, particularly his unwillingness to view Marxism as a scientific method for
reading the world and legitimizing literary work, encountered forceful
opposition in the address delivered by Edoardo Sanguineti. Sanguineti's position rests on the postulate that literature is in essence a
metalinguistic production of ideologies. In other words, literary language and ideology are inseparable inasmuch as a writer's form inevitably corresponds to an ideology (language is always drenched with
ideological paradigms, it is always a codified way of seeing things).[22]
Sanguineti opposes both Giuliani's outlook, centred around the

premise that the avant-garde must privilege the exploration of language over ideological concerns, and Guglielmi's claim for an 'a-ideological' and 'neutral' avant-garde. He states:

> In un testo, non vi è ideologia, esteticamente parlando, se non nella forma del linguaggio. L'avanguardia esprime quindi, in generale, la coscienza del rapporto fra l'intellettuale e la società borghese, portata al suo grado ultimo, ed esprime contemporaneamente, in generale, la coscienza del rapporto tra ideologia e lingiuaggio, e cioè la consapevolezza del fatto che ciò che è proprio dell'operazione letteraria in quanto tale è l'espressione di una ideologia nella forma del linguaggio. (382)

> In a text there is no ideology, aesthetically speaking, if not in the form of language. In general terms, the avant-garde thus expresses the awareness of the relationship between the intellectual and the bourgeois society in its latest development. In general and contemporaneously, it expresses the awareness of the relationship between ideology and language, namely, the realization of the fact that what is intrinsic to a literary operation is the evidence of an ideology in the form of language.

Sanguineti drives the debate in a political direction, foregrounding the dialectical relationship between base (capitalist mode of production, the system of economic relations in bourgeois society) and superstructure, together with the mechanisms that regulate the latter. Sanguineti's politicization of the avant-garde is sustained by his reference to Walter Benjamin's study on Baudelaire, whom he sees as the first modern artist fully aware of the production of 'aesthetic commodities' ('merci estetiche' [381]).[23]

According to Sanguineti, an a-historical approach to the avant-garde, as suggested by Guglielmi, cannot be supported because it does not take into account the condition of the writer within the capitalist-bourgeois society. Sanguineti reverses the position commonly associated with 'vulgar' Marxism, which assigns priority to content over form (it is the content, as an equivalent of the modes of production, that determines forms – the expressions of the superstructure). For Sanguineti, a writer must oppose bourgeois society (contrary to Guglielmi's position, a dialectical negation is still possible) by constructing a 'new rationality' ('una nuova razionalità' [385]) in the form of language. He declares:

> Per essere autenticamente critica, e autenticamente realistica, l'arte deve

energeticamente uscire dai limiti della normalità borghese, cioè dalle sue
norme ideologiche e linguistiche. (383)

In order to be authentically critical, and authentically realistic, art must
exit energetically from the boundaries of bourgeois normality, namely
from its ideological and linguistic norms.

Sanguineti remains loyal to a Marxist revolutionary ethos. In his view,
by espousing forms capable of exploding bourgeois paradigms of normality, the avant-garde can relocate the road to revolution.

As a rebuttal to this proposal to ideologize the avant-garde, Renato
Barilli claims that Sanguineti is still fettered by the post-war notion of a
politically committed literature (*'la littérature engagée'*) which privileges
exclusively 'practical reason' ('ragion pratica') by positing ideology in
'political and economic terms' ('termini politico-economici' [389])
derived from Marxist thought.

Advocating the Kantian category of 'pure reason' ('ragion pura'),
Barilli contends that ideology is also related to 'perception, cognition,
space, and time' ('la percezione, il conoscere, lo spazio, il tempo' [390]),
elements that are fundamental for constructing a view of the world.
Indeed, for Barilli, literature shows many more affinities with questions related to the sphere of psychology, anthropology, or epistemology than with those pertaining to the political or economic order.
Accordingly, literature requires the adoption of an ideological orientation, but not as an embodiment of issues concerning 'practical reason.'
This would heavily impair the literary word's ability to perform an
effective function. Georg Lukács was one critic who, according to Barilli, fell victim to 'practical reason,' for, even though he was culturally
well equipped, he was unable to comprehend the value of the work
conducted by avant-garde artists and writers. The integration of new
cognitive achievements (to which literature is a significant contributor)
into the social structure is seen as a necessary project, but only from a
future-oriented perspective. By shifting modes of perception or cognition, an avant-garde writer contributes, through a series of mediations,
to shaping a new world-view and hence a different future society.

Barilli rejects both Sanguineti's Marxist orientation and Guglielmi's
negation of a literary project of any kind. He proposes to situate the
avant-garde within a dynamic process that is governed by an incessant
relationship between society's rejection of the new and what he terms
'normalization.' The formal innovations and the new consciousness

advocated by works of the avant-garde will inevitably be legitimized by the future society and replaced, in most cases, by other projects that, at first, will appear to be shocking – and on and on, in a never-ending process. Referring to a writer such as Robbe-Grillet, Barilli states:

> Io penso che sia uno scrittore che può resistere, e quindi fra venti, trent'anni, lo vedremo inserito nell'ufficialità; cioè quel suo stile a un certo momento entrerà nella normalità, e ci saranno magari nuove forme artistiche che si rivolteranno contro di lui. (391)

> I think he is a writer who can last and consequently in twenty or thirty years he will be officially recognized. In other words, his style will enter, at a certain point, in the stage of normality and, perhaps, there will be new artistic forms that will revolt against him.

The normalization of the new avant-garde is, for Barilli, a necessity. The new avant-garde writer must perform the role of contributing constructively to the igniting of revolutionary processes at the level of superstructures – that is, the psychological and cognitive levels. Such a writer can add value to the world-view elaborated by the historical avant-garde, integrating it with other alternative projects offered by contemporary culture.

Sanguineti replies by providing a forceful critique of Barilli's notion of normalization. Normalization as an endorsement of the 'normality of otherness' ('normalità autre' [403]) is considered a reformist proposal that implies a constant 'museumification' of the avant-garde. For Sanguineti, the avant-garde, as a politically engaged force that refuses to sever the political from the aesthetic domain, cannot espouse a museumized normality because this would entail the acceptance of bourgeois logic. Adopting Theodor Adorno's concept of museum[24] as a bourgeois strategy for co-opting otherness (which is the equivalent of the legitimation of avant-garde literature through the publishing industry and bourgeois social institutions), Sanguineti declares:

> Il pericolo, al riguardo, sta in un facile eccesso di illusioni: perché questa nuova normalità che ho acquisito e stabilito oggettivamente non può acquisirsi e stabilirsi, oggi, se non nella forma del museo borghese, reificata e neutralizzata. (403)

> The danger here is that there is an enormous excess of illusions: the new

normality that I have conquered and established in an objective fashion, today cannot be conquered and established in any way than in the form of the bourgeois museum, thus becoming reified and neutralized.

For Sanguineti, Barilli's position is dangerously neutral, as is that of Guglielmi. Both Guglielmi's end of ideology and of dialectics and Barilli's inclusivity of otherness in the normality of bourgeois existence cannot but have, in Sanguineti's view, paralysing effects, the unconditional acceptance of the world as it is. Sanguineti's theoretical orientation is opposed not only to the postmodern wing of the *neoavanguardia* but also to its French counterpart, the *Tel Quel* group. Indeed, in the early 1960s, the *Telquelians* rejected the subordination of literature to any political objective and attempted to validate it on the ground of its alternative encounter with language. They searched for a theoretical framework and a literary practice able to establish a distance from notions of moral and political commitment tied to Sartre and the generation of the Resistance. Undoubtedly, the *Telquelians'* radical abandonment of theoretical perspectives linked to notions of Realism, representation, and extraliterary objectives was shared by the postmodern wing of the Italian *neoavanguardia*. Further, the internal divisions of the Italian group were replicated by the French in 1967 when Jean-Pierre Faye left the *Tel Quel* review and founded *Change*, which advocated a literature capable of re-establishing links with issues of political praxis.

Tel Quel was engaged in reassessing the role of Marxism within the theory of literature between 1968 and 1970, when the group participated to two colloquia organized at Cluny by *La Nouvelle Critique*, the first on 'Linguistics and Literature' and the second on 'Literature and Ideology.' If Marxist thought and ideology represented for the *neoavanguardia*, in its early stages, significant issues for debate and divergencies, the *Telquelians* seemed to experience a rapprochement with left-wing political objectives at a later stage, coinciding with the students' revolts and the Maoist cultural revolution. In a more general perspective, however, both groups shared from the start the conviction that it is necessary to place language at the centre of the literary activity, with the goal of subverting the linguistic modalities through which reality is constructed.

The debate inaugurated by the first gathering of the neoavant-garde was followed by the publication of books and articles by many of its members. In the years that followed, between 1964 and 1967, four other gatherings were held. The contentious positions expressed by the group provoked responses by a great number of outsiders, and soon the debate exploded in a literary and cultural confrontation that involved leading intellectual figures of the times.[25]

In order to offer a cohesive analysis of the debate's developments and to avoid cumbersome repetition, the following discussion will not adopt a rigid diachronic approach for the years following the Palermo gathering; instead, it will foreground the group's most prominent positions. To the same end, the views expressed in essays and articles written by members of the group, and that appeared in *Il Verri* – starting with those published in the review's special issue on literature and social commitment – as well as in other journals, newspapers, and books will be integrated here with statements made at other gatherings and set out in various publications.[26]

Guglielmi's positions are further developed in the volume *Avanguardia e sperimentalismo* (Avant-garde and Experimentalism), which appeared exactly one year following the Palermo gathering and included a number of essays already published in journals – the central essay bears the same title of the book and first appeared in *Il Verri* in the special issue already mentioned.

In its general outlook, the volume reiterates the conviction that literature must stop falsifying reality by shrouding it with moral values, prejudices of all sorts, and ideological constructs. The responsibility of a contemporary writer is that of recovering, behind false appearances, a reality in its neutral, physical, material state. Essentially, Guglielmi is searching for a new canon of Realism for which 'there exists no truth prior to reality' ('non esiste una verità antecedente alla realtà' [30]). In writers such as Musil, Kafka, or Joyce, human actions pertaining to the moral, sentimental, or social realms have already been emptied of any ideal function or absolute values. For Guglielmi, this crisis of reality is combined with the futility of calling upon History to uncover a new course of action or to reconstruct a sense of the real. For this reason, he must favour the writer who 'makes an effort to capture [reality] in a primeval state, as a physical matter, prior to any qualifying form of intervention, be it ideological, moral, or sentimental in nature' ('si sforzi di catturarla [la realtà] a uno stadio primigenio, di materia fisica, anteriormente all'intervento di una qualsiasi forma di qualificazione ideologica, morale o sentimentale' [41]).

In order to fend off misleading readings of the term Realism, Guglielmi is keen to clarify that art as representation, or, which is basically the same, as an hermeneutic experience, is a hopeless endeavour. Guglielmi refuses to acknowledge even Eco's notion of art as an 'epistemological metaphor' and the world as an 'open' space of possibilities. His theoretical stand does not admit the existence of any fixed laws governing reality. There can be no exegesis of reality inasmuch as all interpretative tools have fatally collapsed. There exists no longer the separation between words and things. In this theoretical orientation, words are autotelic materials, discrete fragments for constructing their own realities – a position very close to that expressed by Giuliani in his introduction to *The Novissimi*. Guglielmi writes:

> Il poeta, il musicista, il pittore moderno non ci propone immagini della realtà, ma corrispettivi di essa. L'opera d'arte moderna non è uno specchio che, in quanto tale, si pone di fronte all'oggetto che deve riflettere, ma è fabbrica della realtà e, insieme, il suo prodotto. (48)

> The modern poet, musician or painter, does not propose a portrait of reality, but its correspondences. The modern work of art is not a mirror that, as such, places itself in front of the object that it has to reflect, but is the factory of reality and, at the same time, its product.

The principal features of Guglielmi's theoretical discourse, thus far identified with postmodern postures, can be summarized as follows: the devaluation of History, reason, and cognition; the end of dialectics; the relativity of viewpoints and the groundlessness of any truth; the crisis of representation afflicting literature; and the futility of bridging literary work with the life-world. Clearly, the notion of avant-garde, centred on a culture of dissent and antagonism, cannot be situated in Guglielmi's theoretical scheme.[27] Indeed, in his essay 'Avanguardia e sperimentalismo' (Avant-garde and Experimentalism), Guglielmi proposes a distinction between an experimental model of literature and one tied to an avant-garde movement, concluding that the cultural conditions of the times render it impossible for the latter to be put into effect. In the statement that follows, Guglielmi points to pivotal traits of contemporary culture (traits later associated with the condition of postmodernity)[28] that cannot sustain the revolutionary objectives of the avant-garde:

> Una delle caratteristiche essenziali dei nostri tempi è, siamo d'accordo, l'estrema confusione: tuttavia si tratta di una confusione che nasce dal

fatto che nella nostra area culturale tutto è permesso. Cioè è legata in qualche modo a una situazione positiva, di estrema libertà, di estrema tolleranza. Il nostro tempo è fecondo e inventivo quanti altri mai. I prodotti più stravaganti sono accettati e vantano le garanzie più autorevoli. In una condizione del genere, di disponibilità assoluta, quale senso può avere un movimento d'avanguardia? Quali porte vuole aprire, se tutte sono aperte? ... Ormai l'industria culturale fonda la sua prosperità proprio su una produzione di punta. Ostinarsi a comportarsi come se così non fosse è una inutile finzione. Credere che esistano dei nemici da vincere, delle barriere da sradicare, e, insomma, una situazione da capovolgere, nei migliori dei casi è una forma di inconsapevolezza, di insufficienza di coscienza. (54–5)

One of the characteristics of our times, we will agree, is the extreme confusion. However, we deal with a confusion that stems from the fact that in our cultural area everything is allowed. That is to say, it is in some ways tied to a positive situation, one of extreme freedom and extreme tolerance. Our times are as fertile and inventive as any other. The most extravagant products are accepted and boast the most commanding warranties. In this condition of absolute predisposition, what sense can an avant-garde movement have? What doors does it want to open when all doors are open? ... At this stage, the culture industry builds its prosperity on the most innovative products. It is a useless pretence to behave obstinately as if things were otherwise. To believe there are enemies to defeat, barriers to dislodge, or, in short, to believe in a situation that needs to be overturned, it is, in the best scenario, a form of unawareness, an insufficient understanding of things.

There is no doubt that Guglielmi anticipates a theoretical position on the avant-garde that will receive frequent expression only years later. A clear example is Peter Bürger's successful volume, *Theory of the Avant-garde*, in which he claims that the new avant-garde movement represent an 'inautheintic' gesture inasmuch as its project is well integrated in the mechanisms of the culture industry.[29] For Guglielmi, given that the revolutionary objectives of the historical avant-garde are no longer conceivable (it is hopeless to build any bridge between literature and social realities), literature can perform only a role of formal experimentation.[30] The experimentalism advocated by Guglielmi presents numerous features that are commonly associated with postmodern canons. Indeed, it is not only Guglielmi's stylistic and aesthetic insights that provide a lucid view of a postmodern literary orientation. The cultural framework in which he is able to situate literary activity demonstrates a full grasp of political and historical conditions that will be assimilated by North America's theoretical scene much later. The epistemological groundlessness of literary activity claimed by Guglielmi, its inability to provide insights into reality or to offer a redemptive human or social project, are essential elements around which will revolve the explosion of postmodern theory on the North American continent. Indeed, Guglielmi insistence on the end of history, and the death of dialectics, ideology, and the humanist subject are at the core of any postmodern discourse. Nevertheless, some contradictions can be detected.

In Guglielmi's view, the experimental writer must utilize a linguistic laboratory in which materials are extracted from 'the most diverse and widely separated cultural traditions' ('tradizioni culturali più lontane e diverse' [58]). In other words, experimentalism must practise the cannibalization and 'contamination' of conflicting linguistic modes through the 'repêchages' (recycling of existing texts) of materials that cross the boundaries of the most heterogeneous cultures.[31] Intertextuality, hybridization, pastiche are clearly in tune with the dominant tenets that will be identified with postmodern aesthetics. However, it must be pointed out that, if postmodernism cannot be located within the parameters of avant-garde aesthetics (as has been persuasively argued by a myriad of theorists), primarily because it abandons the objectives of an antagonistic culture, Guglielmi's case seems, at least on the surface of things, to display some incongruities.

On the one hand, Guglielmi argues that 'art as intuitive cognition, a synthetic and comprehensive view of the totality of the real, is dead' ('è morta l'arte come conoscenza intuitiva, come visione sintetica e comprensiva della totalità del reale' [82]); on the other, he claims that reality can be recovered – the 'objective of the research is reality' ('oggetto della ricerca è la realtà' [82]), he says in his closing remarks. It seems that Guglielmi does not abandon the hope that literature (unlike postmodernism in general) may discover a sense of authentic reality behind all the simulacra of consumer society and capitalist alienation. Furthermore, he does not seem to renounce completely the conception of literature as a form of adversarial culture. In fact, occasionally he speaks of literature as a field in which it is necessary to apply 'critical awareness' ('consapevolezza critica' [56]) and 'critical acids' ('acidi critici' [61]) in order to generate unbalance and disorder.[32] Although not ideologically oriented, the formal activity of the experimental writer is still somewhat tied to a canon of transgression – even though, it would be fair to say, it is a transgressive action carried out in an exclusively linguistic territory.

One year following the publication of Guglielmi's volume, Sanguineti reignites the dispute with a collection of essays *Ideologia e linguaggio* (Ideology and Language).[33] Here, he reaffirms his position that language and ideology are inseparable in that literature is an ideological activity in the form of language. (The underlying premise is that traditional literature represents the disguised discourses of bourgeois hegemony; essentially, it is an institution that elaborates and legitimizes the ideology, and thus the values, of the bourgeoisie.) In the essay 'La letteratura della crudeltà' (Literature of Cruelty),[34] Sanguineti declares that 'the experience of words conditions – precedes – that of things' ('l'esperienza delle parole condiziona [precede] quella delle cose' [133]). Transformation of reality (things) can occur through the transformation of ideology, which, in turn, can be transformed through the demolition of conventional language. For Sanguineti, avant-garde literature is not a simple epiphenomenon but an activity that, by expressing the dialectical unity of *poiesis* and *praxis*, performs a practical superstructural function. Ultimately, it is a political action. By contesting and destroying the ordered system of traditional language, avant-garde literature throws into question the accepted vision of reality and the dominant ideology. With an indirect reference to Antonin Artaud's transgressive manifesto 'The Theatre of Cruelty,' Sanguineti claims that avant-garde literature 'is not at the service of revolution, but it *is* the revolution at the level of words' ('essa non è al servizio della rivoluzione, ma è la rivoluzione sopra il terreno delle parole' [134–5]). The dialectics between words and things is established inasmuch as the literature of 'cruelty' is based on a 'critical experimentation of the hierarchies of reality as it is *lived* in words' ('una sperimentazione critica delle gerarchie del reale, quale è *vissuta* nelle parole' [134–5]).

Sanguineti seems to set for himself the difficult task of reconciling the Gramscian model of the 'organic intellectual' with the principles of aesthetic autonomy suggested by the Frankfort School – Adorno in particular. Following Antonio Gramsci's commitment to revolutionary praxis, Sanguineti elaborates the figure of an 'organic' writer operating within the context of late capitalism. Sanguineti adheres firmly to the Gramscian principle of the inseparability of theory and practice and assigns to a writer's work on language the function of communicating a counter-ideology capable of supplanting the bourgeois view of the world. (In other words, for Sanguineti, literary transgression allows otherness to speak and to subvert bourgeois discourses on the ground of its difference.) Praxis is identified with the verbal revolution and thus literature maintains its own autonomy with respect to the actions of the political struggle. That is to say, he refuses to subordinate litera- ture to the dictates of a direct political action. Literature delegates its negation of the capitalist system to language – reality does not emerge into consciousness as an cluster of empirical data, as neutral facts, but through a system of signs and codes. This is why language is seen by Sanguineti as praxis. The ruptures of avant-garde writing, as Adorno claimed, denounce the false harmonies and reconciling modes of bour- geois literature, whose function is that of concealing alienation and social contradictions. Sanguineti assimilates Adorno's conviction that the avant-garde produces formal dissonances as messages of dialecti- cal antithesis, as a negation of the present system and as a desire for a new one.

Sustained by Adorno's and Benjamin's analyses on the relationship between art and economic base (the ways it is produced, packaged, marketed, and consumed within a capitalist system), Sanguineti comes to the conclusion that the strategies of late capitalism inevitably reduce all aesthetic works to commodities. According to his theory, the oppo- sition of the avant-garde artist to the commodity condition follows three structurally interconnected stages. The 'heroic aspiration' ('l'aspi- razione eroica') of escaping the market by producing uncontaminated works is followed by the 'pathetic moment' ('momento patetico') in which art is absorbed by the market and reduced to an exchange value. Last is the 'cynical' attitude ('momento cinico'): the artist, with daring innovations, outmanoeuvres competing products by aiming for either immediate or future markets.

The 'heroic' and 'pathetic' attitudes, for Sanguineti, are 'heroically and pathetically blind' ('Il momento eroico-patetico è eroicamente e pateticamente cieco' [65]) in that the avant-garde opposes aesthetic commodification with a full awareness of the ambivalence of its nega- tion. The offer of a 'fetish more mysterious that any other fetish' ('un feticcio più misterioso di ogni altro' [63]) reveals itself to be nothing but an 'astute tactic of competition' ('astuto artificio concorrenziale' [67]). Furthermore, Sanguineti maintains that in the consumer society 'the reality principle tends to coincide with the principle of obsoles- cence' ('il principio di realtà tende a coincidere con il principio di obsolescenza' [74]). It follows that, for the new avant-garde, the escape from commodity fetishism is practically impossible – there is no space for art outside capital. Indeed, inasmuch as the new avant-garde is driven by the 'incessant' search for 'new strategies of subtle aesthetic forms of persuasion' ('sempre nuove strategie di occulta persuasione estetica'), it cannot but express 'a forward thrust towards consumption' ('una fuga in avanti verso il consumo' [74]). In other words, Sanguineti is fully aware of the fact that the new avant-garde's stress on novelty means an acceleration of consumption. The constant search for newness coincides with capitalist modes of production, which are characterized by an endless race for new products and by the concomitant bourgeois desire to create new appetites for consumption. Art enters into a collusive relationship with the market forces. Sanguineti writes:

> L'avanguardia si leva, strutturalmente parlando, contro la mercificazione estetica, e infine ... vi precipita dentro: a livello sovrastrutturale, essa ha il suo nemico dichiarato nel museo, che, da ultimo, come nelle peggiori favole, se la divora tutta tranquillamente. (65)

> Structurally speaking, the avant-garde stands against aesthetic commodification, but in the end ... it falls right in it: on a superstructural plane, it has as a declared enemy the museum, which, ultimately, as in the worst fables, calmly devours it all.

With specific reference to Adorno's investigation on the relationship between market and museum, Sanguineti claims that any avant-garde product is eventually neutralized through the aseptic spaces of the museum or, by analogy, those of the library. He states:

> Il museo e il mercato sono assolutamente contigui e comunicanti, anzi sono le due facciate di un medesimo edificio sociale ... Se il museo è la figura reale dell'autonomia dell'arte, esso è insieme la figura compensatrice della sua eteronomia mercantile ... il museo ha la sua specifica ragion d'essere nella sublimazione che ivi avviene di tutta la realtà commerciale del fatto estetico: è il prolungamento superiore e estremo dell'arte come merce. (81)

> The museum and the market are absolutely contiguous and communicating, indeed they are the two façades of the same social edifice ... If the museum is the real figure of art's autonomy, it is, at the same time, the

compensating figure of its mercantile heteronomy ... the museum has its specific *raison d'être* in the sublimation, that takes place there, of all the commercial reality of the aesthetic production: it is the superior and extreme extension of art as commodity.

On the surface, it would seem that Sanguineti's lucid investigation of an art co-opted by the economic structure of late capitalism shows a postmodernist posture – the avant-garde conceived as part of the system's tactics of consumption and as the ultimate defeat of a culture of opposition. (In this outlook, even the most radical profanation of art accomplished by the Dadaist movement was soon accepted as part of the museum's agenda). However, for Sanguineti, things stand quite differently. If, for a postmodern theorist, such as Jean Baudrillard, economic realities destroy all functions of revolt, dissent, or critique associated with art, Sanguineti, in contrasts, believes that there still exists a space for a negative dialectics.[35]

This project seems to bring Sanguineti close to Georg Lukács's view of Marxism as a dialectical method capable of converting theory into practice, into a vehicle of revolution. Undoubtedly, Sanguineti's attempt to reconcile his theory of literature with a revolutionary praxis, inspired by the principles of historical materialism, mirrors the thesis that Lukács set out originally in *History and Class Consciousness* (1923). However, it must be said that Sanguineti and Gruppo 63 offer a fundamental challenge to the critique of the avant-garde which Lukács presented in *The Meaning of Contemporary Realism*, a volume translated into Italian in 1957 (*Il significato attuale del realismo critico*).[36] For Lukács, avant-garde literature must be condemned because of its inability to reconstruct the totality of human life, which has been destroyed by the fragmentation and the alienation of the capitalist world. Lukács's canon of Realism is meant as a vehicle to recapture the wholeness of life, whereas avant-garde works are seen as decadent and nihilistic expressions of bourgeois culture. Sanguineti's literary transgression is to be interpreted not as a way of directly designing positive values (as in Lukács's case) and juxtaposing them to the dehumanization of life under capitalism, but as the objectification of the negativity of the bourgeois system and as the destruction of its seeming normality. Close to the aesthetic tenets of the Frankfurt School, Sanguineti rejects Lukács's canon of the organic work of art and embraces the principles of allegory, in Benjamin's sense of the term. Whereas the symbol is adopted with the objective of recovering a unity of meaning, a sort of mystical intuition of the univocal and the eternal, allegory promotes the transient, the dismembered, a discontinuous accumulation of objects and events that coincides with the montage technique of avant-garde art. However, it must be said that the montage, fragmentation, and discontinuity advocated by Sanguineti does not imply the outright denial of the possibility of a project of totality, as is the case with postmodern theories. Whereas, for postmodernists, the allegorical practice is seen as the collapse of metanarratives and the dissolution of psychological or social forms of unity, Sanguineti believes that allegory can perform a function of critique aimed at promoting the project of a revolution. The non-organic work presents itself as an artificial construct that simulates alienation under capitalism and thus refuses to provide the reader with the false impression that the world possess harmonious wholeness and order. Indeed, this is in tune with Benjamin's concept of allegory as a form of communication that follows the fall from an Edenic condition and exposes the ruins of History. For Sanguineti, the allegorist is an adversary of capitalism inasmuch as he is able to create the space for a critique, for an art of dissent.[37]

Sanguineti's view of the avant-garde as an expression of political opposition is shared by another Marxist member of the group, Elio Pagliarani. In an address presented at the 'European Community of Writers' convention in 1965 and entitled 'Per una definizione dell'avanguardia' (For a Definition of the Avant-garde),[38] Pagliarani claims that every authentic artist would be considered part of the avant-garde if this movement were perceived exclusively in relation to the innovations of artistic media. Even a text's deliberate critique of specific artistic canons is not sufficient to quality it as an expression of the avant-garde. In his view, an avant-garde artist not only makes the radical innovation of the medium a constitutive feature of his/her work but also offers a critique of the functions connected to the producer and of 'the relationship, between producer and consumer' ('rapporto consumatore-operatore' [340]). For Pagliarani, such a critique inevitably involves issues saturated with social implications. In this sense, the term avant-garde cannot be restricted to a literary and artistic domain. An avant-garde must necessarily feature a 'social critique' ('critica sociale') definable, in a broad sense, as 'cultural' ('culturale') critique (341). (In this perspective, Surrealism cannot but be examined in relation to Marxism, or Russian Futurism in relation to the Bolshevik Revolution.) Furthermore, Pagliarani maintains that, if the avant-garde contests language, a 'social institution *par excellence*' ('istituto sociale per eccellenza' [342]), it must consequently question the dominant and preconstituted messages produced through it. Essentially, the avant-garde cannot be limited to the role of opposition and critique but must rather be a force offering new messages (by contesting the existing ones) and, thus, a new social and cultural project – in short, a counterculture. Pagliarani refuses to confine the avant-garde to the role of critically (or powerlessly) contemplating the ruins of History. Negation of the system is viewed as inseparable from a commitment to other human projects and world-views.

The split between those who viewed the avant-garde as an artistic tendency centred on the critique of language (including the social code and the dominant literary models) and those who saw it as a cultural phenomenon bound to political praxis is articulated by Aldo Tagliaferri – a participant in the second gathering of Gruppo 63 – in an article written for *Quindici* (1968) entitled 'La superstizione della crudeltà' (The Superstition of Cruelty).[39] He argues that Sanguineti's statements on the literature of 'cruelty' are dangerously ambiguous because they do not define whether the dialectics occurs within the realm of words or within that of 'things.' Essentially, his argument goes as follows: if, as Sanguineti claims, literature is the revolution brought about by words (thus a way of overcoming the condition of 'pre-history,' in the Marxist sense of the term), then praxis becomes a superstructure. In Tagliaferri's view, this proposal reverses Marx's relationship between base and superstructure and falls into the trap of believing that ideas can change the world – whereas new ideas, as Marx alerted us, are only substitutes for old ones and leave the world as it is. Even granting that awareness can step outside historical determinants, Tagliaferri concludes that 'the triumphal march of Literature on the road to history is merely a utopia' ('la marcia trionfale della Letteratura sulla via della storia [è] una mera utopia' [359]). Sanguineti's verbal revolution is seen as a flimsy attempt to bridge the gap between those members of Gruppo 63 who defend literature's autonomy and those members who persist in identifying *poiesis* with *praxis*. Tagliaferri is clearly inclined towards a postmodern position. For him, literature is cut off from social and political projects. One falls into the realm of magic and 'superstition' ('superstizione' [360]) either by assigning to literature a positive value based on its revolutionary words or by identifying it with the revolution itself.

Tagliaferri's views were close to those of Giorgio Manganelli, who had participated in the activities of the group since its first gathering. Manganelli summarizes his position in the final chapter of his book

Letteratura come menzogna (Literature as a Lie [1967]). He essentially reduces literature to rhetoric, to a game that, either 'useless' or 'poisonous' ('inutile, velenoso' [172]), ends up being a fabrication, a lie. In a world where children die of hunger, literature is an 'immoral' and 'cynical' activity ('immorale, cinica' [172]). In treating literature as a purely linguistic act, Manganelli demystifies its social and political impact. Basically, this reduction of language to an ontological status detaches it from its social origins and from specific historical conditions. Even though, in his view, literature is driven by an anarchic and utopian spirit, this is a trait dissociated from any tangible project. Indeed, for Manganelli, it is only an 'infantile' and 'irritating' posture ('infantile, irritante' [174]). Manganelli seems to construct a neo-Baroque literary theory by declaring that a writer 'ignores totally the meaning of language' ('ignora totalmente il senso del linguaggio' [175]); he posits that language 'chooses' the writer who becomes a medium through whom it expresses its 'lies, illusionisms, games, and ceremonies' ('menzogne, illusionismi, giochi e cerimonie' [175]). The writer is caught in a web of infinite linguistic subtleties. An encounter with language is an encounter with an oracle. Language, as an oracular god, delivers an ambiguous constellation of meanings. For Manganelli, literary language is surrounded by 'a halo of meanings, it communicates everything and thus nothing' ('un alone di significati, vuol dire tutto e dunque niente' [176]). Here is his closing statement:

> Con le sue proposizioni 'prive di senso,' le affermazioni 'non verificabili,' inventa universi, finge inesauribili cerimonie. Essa possiede e governa il nulla. (177)

> With its 'meaningless' propositions and 'unverifiable' affirmations, [literature] invents worlds and fabricates endless ceremonies. It possesses and governs nothing.

Manganelli's notion of literature as a fictive activity revolves around the assumption that the production of its meaning cannot be grounded in any reality. It is a gratuitous and non-cognitive activity. Literature's verbal constructs do not communicate any truth; they are the result of rhetorical devices engendered by the inner movements of language. Literary signs are enclosed within a verbal space in which there is no possibility of encountering real referents. Undoubtedly, Manganelli's view of literature can be placed within the general orientation of deconstruction and postmoderm theories. His position is thus aligned with that of Guglielmi, Tagliaferri, Giuliani, and, to some extent, Barilli.

As already underlined, this theoretical outlook clashed with the ideas of the Marxist wing of Gruppo 63. Indeed, there is no doubt that Marxism represented the central point of dissension between the modernist and postmodernist camps of the group. In this respect, Sanguineti was the figure who expressed most effectively the innovative contributions of Marxist thought. As noted, Adorno's and Benjamin's reflections on art played a significant role in the development of his position, and Sanguineti must have been familiar also with the aesthetic positions held by other prominent members of the Frankfurt School, like Herbert Marcuse and Max Horkheimer.[40] They, too, viewed aesthetic imagination as a revolt against repressive ideologies and as a utopian response to the dehumanizing conditions of life under capitalism. Avant-garde art, as the 'Great Refusal,' to use Marcuse's phrase, expressed the 'protest against that which is,' generating a 'tension between the actual and the possible' (*One-Dimensional Man*, 63, 61).

The objective here is not to determine all the philosophical, political, or critical factors that contributed to the framing of Sanguineti's theoretical orientation, or that of other Marxist members of the group such as Pagliarani and Balestrini. In any case, it is virtually impossible to establish unequivocally the writings to which Sanguineti was exposed before 1963, when he first formulated his position on ideology and language. Accordingly, the goal here is to place Sanguineti's literary perspective within the general framework of the Marxist culture of the times. Clearly, around the mid-1960s, a number of Marxist philosophers and critical theorists, such as Louis Althusser and Pierre Macherey, were engaged in elucidating the relationship between base and superstructure (including the relative autonomy of the latter) and between literature and ideology.[41]

Sanguineti does not share Althusser's concerns about the gaps or conflicts between the literary text and its ideological subtext. He is unquestionably closer to the genetic structuralism of the Rumanian Marxist critic Lucien Goldmann. In fact, Goldmann centres his research on the ways in which the structure of a text expresses a worldview, an ideology that transcends the author by conveying beliefs and goals of a particular social class. Goldmann's concept of 'homology' is comparable to Sanguineti's position on the relationship between language and ideology.[42]

Another important point of reference for a new Marxist approach to literature was provided by Galvano Della Volpe in the influential volume *Critica del gusto* (Criticism of Taste [1960]). Dissenting from traditional Marxist aesthetics, Della Volpe rejects the principle of the literary text as a reflection of historical realities and instead assigns to it specific cognitive properties that are distinguishable from those associated with scientific knowledge. Poetry is differentiated from the univocal discourse of scientific texts on the ground of its polysemic structure and autonomous formal organization. Della Volpe shifts Marxist aesthetics toward the semantic self-sufficiency of literature by bestowing historical value on its linguistic and stylistic properties. Essentially, he frees Marxist aesthetic theory from a content-oriented approach and recognizes the social dimension of literature in its linguistic fabric. Literature's historical and social properties do not reside in an external realm but are rather to be found within its specific semantic and formal organization. In this view, the mechanical relationship between base and superstructure is supplanted by a far more dialectical approach. Undoubtedly, Della Volpe's reflections provided the Marxist members of Gruppo 63 (Sanguineti in particular) with arguments that could be, and were, grafted onto their general critical orientation.

The issues raised by the Gruppo 63, together with the frequent attacks on conventional literature (successful traditional novelists such as Carlo Cassola, Giorgio Bassani, and Giuseppe Tomasi di Lampedusa were given the appellation of 'Liale del 63,' a term alluding to Harlequin romance writers),[43] became extremely controversial within the literary circles of the times and unavoidably provoked resentments and fierce rebuttals. Indeed, the literary establishment felt threatened by the wave of radicalism and soon launched a counter-offensive. Arguably, the most vocal critics of the group were important intellectual figures such as Franco Fortini, Alberto Moravia, and Pier Paolo Pasolini.[44] Their positions will serve as an illustration of some of the ways in which the new avant-garde's theoretical orientation and literary production were challenged.

Fortini's most vehement attack on Gruppo 63 was articulated in an essay entitled 'Due avanguardie' (Two Avant-gardes), included in the collection *Avanguardia e neo-avanguardia*. In his view, the historical avant-garde is rooted in the attitude of 'contradiction' and 'conflict' which first characterized the Romantic movement. This anarchic and 'irrational' culture ignores dialectics and is thus closed to any form of 'mediation' ('mediazione' [9]). (Fortini poses his argument without paying any attention to the negative dialectics – that is, the impossibility of a final synthesis or mediation – proposed by the Frankfurt School. As a traditional Marxist, Fortini claims that the absence of mediation and of a historical dialectics represents the fundamental ideology of 'new capitalism' ('nuovo capitalismo' [11]). It follows that the new avant-garde and the new capitalism are naturally linked. Furthermore, whereas the historical avant-garde is tied to an art grounded in a tragic world-view and presents some original aesthetic solutions, the new avant-garde merely revisits some of their techniques and submits verbal material to processes of irony, parody, and desecration. For Fortini, these practices mark 'the end of the poetic and artistic institution' ('la fine della istituzione poetica e artistica' [14]) within capitalist society. He argues that the new avant-garde failed to realize that a *real* avant-garde is no longer possible ('le nuove non sono avanguardie' [15]) inasmuch as 'the formal innovations of the avant-garde had become standard practices' ('le innovazioni formali delle avanguardie erano divenute di repertorio' [17]), already integrated into the 'market-museum' ('mercato-museo' [17]). He further argues that a process of homogenization was causing the collapse of the distinction between mass culture and high art. In his view, the avant-garde revolt was assimilated by expressions of mass culture such as 'beatnik conduct' or 'new political anarchism' ('costume beatnik, neo-anarchismo politico' [18]). Fortini concludes that, if the movements of the historical avant-garde stemmed from a state of inebriation, the new avant-garde was programming its entrance into the culture industry in a very sober fashion.

Undoubtedly, Fortini recognizes various traits of the emerging postmodern cultural condition. However, he does not seem to be aware, or pretends not to be, that his objections raised issues that were widely discussed within Gruppo 63, as has already been made clear in connection with Sanguineti's and Guglielmi's positions. Years before the publication of Fortini's essay, Fausto Curi, a critic who participated in the gatherings of the new avant-garde, wrote:

Fra arte d'avanguardia e società neocapitalista non vi è più il distacco netto, la contrapposizione che esistevano un tempo tra avanguardia e società borghese. La società neocapitalista ha 'accettato' l'arte d'avanguardia e l'arte d'avanguardia ha 'accettato' la società neocapitalista. Ovviamente, l'accettazione non implica affatto rinuncia da parte di quest'ultima ai propositi di sfruttamento e mercificazione (anzi li favorisce), né implica il ripudio dell'impegno eversivo da parte della prima. ('Proposta per una storia delle avanguardie,' *Il Verri* 8, 1963, 12)

There is no longer a clear separation between avant-garde art and neo-capitalist society, the opposition once present between avant-garde and bourgeois society. The neo-capitalist society has 'accepted' avant-garde art and avant-garde art has 'accepted' the neo-capitalist society. Obviously, the acceptance does not imply at all the renunciation of exploitation and commodification on behalf of the latter (indeed, it encourages them), but neither does it imply the rejection of a subversive commitment on behalf of the former.

According to Curi, the figure of the *poète maudit*, associated with the anarchism and the desecrating spirit of the avant-garde, has come to an end. However, this is not a big loss in Curi's view. The myths surrounding that avant-garde figure have been unmasked: the total rejection of the social concealed a large dose of 'egotism,' 'individualism,' and an 'aristocratic' sense of spirituality that resulted in purely verbal acts with no real consequences. The irrational and bohemian modes of the first avant-garde has been replaced by a rational, critical, and 'ordered planning of disorder' ('ordinata progettazione del disordine' [13]) that can take place only within a lucid and well-articulated cultural organization. In other words, the protest from the outside of the social has moved into the inside of capitalist institutions. Integrated into the social and economic structure, the new avant-garde can be committed to a 'technical efficiency' and an 'operational effectiveness' ('efficienza tecnica ... efficacia operativa' [14]) that guarantee an impact on all of society's institutions. However, according to Curi, these positive possibilities must be appraised in relation (or in opposition) to the negative outlook of the new avant-garde, with its contention that art cannot 'save humanity' or 'change the world' ('salvare l'uomo ... cambiare il mondo' [14]). Art can no longer be identified with 'the Truth and the Innocence' ('la Verità e l'Innocenza' [14]).

Some of the questions not confronted by Fortini can be framed as follows: Can any form of art escape market forces? How can art play a role within the commodification of all aspects of existence? How can it best put to use its specific tools? Fortini delivers a sermon without addressing these fundamental issues – issues that the new avant-garde not only has incorporated into its awareness of the new historical conditions but has tried to tackle through a significant and intense debate. A simple but effective response to the question of commodification was provided by Eco in an article that appeared in the leftist review *Rinascita*, during the days of the first gathering of Gruppo 63. He wrote:

Il neocapitalismo ha introdotto in un circuito mercantile la protesta d'avanguardia, che quindi non ha più la fisionomia e le funzioni che aveva la protesta delle avanguardie storiche ...; ma il neocapitalismo ha assimilato pacificamente nello stesso circuito mercantile anche tutta l'arte che pretende di esprimere una protesta non formalistica ma rivoluzionaria. ('Per una indagine sulla situazione culturale,' (*Rinascita*, 5 and 12 October 1963; reprinted in R. Barilli and A. Guglielmi, ed., *Gruppo 63: critica e teoria* [Milan: Feltrinelli 1976], 299)

Neo-capitalism has placed the avant-garde's protest in a mercantile circuit, and thus it no longer possesses the features and the functions of the historical avant-gardes ...; but neo-capitalism has peacefully co-opted, in the same mercantile circuit, also all the art that claims to express a protest not in a formal but in a [direct] revolutionary fashion.

In the same article, Eco pointed out a few other questionable aspects of traditional Marxist ideology. According to him, Maxism is often imbued with humanistic paradigms that produce a biased view of the attributes with which a real humanity should be identified. These prejudices are then transposed to the arts and their functions. The result is a form of 'vulgar Marxism' ('marxismo volgare') that expresses a world-view instead of developing a critical method. As well, Eco questions the priority that traditional Marxism attached to the economic base. Art, as a superstructure, follows its own specific dialectics of forms that do not necessarily correspond to historical developments or to economic conditions in a given society. In this perspective, a condemnation of the new avant-garde based on the commodification of its artistic products – as exemplified by Fortini – becomes not only irrelevant but absolutely groundless. If we assign to any art form (not only avant-garde art) a specific function, then it must follow that a relative autonomy from the economic base is necessary.

Another writer, Alberto Moravia, also made this allegation that there was an intrinsic relationship between the new avant-garde and neo-capitalism. In an interview with the magazine *L'Espresso* a few days following the first meeting of Gruppo 63,[45] Moravia described the papers presented in Palermo – as already mentioned, he was present at the gathering – as 'neo-formalist' rather than 'new avant-gardist.' This formalist literature represents, in his view, 'the logical superstructure of the neo-capitalist structure, in the same way as the old formalism of the Fascist period was the logical superstructure of the paleo-capitalist structure' ('logica sovrastruttura della struttura neocapitalistica, allo stesso modo che il vecchio formalismo del ventennio fascista era la logica sovrastruttura della struttura paleocapitalista' [151]). Moravia does not say how works that do not belong to the new avant-garde avoid being expressions of the neo-capitalist structure. Moreover, his vague generalizations lead to obvious contradictions when he claims that the texts of the new avant-garde art are 'prefabricated, planned, programmed' ('prefabbricata, pianificata' programmata, [151]) in that they are based on pregiven literary theories. He compares this deficiency to traditional art, which can be divided, according to Moravia, between that which contains the awareness of Marx and Freud and that which does not. The reasons why Marxist or Freudian theories (which Moravia employed throughout his own narrative work) are not to be considered theoretical grids that determine the nature of creative work are not addressed by Moravia. What he finds intolerable about the young new writers is that they are so concerned with form. For him, questions of form are irrelevant. If they are not treated that way, they are nothing but a demonstration of cultural decadence.

The issue of form as related to the new avant-garde is specifically addressed by Moravia in his article 'Illegibilità e potere' (Illegibility and Power [1967]). The formalist concerns of the new avant-garde and its claim that conventional modes of writing are in crisis is interpreted by Moravia as a deliberate attempt to produce illegible texts. New avant-garde writers pursue illegibility, he states, because they have realized that this kind of writing is marketable. Insatiably looking for new products, the consumer market presents avant-garde texts as fashionable and up-to-date. These texts are surrounded, according to Moravia, by the idea that the illegibility is only temporary. What is illegible today (or legible to the very few) will be legible to most in the future. Moravia then draws a dubious and far-fetched parallelism between the 'political illegibility' ('illegibilità politica' [7]) of totalitarian regimes (Hitler and Mussolini are presented as two cases in point) and literary illegibility. In his view, they both share the same objective: power. The incomprehensibility of the texts implicitly becomes a form of 'oppression' ('sopraffazione' [8]) of the masses, who are made to feel inferior because they are unable to understand at least in the present – what is transparent to the superior writer or to the very few adepts. For Moravia, furthermore, illegibility and power reveal not only an elitist posture but even signs of madness. The avant-garde adopts 'madness' ('follia' [11]) as a method, and, in Moravia's view, there is nothing more easily imitable.

These sweeping observations are neither adequately elaborated nor substantiated by a concrete analysis of the texts. Moravia ends up looking like a rather conservative writer who sees his literary models threatened by young rebels and struggles to protect his turf. He confuses the questioning of standard communicative modes with illegibility, critical provocation with elitism and intellectual power.

As already discussed, every avant-garde movement, to use Barilli's term, is eventually 'normalized.' There is a constant dialectics between innovation and tradition, transgression and norm. Avant-garde art is gradually codified and comes to build its own tradition – its otherness is incorporated into forms and perceptions viewed as standard. This issue was raised on various occasions by Gruppo 63. At the third gathering in 1965, devoted exclusively to the experimental novel, Eco synthesizes the question in a straightforward manner. He declares:

Ogni avanguardia aspira alla tradizione; sarebbe pazzesco se un autore di avanguardia scrivesse per non essere mai, mai, mai capito: scrive invece per rompere una situazione, per comunicare qualcosa di diverso. L'avanguardia 'riesce' quando crea la propria tradizione. (N. Balestrini, ed., *Gruppo 63: il romanzo sperimentale* [Milan, Feltrinelli 1966], 74–5)

Every avant-garde aspires towards tradition; it would be insane if an avant-garde author wrote in order to never, never be understood: instead, he writes to break with a situation, to communicate something different. The avant-garde 'succeeds' when it creates its own tradition.

Moravia made another blunt attack on Gruppo 63 in an article that also appeared in *Nuovi argomenti*, entitled 'Metavanguardia e manierismo' (Metaavant-garde and Mannerism [1967]). Here, Moravia stresses that the historical avant-garde displays a 'morbid sentiment of death' ('sentimento morboso di morte' [6]) because its aim is to destroy art in the same way as 'mortal disease' ('malattia mortale' [6]) had struck European History. Whereas the first avant-garde had expressed a self-destructive, suicidal attitude, the new avant-garde represents a critical rethinking of its precursor. Contemporary culture is witnessing not only the appearance of the 'metatheatre' or the *metaroman* but also the formation of a fabricated avant-garde that coldly reflects on the real avant-garde. In other words, the current movement is a 'metaavant-garde.' Moravia is clever in identifying a major shift in literature towards self-reflexivity (the examples of Butor and Robbe-Grillet are provided), but he is unable to evaluate fully the underlying causes and objectives. For Moravia, because the new literature essentially consists of 'revisiting critically the literature of the past' ('[la] letteratura del passato rivisitata criticamente' [7]), it is a gratuitous form of 'mannerism.' In this sense, he regards Sanguineti's poetry as a manneristic remake of Ezra Pound's works. It follows that, by producing literary texts that imitate other literary texts, the new avant-garde has lost the possibility of imitating reality (the latter is defined as a 'natural object' ('oggetto naturale') and the former, namely the literary text, as an 'artificial object' ('oggetto artificiale' [7]). In fact, Moravia states:

> La polemica della neoavanguardia contro il naturalismo in realtà è una polemica contro la 'natura' cioè contro il rapporto diretto, immediato dell'artista con il reale. (6)

> The new avant-garde's controversy against Naturalism is in actuality a controversy against 'nature,' that is, against the direct, immediate rapport that the artist has with reality.

Moravia grounds his assertions on two questionable assumptions: that nature exists independently of culture, and that the tools employed by the artist are able to transfer the real into the art object. He does not take into consideration the fact that, in the world of art, a change of forms or a critical reflection on its tools can alter the perception of what is defined as real. Moravia's canon is essentially limited to Naturalism and it condemns any artistic solution that does not comply with its dictates.

Pier Paolo Pasolini, in a number of articles, launched the most polemical assaults on the new avant-garde. Two of these articles are particularly significant: 'Nuove questioni linguistiche' (New Linguistic Questions) and 'La fine dell'avanguardia' (The End of the Avant-garde).[46] In the first, Pasolini claims that the new avant-garde is fully integrated in the economic and social perspectives of the times and thus presents no real signs of subversion. Its linguistic protest results in the destruction of all meaning and in so doing, rather than constituting a threat to the system, contributes to the production of a 'cultural void' (12) ('vuoto culturale' [14]). He writes:

> Le avanguardie di oggi conducono la loro azione antilinguistica da una base non letteraria, ma linguistica: non usano gli strumenti sovvertitori della letteratura per sconvolgere e demistificare la lingua: ma si pongono

in un punto linguistico zero per ridurre a zero la lingua, e quindi i valori. La loro non è una protesta contro la tradizione ma contro il Significato: i luoghi da distruggere non sono gli stilemi, ma i semantemi ... il luogo zero delle avanguardie corrisponde a un reale momento zero della cultura e della storia, i luoghi da dove la letteratura si difende non hanno più nessuna corrispondenza con una realtà che si sta modificando. (*EE* 14)

The avant-garde groups of today conduct their antilinguistic action from a base that is no longer literary but linguistic: they don't use the subversive instruments of literature in order to throw language into confusion and demystify it, but they set themselves at a linguistic zero point in order to reduce language – and thus values – to zero. Theirs is not a protest against tradition but against Meaning: the places they destroy are not stylistic but sematic units ... the zero point of the avant-garde movements corresponds to the zero point of culture and history; the positions from which literature defends itself no longer have any correspondence with a reality that is in the process of changing. (*HE* 11)]

It is clear that Pasolini, like other detractors of the new avant-garde, does not assign much consequence to the formal activity of the literary process. Rather, he seems to hold a somewhat debatable idea of the stylistic and semantic properties of literary language. It is as if, for Pasolini, they are two different and unrelated components of literariness. As indicated by the two terms 'passion' and 'ideology,' used as the title of one of his best known theoretical volumes (*Passione e ideologia* [Passion and Ideology]), literature, for Pasolini, is an activity that is antecedent to the writing process. Indeed, the stylistic activity seems essentially divorced from that of the signifieds. It is the passions, the sentiments, and the ideological orientation that constitute for him the core of literature. Forms are neutral containers in which those elements are poured. Conceivably, those same passions and sentiments can be communicated through an essay or a newspaper article, thereby reaching a larger audience and being more useful from a social perspective. Pasolini's positions are dictated by his undialectical conception of signifiers and signifieds. (This is diametrically opposed to Sanguineti's dialectics of language and ideology.) The primacy of the signifiers of the new avant-garde is misread by Pasolini as a cultural aberration. Pasolini gives no credit to a revolution of forms. In fact, as underlined in the first chapter, the language of his own poetry does not depart from tradition (a nineteenth-century poet like Giovanni Pascoli, on whom Pasolini wrote his university thesis, comes to mind), mediated by the linguistic models of *Verismo* and neorealism in which he infuses some of the whining vein of the 'Crepuscular' poets of the turn of the century, without any of their counteracting irony. However, as will be discussed, Pasolini's narcissism is at the centre of his diatribe against the new avant-garde. This is transparent in the second article.

In 'The End of the Avant-garde,' Pasolini laments the crisis of Marxism, the 'decline of ideology,' and the levelling effects of industrialization, all of which, in tandem with other factors, have created a 'transnational' and 'transclassist' social and linguistic condition. This, together with the collapse of all forms of social and cultural commitment on behalf of the bourgeois class, has put a stop to socio-political confrontation and expressions of difference. Undoubtedly, Pasolini offers here an insightful description of societies under late capitalism. Indeed, Pasolini shows enormous foresight in identifying dominant social realities. The problems arise with his evaluation of literature and its functions. For Pasolini, the writers of the new avant-garde are ineffectual 'little friars' (*HE* 126) ('abatini' [*EE* 127]) whose linguistic protest is futile and compromised with the social system. Pasolini accuses the new avant-garde of practising a 'dissociation' between life and literature, since it promotes a conflict with the linguistic modalities of the bourgeoisie that is solely a literary posture and does not attack the rot of that social class. Furthermore, Pasolini insists, the demolition of language is a form of suicide. The 'destruction' of language is translated into the 'self-destruction' of the poet. He writes:

> Ora, ogni distruzione e sostanzialmente un'autodistruzione ...: distruggendo i valori sociali (letterari) della lingua, distruggendo la forza significativa e metaforica della parola, distruggendo infine la propria scrittura o la propria tentazione di scrittura – il poeta distrugge se stesso ..., e diventa insignificante come attore di una semplice e assoluta protesta. (*EE* 129)

> Now, every destruction is essentially a self-destruction ...: by destroying the social (literary) values of the language, destroying the significative and metaphoric force of the word, finally destroying his own writing or his own temptation to write – the poet destroys himself ... and also becomes insignificant as an actor [protagonist] of a simple and absolute protesti (*HE* 128)

What Pasolini fears most is a form of literature that keeps the 'I' at bay. For him, literature is a narcissistic space in which the 'I' contemplates itself. The 'I' can even transform social and political issues into a platform from which to secure its identity. Indeed, the epic intent of his poetry is constantly undermined by the overwhelming presence of the autobiographical.[47] That the 'I' is at the centre of Pasolini's interests is explicitly revealed when he comments on Sanguineti's poetry. He asks himself: 'But what do I know about the author of that text? Ah, here, absolutely nothing' (*HE* 130) ('Ma cosa vengo a sapere dell'autore di quel testo? Ah, qui, assolutamente nulla' [*EE* 131]). Pasolini mistakes the apparently impersonal technique of assemblage with the disappearance of the 'I.' What is the relationship between language and subjectivity? How can subjectivity exist within an alienated linguistic code and a worn-out literary tradition? Does literature simply anchor conquered states of consciousness to written words? To state the matter differently: Is meaning an *a priori* realization simply transferred to the page? Astonishingly, Pasolini does not pose any of these fundamental questions. He merits all our respect for having passionately pondered the effects of homogenization and repression under late capitalism, but he is unable to problematicize this condition within a literary context. Pasolini possesses a rather dubious conception of the relationship between art and representation. Let us examine the following statement:

> Il cinema è una lingua ... una lingua che costringe ad allargare la nozione di lingua. Non è un sistema simbolico, arbitrario e convenzionale ... Il cinema non evoca la realtà, come la lingua letteraria; non copia la realtà, come la pittura; non mima la realtà, come il teatro. Il cinema *riproduce* la realtà: immagine e suono! ... Il cinema esprime la realtà con la realtà ... Altro che fare la 'semiologia del cinema': *è la semiologia della realtà che bisogna fare!* ... Il cinema ci fornisce dunque 'una semiologia in natura della realtà.' Perché ho fatto tutto questo stravagante discorso. Perché mi ci è voluto il cinema per capire una cosa enormemente semplice, ma che nessun letterato sa. Che la realtà si esprime da sola; e che la letteratura non è altro che un mezzo per mettere in condizione la realtà di esprimersi da sola *quando non è fisicamente presente*. Cioè la poesia non è che una evocazione, e ciò che conta è la realtà evocata che parla da sola al lettore, come ha parlato da sola all'autore. (*EE* 135, 137)

Cinema is a language ... which compels the enlargement of the concept of language. It is not a symbolic, arbitrary, and conventional system ... Cinema does not evoke reality, as literary language does; it does not copy reality, as painting does; it does not mime reality, as drama does. Cinema *reproduces* reality, image and sound! ... Cinema expresses reality with reality ... Something other than making the 'semiology of cinema.' *It is the semiology of reality that must be made!* ... Cinema thus furnishes us with 'a semiology of reality in nature.' Why have I made this extravagant speech? Because cinema was necessary for me to understand an enormously simple thing which, however, no man of letters knows. That reality expresses itself with itself, and that literature is nothing more than a means of allowing reality to express itself with itself *when it isn't physically present*. That is, poetry is not only an evocation, and what counts is the reality evoked, which alone speaks to the reader, as it spoke alone to the author. (*HE* 133, 135)

Cinema cannot be regarded as a semiotic system? Cinematic iconic signs are true reproductions of raw reality? (Not to speak of painting seen only as a copy of reality.) The intent here is not to provide a detailed critique of Pasolini's film theory, but it must be emphasized that he fails to take into consideration the syntagmatic articulation of cinematic images and thus the role of montage as an adulterating technique of reality. Pasolini commits the imprudence of not separating cultural conventions ('secondary modelling systems,' to use Yury Lotman's definition of art objects)[48] from natural objects. He does not investigate adequately the complex relationship between a signifier and a signified, a signified and a referent. Pasolini indirectly questions the work on the semiotics of film being done in those years by Christian Metz, but without developing an overall theory of cinematic language.[49] He refuses to acknowledge Saussurean and semiotic notions of the sign – or Marshall McLuhan's analysis of media – and remains entangled in somewhat unsuspecting concepts on the relationship between signifiers and reality.[50]

Pasolini's statements on literature are equally dubious. That literature is a medium to represent a physically absent reality – a simple reproduction of reality – is indeed a questionable tenet. One point must be stressed: what separates Pasolini's stances from those of the new avant-garde is not so much literary taste as significant cultural perspective. The new avant-garde elaborates its debate on literature through phenomenology, structuralism, neo-Marxism, new physics, information theory, and aesthetic models adopted from serial music or visual arts, whereas Pasolini shows a more restricted scope of interests.

He certainly possessed acute sociological and anthropological anten-
nae, but they were not sufficient to enable him to make a radical and
innovative contribution to literary debate. He often resorts to insults as
a way of scoring points, as when he writes that the authors of the new
avant-garde are 'young and petulant idiots' who speak about 'the anti-
novel as if they were speaking about Parma prosciutto' (*HE* 134) ('gio-
vanotti cretini e petulanti parl[ano] di antiromanzo come se parlassero
di prosciutto di Parma' [*EE* 136]).

Essentially Pasolini confronts Gruppo 63 with outdated principles of
literature and its functions. To put it succinctly, he is unable to engage
in a fruitful exchange on the specificity of literariness and on the relationship between the autonomous and heteronomous levels of the literary activity. Pasolini's stance in favour of a literature oriented towards
sociological analyses, his embrace of aesthetic principles based on representation, and his assigning of a cognitive function to literature cannot but clash with the ideas of the postmodern camp of the new avant-
garde. However, Pasolini refuses to recognize the significance of its
modernist wing – and of Sanguineti in particular, against whom he
launches his most poisonous attacks.[51] The worse comes when he
accuses all the members of Gruppo 63 of being 'petit-bourgeois' (*HE*
130) ('piccolo-borghesi' [*EE* 133]). This charge sounds somewhat amus-
ing if we consider many traits of Pasolini's literary and filmic production. In fact, much in tune with the decadent tradition of Gabriele
D'Annunzio, he continues the bourgeois process of the aestheticization
of life – in his case, of the lower classes in particular. As mentioned in
the first chapter, Pasolini aestheticizes and mythologizes the peasants'
and subproletarians' adversities, transforming them in idyllic and ero-
ticized portraits of a vanishing world. His nostalgic longing for a pre-
industrial and pre-bourgeois society tints his anticapitalism with rather
romantic overtones.[52] The sad story Pasolini refuses to acknowledge is
that all of literature, as we have known it for centuries, is a bourgeois
institution formed by bourgeois men and women. The project of the
avant-garde and of the new avant-garde is that of a revolt waged from
within the institution. Pasolini predicts the end of the new avant-garde,
but for the wrong reasons. In his view, it had to come to an end because
its dissent was strictly verbal, a futile 'antiliterary protest' that makes
use of harmless 'paper bombs.'

However, when students revolted in 1968 (joined by workers, in
1969, during the so-called 'Hot Autumn'), they saw Gruppo 63 as their
ally. The new avant-garde revolted against literary order and the stu-

dents against social order. For many left-wing militants, *Quindici*, the journal of the new avant-garde, soon became the platform from which to spread the project of the revolution. The postmodern camp interpreted this alliance as the end of its literary projects, while the modernists saw it as an opportunity to join forces with the revolution. The editorial board of the journal became so polarized on this issue that all attempts at reconciliation proved futile. In August 1969 the journal published its last issue and with its disappearance Gruppo 63 died as well. However, as Eco has claimed, it was more a suicide than a death.[53] The creation of a bridge between literary activity and subversive praxis turned out to be an impossible proposition.[54] If it is undeniable that literature is a unique space for promoting cultural critique, it is equally true that aesthetic projects can neither compensate for the realities of the world nor take the place of direct political action in changing our social condition.[55]

3 The Gestural and Schizoid Language of Alfredo Giuliani

The most striking feature of Alfredo Giuliani's poetry is the search for a language rid of sentimental and autobiographical tones.[1] Giuliani strives to challenge a whole tradition that for centuries has identified the primary source of poetic communication with the inner activities of the 'I.' To put it synthetically, his goal to dislodge the centrality of the 'I' coincides with his urgent quest for a radically anticonventional poetic language. This project began during the years of Giuliani's involvement with *Il Verri* and came to maturity with his edition of *I Novissimi*. It is important to underline, however, that Giuliani revealed a strong desire for innovation even before the period of his involvement with that review, a desire expressed most clearly in his first poetry collection, *Il cuore zoppo* (The Lame Heart [Varese: Magenta, 1955]).[2]

In fact, in spite of the presence of an analogical language reminiscent of the Hermetic tradition, Giuliani's first collection already discloses his ambition to venture outside the poetic forms of Italian tradition. He finds much inspiration in the image-oriented poetry of Dylan Thomas. This early stage of Giuliani's poetry is pervaded by sudden explosions of images and hallucinatory symbols, combined with a visual and sensuous language that owes its debt to the Welsh poet. Thomas's ambiguous diction and transfiguration of reality into fantastic, chromatic images are adapted by Giuliani with a vital tension that oscillates between adolescent vigour and menacing anticipations of death ('In my blood the woods resurge / The blackberry the strawberry the bramble / For the boys' sweet pillage ... My root urges under the pavement / It lauds the wind nurturing walls and leaves / For my climbing heart' [trans. Vittoria Bradshaw, 1971]) ('Nel mio sangue risuscitano i boschi / La mora la fragola la spina / Per il dolce saccheggio dei ragazzi ... La mia radice urge sotto l'asfalto / Loda il vento che nutre muri e foglie / Al rampicante cuore).

As in Thomas's poetry, the 'I' in Giuliani's work is often assimilated into the life of the objects, thus deterring direct self-analyses. In poems such as 'Resurrezione dopo la pioggia' (Resurrection after the Rain) and 'Grigie radure s'accendono' (Grey Clearings Light up), emotional or introspective statements are constantly averted by the narration of events or by the pervasive presence of the landscape ('It was in the calm resurrection after the rain / the asphalt reflected all our stains / a long goodbye flew like an acrobat' [*I Nov*, 147]) ('Fu nella calma della resurrezione dopo la pioggia / l'asfalto rifletteva tutte le nostre macchie / un lungo addio volò come un acrobata [*VN*, 19]); ('Work underway behind the fence keeps moving / With the churning of cement-mixers, pouring with asphalt, / Shaving the sky with electric saws; / The silent tower is razed to the ground' [*I Nov*, 149]) ('Il lavoro è già dietro lo steccato, avanza / Col tonfo delle betoniere, cola con gli asfalti / Spela il cielo con la sega elettrica; / Al suolo è rasa la muta torre' [*IN*, 78]).

Two poems, 'I giorni aggrappati alla città' (The Days Clinging to the City) and 'Compleanno' (Birthday), are particularly significant for their anticipation of a number of issues around which will revolve Giuliani's poetic search. In the first, a pervading awareness of futility and a sense of anxiety ('The days clinging to the city and disinherited, / the empty furnace blasts the dead slag' ('I giorni aggrappati alla città e diseredati, / la vuota fornace ribrucia scorie morte') are juxtaposed to reflections on language and poetic communication ('My lands grazed / by deadly silence, I see my words line up / beside the final hour of the day harangued by sails, / and summon me again' [*I Nov*, 147]) ('Io vedo le mie parole, / le mie terre brucate dal silenzio mortale / schierarsi / lungo l'ultima ora del giorno tormentato di vele, / e rievocarmi' [*VN*, 27]). In the second poem, allusions to linguistic and mental disintegration, or to the senselessness of everyday communication, announce pivotal aspects of Giuliani's future poetry ('When you say   the mind goes to pieces, life / is sad with prattle ... the tongue pressed between a wall and a coin // Behind the syllables the Enemy slashes ... in my thoughts I will wring out a road / to the toughest Spring' [*I Nov*, 153]) ('Quando dici: – la mente si disfà, la vita / è triste di ciarle / ... // la lingua premuta tra un muro e una moneta. / Sempre dietro le sillabe che il nemico lacera / ... / dei miei pensieri torcerò una strada / fino alla più ardua primavera' [*VN*, 29]).

As pointed out in chapter 1, in the mid-1950s, following the publication of *Il cuore zoppo* (The Lame Heart), Giuliani developed a phenomenological orientation that would eventually lead to the poetics of the 'reduction of the I' and 'schizomorphism.' During this period, he paid close attention to poets like Eliot, Pound, and Olson. Giuliani must have these poets in mind when he remarks that the objective of his poetry is 'to allow thoughts to emerge visibly, like things, not as discursive topics' (*I Nov* 31) ('far diventare i pensieri visibili come cose, non quali argomenti' [*IN* 25]). He is also attracted to the unconventional traits of a writer such as Alfred Jarry, whose farcical and grotesque theatrical language undoubtedly played a role in stimulating a search for new poetic solutions.[3] The artistic experiences of the first avant-garde (Dadaism and Surrealism in particular), as well as coeval developments in the fields of figurative arts and music (see chapter 1), contributed in guiding Giuliani towards the rejection of established canons of lyricism and of ordinary poetic language and structures.

He begins to privilege a schizoid and paranoid language that, on the one hand, gives voice to the senselessness and the dementedness of the quotidian, and, on the other, provides new formal possibilities. Pathological language disrupts rational associations or logical linguistic sequences and performs the function of exploring an alternative verbal space. Mental and linguistic derangements are constructed, in a methodical fashion,[4] with the intent of fracturing the centrality of the 'I' and of foregrounding imaginary and hallucinatory events, occasionally extracted from the repertory of unconscious symbology and archetypes.

In *Povera Juliet e altre poesie* (Poor Juliet and Other Poems [Milan: Feltrinelli, 1965]), Giuliani starts to shatter the monologic structure of traditional lyricism by offering a montage of voices, personas, and characters who often seem to put in motion a chain of absurdities and delusions. It is as if he is searching for meaning through an investigation of the senseless. Indeed, Giuliani's goal is to dissociate and disintegrate the 'I' so that deviant views of the world can emerge. He strives to open up poetic spaces not colonized by hegemonic linguistic communication. In its most radical moments, this poetry admits no interdictions. It is a revolt against institutionalized language with its functional and utilitarian practices.[5] As a linguistic experience of limits, bordering on pathological patterns and structures, Giuliani's work is close to George Bataille's concept of poetry as a medium of subversion and violation. Poetry has to express a silenced language, one consisting of culturally prohibited words.[6] In this respect, some of Giuliani poetic practices can be seen as an enactment of what psychologist Lev Vygotsky defines as 'interior language' (limited to the individual), in contrast to 'exterior language' (used as a social medium). With reference to this principle, Giuliani comments that poetry can be seen as 'the laboratory of the words' senses and nonsenses ... a place where signs and meanings are manipulated, invented, both consciously and unconsciously' ('il laboratorio dei sensi e dei nonsensi delle parole ... il luogo dove i segni e i significati vengono manipolati, inventati, consciamente e inconsciamente').[7]

The poetic imagination has to be free of established hierarchies. It does not follow preconceived or preordered thoughts. Poetry stems from the process of writing, from the internal vitality of language, and is capable of unfolding hypnagogic visions suspended in a state between dream and waking:

> Così la sera ci lascia con le sue zampe morbide sul terriccio degli insepolti
> e il sostrato assoluto e relativo si costituisce al passaggio di toni violacei
> in bruni sempre più somiglianti alla cellula originaria del giudizio (ti).
> Sgorgano tutti i pensieri disidentificati dalla coniugazione del giorno, la
> sonata in fa, l'acqua alle piante, la vacca bruca dietro i vetri ('Il Professor
>   PI esperisce la logica metasessuale,' *Povera Juliet, VN*, 57)

> So the evening leaves us with its soft paws on the peat of the unburied /
> and the absolute and the relative substratum is constituted at the changing of violet-like tones / in brown ones looking more and more like the original cell of judgment (ti). / All thoughts gush out dis-identified by the conjugation of the day, the / sonata in F major, water the plants, the cow that grazes behind the glass. (Professor PI Practices the Metasexual Logic)

Particularly significant are the clusters of meaning generated by recurrent homophonic devices. It seems that the contiguity of the terms is solely determined by phonetic equivalences. An example is the poem 'Azzurro pari venerdì' (Friday, You Look Blue). In this case, the homophony enters into conflict – in a rather provocative fashion – with conspicuous semantic antitheses and contradictions. The reader is faced with a sense of ambiguity that, on the one hand, fosters a dynamic hermeneutic effort and, on the other, hinders the handing down of ready-packaged and easily digestible world-views. Here are a few lines of the poem:

E lo psichiatra disse: (a proposito del sogno): l'immagine
del bambino con la merda in mano è il mondo
largo luminoso vuoto stretto oscuro colmo elevato profondo
mobile impuro immobile sudicio contagioso disgustante
accogliente minaccioso illimitato doloroso
velenoso vischioso decomposto penetrante
fisiognomico ignominioso numinoso è il mondo
sanguinoso tagliente spermatico molle terrificante
dissipante vertiginoso appropriante metamorfico (*VN*, 50)

And the psychiatrist said: (in reference to my dream): the image / of the baby with shit in his hand is the world / vast luminous empty narrow dark overflowing elevated profound / mobile impure immobile filthy contagious disgusting / accommodating menacing boundless painful / venomous viscous rotten penetrating / the word is physiognomical ignominious numinous / bloody sharp spermatic soft terrifying / dissipating vertiginous adaptive metaphoric. (Trans. Lawrence R. Smith, *The New Italian Poetry* [Los Angeles: University of California Press, 1981], 323)

The semantic displacements and the agitated rhythms of this poetry produce raving, delirious effects that, when examined closely, reveal a state of tension and anxiety. This is clear in a poem such as 'Il vecchio' (The Old Man) where an overwhelming sense of dread obscures any attempt of the character to find probable or rational solutions:

Barcolla nella ruota che invecchia l'aria,
velocemente, i polsi lenti incespicano ...

Siamo davvero pazzi di paura. Se il cielo esagera,
sottrai la gabbia alla plumbea alleanza.

Cicli s'annientano contro una ragione ostile.
Evadi, pensa la luna che si strofina il dorso
ai ruscelli primaverili. In Cina, sai, i cani,
è quasi l'ora di cena, sì, li frollano vivi. (*VN*, 49)

He staggers on the wheel that ages the air, / quickly, his slow pulse stumbles / ... / We are truly wild with fear. If the sky exaggerates, / remove the cage from the laden alliance. // Cycles clash and die against hostile reason. / Escape, think the moon rubbing its back / on the brooks of spring. In China, you know, the dogs, / yes, it's almost suppertime, they age them alive. (*I Nov*, 161, 163)

The existential agitation and malaise of the characters or personas (a sort of neurotic state of the mind torn between fears and desires) becomes infused with a sense of social discontent, creating a correlation between psychological and historical conditions. A case in point is the poem 'È dopo' (It's After), where Giuliani expresses, rather transparently, a cultural and ideological antagonism towards the state of void and the contradictions ('sorrowful suspension') in which the individual and the social psyche seem to be engulfed:

I latrati, che vogliono dire? nella bruma,
non abbiamo intenzione, è l'insorgenza
del caso, quella vecchia infingarda sa
la cosa, ha cessato di essere privata, la
tua paura legge col cavo dell'occhio, la
tua paraforia intende nel cerebro vuoto.
Ma io-qui-ora, dolorosa sospensione, so (*VN*, 47)

What's this barking supposed to mean? in the mist, / we have no intention, it's the surging / of fate, that sluggish old dame knows / something, she's stopped being private, she / reads your fear with the eye-socket, / understands your paraphoria in her empty cerebrum. / But me-here-now, sorrowful suspension, I know (*I Nov*, 175)

The sclerotic social condition is marked by abnormal perceptions ('paraphoria') and a sense of unreality ('simulacra'), to which Giuliani opposes, as an active agent, the regenerating effects of a storm – an emblematic vision embodying the desire for difference and utopia ('Different logic'; 'utopia is truer / than nostalgia' [*I Nov*, 177, 179]) ('Altra logica'; 'utopia è più vera / della nostalgia' [*VN*, 47–8]). Another significant text centred on social decay is 'Altrimenti non si spiega' (*VN*, 51–2) (Otherwise You Cannot Explain It), where the presence of worms and insects, associated with the putrefaction of corpses, becomes emblematic of a historical situation – disgust with bourgeois existence, social hatred, war, violence. In this respect, Giuliani's poetry is marked by two interrelated conditions: a fragmented and repressed personal identity, and an alienated, mystifying collective reality that needs to be brought to consciousness through the process of writing. In the introduction to the Novissimi, referring to his own poetry, Giuliani affirms:

> Io non voglio esprimere me stesso, ma l'esperienza che il 'me stesso' fa rispecchiando e anche *resistendo* al rispecchiamento, determinandosi *sopra* la determinazione storica. L'esperienza non è il risultato, è biografia della coscienza. (*IN*, 25)

> I don't want to express myself, but rather the experience 'My self' undergoes in reflecting and also *withstanding* reflection, determining itself *over* and *above* historical determination. Experience is not the result, it is the biography of consciousness. (*I Nov*, 31)

Through constant textual fragmentation, which, with its mobile and fluid construction, precludes any cohesion or progression of discourse, Giuliani embarks on a linguistic and existential journey totally guided by the desire to explore the inner movements of language. However, paradoxically, the poet soon realizes that the proliferation of images without a beginning or end, the vertiginous verbal adventure, is a constant reminder of the impossibility of arresting the flux, of finding reassuring linguistic crystallizations. Language's vitality paradoxically seems to coincide with its own annihilation. The endless movement from one image to another cannot but effect the dissolution of any possible unity. (The linguistic flux with its effects of instability coincides with the instability of the subject and identity.) A number of texts, such as 'La cara contraddizione' (The Dear Contradiction), present a poetry torn between presence and absence, voice and silence, inevitably divided between the search for an authentic reality free from a priori schemes of perception and the unsurmountable mediation of language. Closed unto itself, within its tautological movements, language runs the risk of being intransitive, dangerously sliding towards its own nothingness:

> Molti nomi ha la terra. Pochi suoni
> colmano l'ora, traboccano per dire
> alla viva quiete moto rivelazione
> di semi e figure che sùbito abbandoni.
>
> Parola fu in origine voce dell'assente;
> ne tu l'ignori che, l'ombra capovolta,

scendi per l'aria ferita dal rompito dei motori
e tumultuare ascolti dal muto frangente ...

Viene l'enorme silenzio da sorpassare,
inevidenza assoluta s'accende nei dilegui.
Non sapere dove la svolta conduce
è il modo buono di pensare.

Vagabonda scarabocchia la terra,
chi ha temprato la punta della mente?
La carta vetrata dei giochi, l'adulto coltello
che sbucciò l'evidenza dal niente. (*VN*, 36–7)

Many names hathe the earth. A few sounds slake / the hour and overflow
to bespeak / the living quiet movement revelation / of seeds and figures
you instantly forsake. // In the beginning word was the voice of
absence; / nor with shadow turned do you pretend not / to descend
through air wounded by coughing motors / to hear rioting from a reef of
silence / ... / Up looms the huge silence to ring, / absolute lack of evidence lights up in trickles. / Not knowing where the turn may lead / is the
best way to think. // Oh earth, you vagabond scribble, / who sharpened
the point for the mind? / The toy sandpaper, the adult knife / that peeled
the evidence from nil. (*I Nov*, 143, 145)[8]

Vitalistic and nihilistic at the same time, this stage of Giuliani's
poetry hopelessly attempts to reconcile word and silence, life and
death. In search of a transparent contact with the world, he also
explores the dimension of the animal instincts, of the regression to a
precognitive state which could provide access to a direct, primordial
awareness. The recurrent references to the natural state of animal realities, in poems such as 'Penuria e fervore' (Penury and Fervour), 'È
dopo' (It's After), and especially 'Predilezioni' (Predilections), with its
lycanthropic images, reveal Giuliani's desire to recover a genuine
vitality, a liberating and immediate experience of the world:

Prendi il nero del silenzio, tanto parlare
disinvoglia la nuca, in sé pupilla, palato
di cane, oppure pensa le notti che risbuca
nel gelo il firmamento dei gatti, amore. (*VN*, 39)

Take the black of silence, such talking / dissuades the eye behind the neck, palate / of dog, or else think the nights the firmament / of cats popping out of the cold, my love. (*I Nov*, 159)

In phenomenological terms, Giuliani's poetry intends to unfold the immediate givens of consciousness, a state of 'sympathy' with externality, or, to use Minkowski's words, a 'lived syntony' with the world (70). However, there is no escape from the prison of language and from the alienating condition of existence: in the miserable struggle 'there is no cure for our bad directions, / for the stench of roses ... and there is no honour, no calm, no truce' ('Non c'è rimedio a questi nostri disguidi, / al lezzo delle rose ... e non c'è onore, né calma, né tregua').

Beginning with 'Prosa' (Prose) and 'I mimi mescolati' (Mixed Mimes), Giuliani enters a new phase, experimenting with poetry constructed as collages of everyday dialogues. Here are a few lines from the first poem:

> particolarmente intensa delle regole elementari, la prescrizione è
>   contenuta
> nel prodotto (è un nitrito, potrebbe essere), se ne sta ai giardini a leggere
> l'Ordine Pubblico o Il Cavallo. Inutile lamentarsi. Avrà la pensione
>   (*VN*, 53)

> intense fluxion of elementary rules, the prescription is contained / inside the product (it's whinnying, could be) he's in the gardens reading / the Ordine Pubblico or Il Cavallo. No use complaining. He'll have his pension (*I Nov*, 165)

Held together only by the metrical and rhythmical order of the sequences, devoid of any logical semantic articulation, these poems do not simply mirror the reified condition of contemporary language. Through a daring montage of heterogeneous linguistic scraps, Giuliani on the one hand, tries to reduce language to a non-referential, material entity; and, on the other, shows a desire to reactivate its power for creating new possible realities. The attention given to objects in the previous poetry is now radically supplanted by the centrality of the linguistic sign.

These experiments with collage led to *Chi l'avrebbe detto* (Who Would Have Said It) (Turin: Einaudi, 1973), a collection of poems written between 1952 and 1966 and described by Giuliani as 'theatre poetry' ('poesia di teatro'). In texts such as 'Io ho una bella pera, e tu cos'hai?' (I Have a Beautiful Pear, and What Do You Have?) and 'Povera Juliet'

(Poor Juliet), Giulani wants to abolish the representational dimension of theatre in order to reduce the linguistic sign to pure movement, action, gestural invention – not the arbitrary entity that replaces or represents, as a double or as a mirror, objective reality. This is not to say, however, that the self-sufficiency of the poetic performance is irrevocably severed from an outside world. Social neuroses and pathologies are there as a constant backdrop. The aesthetic matrix of this operation includes the theatre of Artaud or the Living Theatre, if not Dadaistic experiments. Here are a few examples of dialogues from 'Povera Juliet':

– scusa, che si fa con l'idea di idee? (ribatte l'onorevole) /
  e lui: portatemi a mangiare: muoio di fame / ... /
– se uno può non nascere, dov'e la verità? / la vecchia che scivola non
  vuol dire marxismo / ... /
– in solitudine / dopo una scelta al buio / vedersi / parlarsi / conoscersi
– ormai si vede dal giardino / un sinistro volo di uccelli / una calza di
  seta / lenzuola
– ghiottoni
– ma c'è dell'altro. (VN, 61, 63)

– excuse me, what does one do with the idea of ideas? (rebuts the member of parliament) / and he: take me to eat: I am starving / ... / – if one can not be born, where is the truth? / the old woman who slips does not mean marxism / ... / – in solitude / after a choice in the dark / to see oneself / to talk to oneself / to know oneself / by now one can see it from the garden / a sinister flight of birds / a silk sock / linens / – gluttons / – but there is more.

In his obsessive search for a verbal sign in its pure state, Giuliani is providing a poetic equivalent of avant-garde music as practised, for instance, by Cage in his experiments with noises, environmental sounds, or sounds of nature. Besides his relationship with avant-garde music, as mentioned in chapter 1, Giuliani came into close contact with a group of Roman artists, including Gastone Novelli, Toti Scialoja, and Achille Perilli, who were pursuing an abstract form of painting based on the medium itself, specifically, on the gestural treatment of pictorial signs adopted as pure signifiers. In a poem titled 'Una conferenza di Jorge Luis Borges' (A Lecture by Jorge Luis Borges), Giuliani carries his attempt so far as to reduce the word to dismembered phonemes, absolute noise:

KRAKUAC.boc.bok.Kuakk.uuus ... bok.KUAKUARS.u
KK.uuu(!!!.....................!!...) uUuuAuau
AuAuUu.boc. **Martin Fierro** / boc.bok.KUAKUAS.UKK.
paisaje / uuUuuuauauauauuuuUUUUU.KUAskkc. **pampa**
(*VN*, 83)

Poems such as 'Invetticoglia' and 'Yé-Yé coglino' which close the
collection, seem to approximate pure invention. In some instances, the
almost total collapse of the referential function of language allows for
an exploration of its internal resources – verbal acrobatics guided
solely by a linguistic excitement that creates puns, double entendres,
neologisms, etymological games, and phonic equivalences of all sorts.
Poetic writing invents its own worlds. Behind the gratuitous, ludic,
and clownish postures lies an intent of linguistic disalienation that,
with its demystifying effects, involves the area of the subject.[9] That is
the case with the latter poem, in which the fragility and splintered
multiplicity of the 'I' (or its disappearance, 'you are nobody') is
presented through a series of puns and linguistic inventions that
defy translations. Here is the first part of 'Yé-Yé coglino,' only in the
original:

> sei uno sei uno sei uno sette con due o sei nessuno
> pinco di menelicche cocuzza schizzetto cecio lupino
> catenella coda ovotinto spolvero scimmio tamburino
> sei uno sei uno dopo e prima o sei nessuno
> barlaccio bìsciola grifo cuccoberlicche rampichino
> muffo muffione paletta misicala callalessa cartoccino. (*VN*, 100)

The joyous carnival of words (which reaches limits of transgression in
'Invetticoglia'),[10] is opposed by Giuliani's critical awareness: just as
poetry cannot become pure animal utterances, so it cannot escape from
culturally predetermined linguistic signs. In 'Le radici dei segni' (The
Roots of the Signs), which opens, as a prologue, both *Povera Juliet* and
Chi l'avrebbe detto, the claim that 'cultures are alphabets' ('le culture
sono alfabeti') reveals the impossibility of going beyond the linguistic
sign, the hiatus that unavoidably marks the distance from an unadul-
terated contact with reality. In fact, the first verse equates the verbal
sign to an abyss: 'All signs are indeed in danger, AAAABBBYSS' ('Come
sono in pericolo tutti i segni, AAAABBBBSSOO'). The chasm provoked by
the sign prevents the experiencing of life in a transparent fashion:

... quasi il ronzio monotono
della matita sui nervi dell'impazienza, e la mano non puoi lasciarla
carezzare la vita, né l'occhio è mai pagato o goduto se non per leggere
e rifare questi tuoi segni, schioccanti a sorsi di forti gradazioni ...
  (*VN*, 96)

almost the monotonous buzzing / of the pencil on the nerves of impa-
tience, and you cannot let / the hand caress life, nor the eye is ever paid
or enjoyed if not / for reading / and redoing these signs of yours, smack-
ing in sips of strong / gradations ...

This poetry displays a conflict that can be examined in terms of the
philosophical positions expressed, on the one hand, by Husserl's phenomenological standpoint and, on the other, by Wittgenstein's lan-
guage-centred orientation. (It is worth noting that the ambivalence, the
antithesis, or the contradiction are recurrent features of Giuliani's
poetry, tied also to the conflicts of neuroses and schizoidism. In a the-
atre-poem, 'Urotropio,' he explicitly writes that 'the necessity for
which the intellect / produces antinomies was discovered by Kant' ['la
necessità per cui l'intelletto / produce antinomie fu scoperta da Kant
(*VN*, 65)]. Giuliani's phenomenological reduction aspires to encounter
the world as a self-given inasmuch as it attempts to access the object
and the flux of the life-world without assumptions and presuppositions. Conversely, in a way close to Wittgenstein's philosophy,
Giuliani perceives the contact with the object as a languageified experience, as a process inseparable from the conceptual frames rooted in the
system of language. Since there is no 'I' that is independent of the
world, there is no 'I' or consciousness independent of language. If reality is framed by language, consciousness inhabits language. Fixing its
gaze on things-in-themselves, poetry finds uneasiness in the realization that they are firmly embedded in linguistic signs.[11]

Giuliani's next collection, *Il tautofono* (The Tautophone), comprises
poems written between 1966 and 1969 (Milan: Feltrinelli, 1969). As the
title suggests – it is a combination of the Greek words *tautó* and *phoné*,
meaning the same sound – the reader enters into a linguistic realm in
which the differentiating elements of language are absent. In a short
preface to the volume, Giuliani points out that *tautofono* represents a
poetic equivalent of the Rorschach Inkblot Test. The inkblots are
replaced by dismembered sentences, amputated narrative sequences
which, in their nonsensical flow, indicate that there is no possibility of

semantic coagulation – there is no possibility of meaning. Unlike the Rorschach Test, however, the projective technique does not allow for absolute free associations. The poet guides the interpretations of these meaningless sounds. In this epos of death and nothingness we witness the total collapse of reality – human identity is no longer possible. In a psychotic delirium, an 'hominicanoid' ('ominicànide') (an anti-hero who cannot be defined as a human) moves in a labyrinth of signs that speak only of the death of all meaning. In Giuliani's hallucinations, the distinctive features of vegetal, animal, or human realities no longer exist. The hominicanoid, in its voyage through spaces populated by 'fizzy corpses' ('cadaveri frizzanti'), 'horrible embryos howling with the tail' ('orribili embrioni con la coda urlanti'), encounters 'hairy grass' ('erba pelosa'), 'nasal vegetation' ('vegetazione nasale'), 'a worm with swollen feet' ('un verme coi piedi gonfi'), and 'tortoise vineyards' ('vigneti di tartaruga'). In a world degraded to a garbage dump full of excrement, a world in which only absurd animalistic rites and onanistic acts are performed, 'nature no longer exists' ('la natura non c'è più' [*VN*, 121]). The absence of nature declares the absence of authenticity and the impossibility of real existence.

As descriptions of this surreal voyage, a voyage that uncovers the meaningless rituals of our daily existence, poems such as 'Avventure di quando vivevo proprio in quel tempo' (Adventures of When I Was Living Right at That Time) and 'Fuga in famiglia' (Family Escape) are particularly revealing. *Tautofono*, however, should not be read solely as an epos guided by an anarchic, destructive neo-Dadaistic anti-discourse. With his collages, his accumulations of fantastic and heterogeneous materials, Giuliani is providing, at the same time, a mimicry of Surrealistic procedures: images are constructed and then, with a sort of clownish gesture, erased. Signs remain an illusion of meaning and inevitably cannot but reveal their ambiguous state, as in 'Il canto animale' (Animal Song):

> ho rivisto il nostro cantante a me piaceva lo stesso i lunedì mattina come
>   sono
> belli i lunedì io gli toglievo il fiato esplodendo le vocali dal naso comple-
>   tamente
> libero di labiali e dittonghi genuini insomma quando non canta è uno
>   spettacolo
> e appena non canta più è una creatura forse soltanto le gengive più
>   erotiche e minerali

la nostra piccola atmosfera soffre di un accumulo di onde disritmiche e ci
  perturba
più del barrito degli elefanti e poi c'è la grande lezione silenziosa dei gatti
  dio
com'era bello con la ventosa della gola godere le strisce d'aria e sputare
  sul sole
quanto mi piace il muso ottuso dell'amore che respira muto tra la vegetazione nasale. (*VN*, 111)

I saw our singer again I liked him as much as ever Monday mornings
how / beautiful the Mondays are I took his breath away the vowels
exploding from his nose completely / free of labials and genuine diph-
thongs that is when he doesn't sing it's a real performance / and as soon
as he stops singing he's a creature perhaps only the most erotic gums and
minerals / our small atmosphere suffers from a build-up of arhythmical
waves and it bothers us / more than the trumpeting of elephants and
then there's the great silent lesson of cats goodness / how beautiful it was
with the suction cup throat to enjoy the layers of air and spit on the sun /
how I do like love's blunt snout which breathes silently in the nasal vegetation. (Trans. Lawrence R. Smith, *The New Italian Poetry*, 326)

Closed within its own verbal space, *Tautofono* once again reveals the
dualistic movement of Giuliani's poetry: the orgiastic vigour of the linguistic sign and the solitary void of its narcissistic nature.

The collage technique is also employed in *Il giovane Max* (The Young
Max), a series of texts written between 1969 and 1972. Grotesque and
linguistically eccentric, *Il giovane Max* defies any traditional classification: it is neither a poem nor a novel. It is, perhaps, as Giuliani says in
the volume's opening section, a collection of 'Poems without verses'
('Poesie senza versi'), a pasting together of fragments of alienated and
desemanticized language.[12] *Il giovane Max* can be read as a sort of
mock-narrative, a derisive, burlesque imitation of narration itself.
Again in this collection, faced with a standardized and automatized
linguistic code, Giuliani does not find any road leading to a subjective
and authentic use of language. Experimenting with an alienated,
pathological language seems to be the sole possibility left open to literature. Farcical and carnivalesque, *Il giovane Max* subverts literary
norms and, in its perversion, refuses to reduce literature to a regurgita-
tion of social and political discourses. With its constant semantic
obstructions and linguistic absurdities, this collection reaffirms

Giuliani's courageous defence of literature against all the pressures to transform it into an instrument other than itself. For Giuliani, poetry must turn inward, providing an imaginative exploration in the realm of language. When it does so, it produces its own representations capable of inversions and subversions. For Giuliani, poetry and literature can be nothing else.

4 Collage, Multilingualism, and Ideology: Elio Pagliarani's Epic Narratives

From his first publication, *Cronache e altre poesie* (Chronicles and Other Poems [Milan: Schwarz, 1954]), Elio Pagliarani displayed an urgent desire to move away from the lyric genre to pursue a narrative form of poetry steeped in social realities.[1] This attraction towards narrative verse can be explained by two key factors: Pagliarani realized that the lyric tradition, with its inner diaries and transcendental yearnings (as epitomized by Hermeticism), had reached a state of linguistic and thematic exhaustion; and the post-war social and linguistic realities offered poetry opportunities for innovation. Undoubtedly, behind this poetic orientation there lies an ideological outlook that privileges the collective over the private, externality over the necessities of the 'I,' the epic over the subjective. This is not to say, however, that the 'I' is disbarred from making appearances. The 'reduction of the I' – advocated by Giuliani as the fundamental common ground upon which rests the new poetics of the Novissimi – is achieved in Pagliarani's poetry mainly through the creation of characters and the narration of chronicles dealing with the squalid conditions of Italy, a country undergoing at the time a drastic passage from a predominantly agricultural society to an urban and industrialized one. This poetic material clearly decentres the 'I' but does not result in its effacement. The 'I' in fact attests its presence either by performing a dialogic function in its encounter with others or by resorting to the role of a chorus – a commentator on actions and events, as in dramatic poetry.

Even though the rejection of the lyric tradition places Pagliarani within the new avant-garde, other elements of his writing set him apart. His inclusion in the anthology of the Novissimi and his subsequent participation in the activities of Gruppo 63 call for some elucidation. With a few exceptions, Pagliarani does not adopt the language of pathology and disorder to the same extent as Giuliani and Sanguineti. His aim of telling a story requires a certain degree of narrative flow that cannot endure the semantic and syntactic fragmentation, or the aphasic features, present in the poetry of the other two poets. Pagliarani's poetic narration and epic vein can be traced as far back as the Scapigliatura and Verismo movements, which adopted literature as an anti-rethorical documentation of social life and human oppression.[2]

A chronologically closer model is Cesare Pavese's narrative poems in *Lavorare stanca* (Hard Labour, 1936),[3] which features a prosaic linguistic register intended to capture everyday experiences of peasant, proletarian, or marginalized characters (prostitutes, drunks, drifters). Pavese's elongated verse, with its everyday syntax and lexicon, and his desire to draw into literature the ordinary lives of common people unquestionably played a central role in inspiring Pagliarani's early poetic experiments. In this respect, in fact, he is close to Pasolini and the *Officina* group, with their representational poetics and social commitment. Pagliarani's attention to the changing social realities of Italy and his determination to observe the private realm within a political perspective – particularly the effects of urbanization and industrialization on the proletariat or petit bourgeoisie – tied to a view of literature as a vehicle of critical realism and as a project for ideological renewal – underline his affinities with the experimentalism of the *Officina* group. Indeed, that journal showed a constant critical appreciation of Pagliarani's early works and welcomed him as a contributor. However, Pagliarani's connections to the new avant-garde are equally strong and convincing.

Pagliarani is not a poet whose realistic slant can be explained in terms of a descriptive and unified language that aims at representing externality. In other words, he does not share with the *Officina* group the intent to create a homogeneous literary style. Pagliarani's formal experiences, starting particularly with the epic poem *La ragazza Carla* (The Girl Carla), are centred on the technique of collage and multilingualism. The collage of verbal cut-ups selected from a variety of sources responds on the one hand, to the need of representing the differentiated speeches of our linguistic realities and, on the other, aligns itself with the new avant-garde objective of creating textual disruptions, disorder, and asyntactism as a strategy of resistance to the conventions of traditional forms which, with their pacifying effects, can be consumed so easily by the reader. Pagliarani's heteroglottic approach to poetry underscores that language is a social medium immersed in class divisions and susceptible to political and ideological conflicts. (In an article written in the late 1950s, Pagliarani claims that a poet's end is to 'transfer in the poetic language the contradictions present in the language of social classes' ['trasferire nel linguaggio poetico le contraddizioni del linguaggio di classe'].[4]) As a social heteroglossia, poetry's language can neither be reduced to the homogenizing linguistic constrictions of the poetic 'I' nor exempted from tensions, juxtapositions, and disconnections. Yet it still must be emphasized that, in spite of its disjointed traits, Pagliarani's organizational structure of the poetic text maintains a communicative goal that is abandoned only in some extreme instances. In Pagliarani's case, the necessity of communication is grounded in the view that poetry and literature have a social function to perform and that they can turn their critical outlook on the world into a project of emancipation and political transformation. The necessity of maintaining a constant link between literary codes (their formal organization) and extraliterary ones indicates that the former are closely tied to social action. Literary work on the linguistic sign cannot be separated from the production of social and political confrontation.

The early poems of the 1950s, collected in *Cronache e altre poesie* (Chronicles and Other Poems), exhibit primarily social themes and urban landscapes. Without doubt, they also herald the narrative features of Pagliarani's poetry but are bound to a linguistic and formal organization that cannot yet be fully situated within the avant-garde perspectives of his mature collections.

These chronicles narrate unassuming events in the lives of humble people (a seamstress, a street sweeper, a miner, a factory worker, night-school students) caught in their daily existence. What follows is the opening section of 'I goliardi delle serali' (The Goliards of Night School), which presents an ironic portrayal of a group of working-class students whose cheerful and carefree attitude is contrasted with their economic constraints. They share the burden of a social condition that erases their individual differences – they all must hold a job during the day and attend school at night:

I goliardi delle serali in questa nebbia
hanno voglia di scherzare: non è ancora mezzanotte
e sono appena usciti da scuola
                    'Le cose nuove e belle
che ho appreso quest'anno' è l'ultimo tema da fare,
ma loro non si danno pensiero, vogliono sempre scherzare.

Perché il vigile non interviene, che cosa ci sta a fare?

È vero però che le voci son fioche e diverse, querule anche nel riso,
o gravi, o incerte, in formazione e in trasformazione,
disparate, discordi, in stridente contrasto accomunate
senza ragione senza necessità senza giustificazione,
ma come pel buio e il neon è la nebbia che abbraccia affratella assorbe
   inghiotte
e fa il minestrone,
                  e loro ci guazzano dentro, sguaiati e contenti. (*IN*, 39)[5]

The goliards of night school in this fog / feel like joking: it's not yet mid-night / and they got out of class just now / 'The new and lovely things / I learned this year' is the last essay to hand in, / but they don't think about it, they just want to joke. // Why doesn't the constable step in, what's he is waiting for? // It's true though the voices are hoarse and varied, pee-vish even in laughter, / or serious, or uncertain, in the making or muta-tion, / disparate, discordant, in shrill contrast, come together / without reason without necessity without justification, / but as with darkness and neon it's the fog that embraces fraternizes absorbs swallows / and makes a stew, / and they wallow in it, crude and happy. (*I Nov*, 67)

The urban outskirts of the industrial centres of northern Italy (Milan, where the poet resides, becomes a constant point of reference) make up the setting of the stories: desolate surroundings crossed by trains, buses, and trolleys; dull-looking factories with cranes, sirens, and chimney stacks; squalid cinemas or game-stands on fairgrounds where people spend aimless Sunday afternoons. This bleak landscape is made even more dismal and melancholic by the occasional presence of rain and fog. For Pagliarani, the urban centre is an inhospitable place dominated by the ethics of work and the logic of money and profit. Consider this text in 'Due temi svolti' (Two Topics Are Explored): 'I remember my grandfather / who did not want to see me play happily: "children must cry / men must work"' ('mi ricordo mio nonno / che non voleva vedermi giocare / contento: "i bambini devono piangere / gli uomini lavorare"') (9). Or this one in 'Trascrizione' (Transcription): 'We have built so much fixed / capital with a high potential for growth / ... / but there is a crisis of production and it's spreading / the fur-naces are shut down /... / I am Fiat Ford General Motors / a very solid chimney stack /... / The structures are built in / reinforced concrete where wood-worms / don't nest, the mechanism is guaranteed and it does not allow / for deviations, the siren does not whistle // no fruit to reap' ('Abbiamo costruito così tanti / capitali fissi ad alto potenziale / ... / ma c'è crisi di produzione e circolante ormai, / i forni sono spenti / ... / Io sono la Fiat la Ford la General Motors / un solidissimo comignolo / ... / Le strutture sono in cemento armato dove non / annidano tarli, il meccanismo è garantito e non consente / deviazioni, la sirena non fischia // niente frutti') (19).

A transparent correlation is established between the dreariness of the external landscape and the interior sterility of the characters, often caught in inane gestures and monologues. Here, in 'Due temi svolti' (9), are the aspirations of a young working-class student:

Adesso studio nelle commerciali
ma da grande farò lo spazzino
all'aperto, perché ci voglio bene, a Milano
e le strade le voglio pulite
e mi piacciono le tute
e darò una mano all'agente
se una coppia calpesta il giardino
e picchierò i bambini che saltano.

Now I attend a vocational school / but when I grow up I will become a street sweeper / because I love Milan / and I want the streets to be clean / and I love overalls / and I will give a hand to the constable / if a couple walks on the grass of a public garden / and I will beat up the children who jump.

The theme of love, recurrent in poems such as 'Canto d'amore' (Love Song) or 'Viaggio N. 2' (Trip N. 2), is treated either in the form of carnal desire (sexuality, however, is also explored in its repressive aspects) or as a hopeless quest for fulfilment. The general state of internal emptiness is embodied in the figure of the puppet that appears in the opening poem of the collection, 'Due ottave dal diario milanese' (Two Octaves from the Milanese Diary): 'the mechanical / puppet urged: Shoot, shoot, / three ball for one penny and a bottle for a prize. / But my face, mother, resembles his' ('il pupazzo / meccanico invitava: Tira, tira, / tre palle un soldo e in premio una bottiglia. / Ma la mia faccia, mamma, gli assomiglia' [5]).

The most significant formal aspects of this collection centre on the use of a prosaic and denotative language that departs both from symbolic-metaphoric practices and from the stylized diction of poetic lyricism. Pagliarani foregrounds a colloquial lexicon and a syntactic construction that at times exploits regional linguistic nuances. He adopts free direct speech, monologues, and dialogues that bring into the narration an element of dramatization (cf. in particular, 'Domenica' [Sunday] and 'Viaggio N. 2.' In turn, these strategies contribute to create syntactic and rhythmic dissonances and an overall jarring effect on the narrative. Combined with the occasional use of ready-made linguistic fragments ('Romanza sotto la pioggia' [Song under the Rain] even presents clips of a popular song), all these aspects are an indication that Pagliarani is looking for innovative poetic language and genres, a search that, intensified by the theoretical and cultural climate brought about by the new avant-garde, will eventually lead him to more radical practices.

A short collection of the late 1950s, *Inventario privato* (Private Inventory [(Milan: Veronelli, 1959]), seems to be somewhat anomalous among Pagliarani's poetic works.[6] The unifying elements of this collection are the theme of love – often seen as a possible but constantly frustrated remedy to the inadequacies of life – and an epigrammatic and aphoristic language that is not immune from the memory of classical diction associated with such a poetic genre. Here is one untitled poem:

> È già d'autunno, altri mesi ho sopportato
> senza imparare altro: ti ho perduta
> per troppo amore, come per fame l'affamato
> che rovescia la ciotola col tremito.
> (*La ragazza Carla e nuove poesie*, 112)

It's already fall, other months I endured / without learning anything: I lost you / for too much love, as for hunger the starving man / tips over the bowl trembling.

Perhaps, a line of continuity with respect to the previous collection can be detected in the everydayness of the episodes and of the sentimental encounters (an event at the train station, the work at the office, a telephone call), together with the dialogic structure of many verses. Even these private accounts of longings and anguish are treated in an intersubjective fashion that does not only involve the object of desire but draws into its discourse conversations with others – a sort of choral

interpretation of events and emotional states usually offered by friends ('I don't leave you with an alibi, I love you / with the necessary cruelty to risk / your life because mine is not at stake // but by instinct you withdrew / Luciano says you don't have sufficient / vitality' ['Io non ti lascio alibi, ti amo / con la crudeltà necessaria per rischiare / la tua vita perché la mia non è in gioco // ma d'istinto ti sei ritratta / dice Luciano che non hai sufficiente / vitalità']) (114).

The epic drama *La ragazza Carla* was written between 1954 and 1957. It was first published in its entirety in *Il Menabò* (n. 2, 1960); the following year, selections were included in the anthology of the Novissimi. The first edition, in the form of a book, appeared in 1962 under the title *La ragazza Carla e altre poesie* (The Girl Carla and Other Poems [Milan: Mondadori]).

The poem is set in 1948. However, it is closely tied to the period when it was written, the time of the so-called 'economic miracle,' during which Italy underwent unprecedented economic growth and witnessed the beginnings of a consumer society. Economic expansion came at a heavy price, however, which was paid disproportionately by the working class: exploitation, inadequate working conditions, crowded dwellings, and psychological hardship. It is in the embryonic stages of these social and economic transformations that the protagonist of Pagliarani's poem, Carla Dondi, a seventeen-year-old girl, has to face the 'cement forests' ('boschi di cemento' [I, sec. 1]) of Milan, social adversity, and the insecurities that unavoidably are connected to the passage from adolescence to adulthood. (The impact of these conditions is so grievous that the narrator finds it necessary to link, in an epigraph, his story with a 'real' case recounted to him by a psychiatrist. A girl, finding herself in a predicament similar to Carla's, decides to take sleeping pills during weekends in order to stay asleep until going back to work on Mondays. In dedicating the poem to this anonymous youngster, Pagliarani underscores the solid connections of his story with externality.)

The poem is divided into three parts, each constituted by various sections. It opens by introducing the protagonist, who lives in a crammed space of a home she shares with her mother, her sister, Nerina, and her brother-in-law, Angelo. Milan's industrial outskirts, with their trains, trucks, and bridges, function as a backdrop:

Di là dal ponte della ferrovia
una traversa di viale Ripamonti

c'è la casa di Carla, di sua madre, e di Angelo e Nerina.

Il ponte sta lì buono e sotto passano
treni carri vagoni frenatori e mandrie dei macelli
e sopra passa il tram, la filovia di fianco, la gente che cammina
i camion della frutta di Romagna. (I, sec. 1)

On the other side of the railroad bridge / a street off Viale Ripamonti / is Carla's house, her mother's, Angelo's and Nerina's. / / The bridge just sits there and underneath pass / trains cars wagons brakemen and cattle for the slaughterhouse / and above the tramway and the trolley bus alongside, people walking / the fruit trucks from Romagna. (IN, 81)

Carla helps her mother with the housework and makes slippers while attending night school to become a typist. She is portrayed as a victim both of her social conditions and of the fact that she is a woman – suffering economic strains, trapped in her domestic role within the family (cf. I, sec. 6), and subjected to sexual harassment in the outside world ('two hands / that swoop on your breast / ... / the thorny infection of the hand' [I Nov 83]) ['due mani / che biombano sul petto / ... / il contagio spinoso della mano' (I, sec. 1)]). Carla also experiences a perturbing awareness of sexuality when she hears the squeaking of her sister's bed at night-time. She reacts to this with ambivalent and conflicting sensations ('sweat, / and goose bumps and shivers and hot flashes' ['sudore / e pelle d'oca e brividi di freddo e vampe di calore (I, sec. 3)]). Similarly, when the owner – Signor Praték – of an import-export company where she has found work makes advances towards her, she feels revulsion – both towards sex and towards life itself:

No, no, no, – Carla è in fuga negando ...

Ho paura mamma Dondi ho paura
c'è un ragno, ho schifo mi fa schifo alla gola
io non ci vado più ...
Schifo, ho schifo come se avessi
preso la scossa
          ma sono svelta a scappare
io non ci vado più. (III, sec. 1)

No, No, Carla is on the run denying / ... / I'm afraid, mamma Dondi I'm

afraid / there is a spider, it disgusts me I'm disgusted in my throat / I
won't go there anymore / ... / Disgusting, I'm disgusted as if I had / got-
ten a shock / but I'm quick to run / I won't go there anymore. (*I Nov* 115)

Carla is overwhelmed both by her socio-economic conditions and by
her entry into the world of adulthood. She feels 'estranged from life'
('straniera alla vita' [I, sec. 4]) and see herself as a 'fugitive' ('fuggitiva'
[I sec. 1]) in a world with which she is unable to come to grips (Carla
wonders how others can have confidence in themselves and the
strength to survive such turmoil; cf. II, sec. 7). However, in her work
environment, Carla is gradually forced to take the necessary steps
towards the acceptance of life's harsh realities ('As a clerk you learn
many things / here's the real school of life / some things you've got to
learn them fast / because that means you know how to live' [*I Nov*,
101] ['Negli uffici s'imparan molte cose / ecco la vera scuola della vita
/ alcune s'anno da imparare in fretta / perché vogliono dire saper
vivere' (II, sec. 3)]). She discovers Praték's greed and his power over
others because of his economic position, as well as Monsieur Gold-
stein's easy profits as a money-trader, in contrast to her family's struggle to make ends meet (cf. II, secs. 3, 4). When a co-worker, Aldo, starts
to court her, Carla slowly becomes receptive to his advances. She
learns to put on lipstick and begins to wear a pair of nylon stockings,
both signs of adult life (III, sec. 7). In her relationship with Aldo, Carla
expands the boundaries of her social space: she witnesses a workers'
demonstration and a political speech in the piazza (cf. III, secs. 4, 5).
Nevertheless, at the poem's end, she is not yet politically aware of her
social condition. Carla has discovered the physical qualities of her fem-
ininity and she has begun to tap into her desires; she has constructed
the basic requirements for a dialogue with others (including, perhaps,
a sense of her own morality); she has opened herself to life's chal-
lenges. All that said, however, she remains essentially unaware of the
boundaries of her social class. Far from acquiring a political consciousness, Carla accepts her life as a matter of fate. Survival in the city-forest
becomes her goal ('survives / in fact, only who learns to live' [*I Nov*,
123] ['sopravvive / difatti, solo chi impara a vivere' (III, sec. 5)]). There
is no way of eluding one's own life:

È nostro questo cielo d'acciaio che non finge
Eden e non concede smarrimenti,
è nostro ed è morale il cielo

che non promette scampo dalla terra,
proprio perché sulla terra non c'è
scampo da noi nella vita. (II, sec. 2)

It's ours this steely sky that does not pretend / Eden and does not allow lapsing, / it's ours and moral the sky / that does not promise escape from the earth, / just because on earth there is no / escape from us in life. (*I Nov*, 101)

La ragazza Carla is not confined to the narration of the tale of a young girl caught within the web of an alienating social world. The poem is marked by a constant contamination of genres and a collage technique that involves heterogeneous materials and a plurality of linguistic registers. In fact, the poem does not rest solely on an epic and narrative mode that links the personal with the collective, the individual with the social. Pagliarani breaks the narrative plane of the poem with structures that draw both from drama and from melodrama. They include dialogues and monologues (e.g. I, sec. 9; III, sec. 1), with constant shifts from the narrative to Carla's stream of consciousness to segments of conversations. To this second plane of the poetic structure is added a lyrical dimension that, exploiting a device similar to the function of a chorus, serves as the author's commentary on the actions of the characters and expresses his moral and political solidarity with the oppressed. In this realm, Pagliarani's ideological and political tensions emerge quite directly, confirming the presence of the 'I' and its social vocation. In turn, this component affects the linguistic register. If the narrative and dramatic levels of the poem rely on a referential and prosaic language, the lyrical level utilizes a figurative speech that admits even the conventions of metaphor. The following are two examples excerpted from the last part of the poem:

Autour des neiges, qu'est-ce qu'il y a?
Colorati licheni, smisurate
impronte, ombre liocorni
laghi celesti, nuvole bendate,
risa dell'eco a innumeri convalli
la vita esala fiorisce la morte
solitudine ìmperio libertà. (III, sec. 4)

Autour des neiges, qu'est-ce qu'il y a? / Colored lichens, immense / footprints, unicorn shadows / cerulean, blindfolded clouds, / the echo's laugh at numberless vales / life exhales death flowers / solitude dominion freedom. (I Nov 121)

Quanto di morte noi circonda e quanto
tocca mutarne in vita per esistere
è diamante sul vetro ...

Ma non basta comprendere per dare
empito al volto e farsene diritto:
non c'è risoluzione nel conflitto
storia esistenza fuori dell'amare
altri, anche se amore importi amare
lacrime, se precipiti in errore
o bruci in folle o guasti nel convitto
la vivanda, o sradichi dal fitto
pietà di noi e orgoglio con dolore.
(III, sec. 7)

How much death surrounds us and how / much must be turned to life to exist / its diamond on glass / ... / Yet understanding is not enough to give / impetus to the face and make it law: / there is no solution to the conflict / history existence outside of loving / others, even if love means loving tears, if it falls into error / or burns in neutral or food rots / at banquets, or from the thick yanks pity / for ourselves and painful pride. (I Nov, 133)]

There is no doubt that Pagliarani's objective is to shift poetry towards the modern epic and dramatic verse (inspired by Pound, Eliot, and Majakovskij), but without totally suppressing his own voice. The contamination of genres corresponds to the heteroglottic structure of the poem and to the multiplicity of voices that interact within the text. The poem follows a discontinuous and fragmentary organization that depends not only on techniques of flashback and syntactic and rhythmic ruptures (the hendecasyllablic verses are contiguous to seven-syllable lines and to shorter or much longer ones, the traditional metre to the atonal verse) but also on cut-ups and lexicon derived from a variety of specific linguistic sources. The social tensions and conflicts are mirrored in the linguistic clashes produced by the poem. Definitively, Pagliarani's text is not built on a random and aleatory accumulation of linguistic fragments extracted from industrial society. A critical perspective is constantly maintained both in the ironic treatment of the material and in the general rejection of the social and phycological climate in which the characters move.

La ragazza Carla presents a plurality of linguistic planes that include the jargon of advertisement (II, sec. 1) and of technical handbooks (I, sec. 7), legalese (II, sec. 6), and the vocabulary of commercial transactions (II, sec. 4). Such linguistic registers, traditionally considered unpoetic, become a substantial part of the linguistic structure of the poem. The deviation from poetic norms results in a collage of linguistic registers and styles that incessantly produces frictions and contrasts. In one instance, Pagliarani even employs the linguistic modes of nursery rhymes (II, sec. 7), which, with their merriness and simplicity, contradict the grave conditions and social adversities set out in the poem. Here is an example of the language used in Carla's handbook for typists (note the ironic contrast between the promises of the handbook and the protagonist's uncertainties):

> *Guida tecnica per l'uso razionale*
> *della macchina*
> > la serale
> di faccia alla Bocconi, ma già più
> > *Metodo principe*
> > *per l'apprendimento*
> > *della dattilografia con tutte dieci*
> > *le dita*
> non capisce se è un gran bene, come pareva in casa
> > spendere quelle due mila lire al mese
> > *Vantaggi dell'autentico*
> > *utilità fisiologica, risultato*
> > *duraturo, corretta scrittura*
> > *velocità resistenza*
>
> PIANO DIDATTICO PARAGRAFO PRIMO ...
>
> *Quando il dispositivo per l'inversione*
> *automatica del movimento del nastro, o per difetto*
> *di lubrificazione o per mancanza*
> *del gancio*
> > *non funziona.* (I, sec. 7)

Handbook for the Smart Use / of the Typewriter / nightschool / across the

street from Bocconi, but she no longer / *World's Finest Method* / *for Learning* / *Typing with All* / *Ten Fingers* / understands the big advantage, as it
seemed at home, / spending those two thousand monthly / *Benefits of the
Authentic* / *Physiological Practicality, Lasting Results, Precision Writing* /
Speed Endurance / / LESSON PLAN PARAGRAPH ONE ... / / *When the device for
the automatic* / *reversal of the ribbon, either from insufficient* / *lubrication or failure* / *in the catch* / *does not function* (I Nov, 85, 87)

La ragazza Carla's linguistic clashes create a Brechtian alienation-
effect and a tension that send clear socio-political signals. This poem,
with its juxtaposition of colloquialisms and technical lexicon, lyrical
and narrative styles, referential and figurative language, and traditional and atonal verses, represents the fertile and creative possibilities
for an avant-garde aesthetics that does not renounce social issues and
commitment.

Pagliarani's most daring and provocative poetic venture was
undoubtedly the collection *Lezione di fisica* (Physics Lesson), first published in 1964 and subsequently reprinted in an expanded version
under the title *Lezione di fisica e fecaloro* (Physics Lesson and Fecalgold
(Milan: Feltrinelli, 1968]). In this collection, Pagliarani reaches the limits of the possibilities for constructing poetry with materials procured
from fields and contexts shunned by poetic conventions. He works
with cut-ups and quotes taken from a variety of sources – books,
essays, newspaper articles on quantum mechanics, logical positivism,
statistics, linguistics, political economy. The semantic and syntactic
incongruities are much more accentuated than in previous works, with
the result that, particularly in the second part of the collection, the narrative mode is kept at a minimum or collapses altogether. The effect is
one of total discontinuity accompanied by a sense of linguistic and
mental chaos. This is not to say, however, that the reader experiences a
total loss of signification. Meaning is constantly frustrated; it becomes
problematic and complex. Messages are not devised in the customary
form of a discovery that the author offers to the reader. Instead, Pagliarani creates his poetry from the process of investigation and questioning of the materials at hand. He approaches them with inquisitive
reasoning and ideological-existential intensity that involves, at the
same time, the reader, who is called to sift through the tangled discourses with an analytic and discriminating perspective. Poetry rejects
the prepackaged and ready-made messages of consumer society and
becomes a language of critique and interrogation.

The poems are written in the form of letters intended to establish a dialogue with a number of people, mostly artists and intellectuals, by raising issues and posing questions. Pagliarani revives the form of the eclogue in order to experiment with an intersubjective construction that leaves unanswered, both for the author and the reader, questions and comments. In other words, Pagliarani discusses – in an epistolary fashion – with his readers topics that are close to the interests of his addressees, but, evidently, without the possibility of their replying. This formal organization confers on the poems an open structure that rebounds on the readers, compelling them to participate in the 'discussions' and to formulate their own responses. (Indeed, these poems are structured as recitatives whose segments are interchangeable. In one poem, 'Trying to Focus' (titled in English), Pagliarani advises the readers that the 'refrain can continue' ('Refrain: può continuare').

Pagliarani's social and political vocation is apparent from the numerous issues on which he focuses his attention: the Cold War, the threat of an atomic explosion, racism, colonialism, Mao's politics, the new guises of fascism, the political superficiality making its way into left-wing attitudes, politics and the Third World, Italy's 'Southern Question,' class tensions, John F. Kennedy's assassination, the role of the church, and many more. There is no doubt that these poems convey Pagliarani's strong commitment to civil activism, but they never degenerate into fixed statements. On the contrary, they are animated by a spirit of contradiction and dialectics that is inflamed by constant irony and a sense of anarchism ('the anarchic tradition is fresh' ['la tradizione anarchica è fresca'] is the closing line of 'Come alla luna l'alone' [38] [Like the Halo to the Moon]). Irony strikes on the figure of the poet and on poetry itself:

L'angoscia intellettuale della gioventù quando scopre insufficiente
l'intelletto, cioè la capacità della ragione di distinguere
com'è lontana, Franco: era quella che chiamavamo
angoscia esitenziale? Fosse o no un male
alla milza, solo per ricchi voglio dire, né di essa m'addoloro
né della sua lontananza.
('Proseguendo un finale,' 11)

The intellectual anguish of youth when it discovers the intellect / insufficient, namely the ability of reason to distinguish / how distant it is, Franco: was that what we used to call existential anguish? If it were or not a pain / in the spleen, only for rich people that is, I am neither grieving for it nor for its distance. (Following a Finale)

Che sappiamo noi oggi della morte
nostra, privata, poeta?
                    Poeta è una parola che non uso
di solito, ma occorre questa volta perché
respinti tutti i tipi di preti a consolarci non è ai poeti che tocca dichiararsi
sulla nostra morte, ora, della morte illuminarci?
('Oggetti e argomenti per una disperazione,' 20)

What do we know today of our / death, our private death, poet? / Poet is a word that I usually don't use, / but it's necessary this time because / rejected all kinds of priests to console us is it not the poets' / turn to take a stand / on our death, now, to enlighten us on death? (Objects and Topics for a Despair)

Irony befalls poetry itself. In its self-reflexive investigation, the language of literature undergoes the same process of demystification that is practised on other linguistic codes. Poetry starts devouring itself and questioning its own status – the possibilities of its social functions. It cannot resolve within itself the contradictions of reality. As Pagliarani writes in the closing lines of 'La pietà oggettiva' (The Objective Pity), 'I would like to see that it were not like this / that one achieved in verses a sufficient catharsis' ('vorrei vedere che non fosse così / che si compisse nei versi la catarsi che bastasse'). With its lost innocence, poetry is forced to shun the temptation of re-establishing a conciliatory and peaceful relationship with itself and the world ('the verse becomes self-satisfied, nothing is easier than this but I break it' [Like the Halo to the Moon] ['il verso si fa compiacente, niente è più facile di questo ma io lo spezzo ('Come alla luna alone,' 37]).

The poem 'Lezione di Fisica,' which is also the title of the entire first part of the collection, is particularly remarkable. It discusses Max Planck's quantum theory, making reference to his study of light and heat emitted by black bodies in relation to radiation energy and emission of wavelengths. Other reference are made to Louis de Broglie's observations on the wave properties of radiation and to Werner Heisenberg's 'Principle of Uncertainty,' specifically to his thesis that an object's characteristics are altered by the process of any experimentation. These theories of nuclear physics are then connected to the atomic bomb and its potential for devastation, as illustrated in a statistical study by Herman Kahn. (The poem make allusions to President Franklin Roosevelt and the atomic project and uses quotes from Albert Einstein.) The detached scientific language, together with the dispassionate account of an anticipated atomic explosion, clashes with the emotional language of love and human dialogue – the poem is addressed to Elena, a woman with whom Pagliarani is clearly involved:

> E io qui sto
> e io qui sto Elena in gabbia e aspetto
> il suono di un oggetto la comunicazione dell'effe to
> su te, delle modifiche
> > Non sono io
> che ti tradisco, chi ti prende alla gola è la tua amica
> la vita. ('Lezione di fisica,' 26)

And here I am / and here I am in a cage Elena and I wait / the sound of an object the communication of the effect / on you, of the modifications / I am not the one / betraying you, who takes you by the throat is your friend / life.

In constructing a collage of thoughts and questions, Pagliarani bridges the social with the private, the scientific with the emotional, in such a way as to defy ordinary modes of communication and to employ the resources of poetry in shaking the passive acceptance of social linguistic platitude and stereotypes.

The second half of the collection, 'Fecalgold' ('Fecaloro'), comprises six poems, set in lines that run lengthwise on the pages without, on first impression, any rhythmic or phonological patterns. The absence of linguistic markers allows the lines to flow in an arbitrary and disorderly movement that seems to abjure all laws of homophony and rhythmicity traditionally associated with poetry. However, a closer examination of the poems reveals rhymes, other phonological devices, traditional metres, and syntactic repetitions, such as the figure of the anaphora. The problem is that they are not clearly evident but rather dispersed in the general clutter of linguistic fragments.

This calculated disorder and pervasive asynchronism does not rely simply on the effect of shock or on the need to deautomatize the reader's habituated responses. Defamiliarization and the alienation-effects are unquestionably there, but they do not explain the entire picture. Pagliarani seems to identify poetry not with a finished product but with a working process that, on the one hand, searches for a poetic language, and, on the other, hides and frustrates it. This discordant perspective cannot but stem from the fear of the sublime or from its present impossibility. For Pagliarani, the seductive beauty of aesthetic forms is compromised not only by their obsolescence and fossilization but also by their consolatory and reconciling effects. Poetry, then, must be engaged in producing forms of anti-sublime and, through them, it must protest against both its own history and that of the world.

The formal provocation and desecration are mirrored by the iconoclastic treatment of materials and issues. The fragments range from a study of Ferruccio Rossi-Landi on language as a production of goods to an interview with Mao in a French newspaper and essays on the theory of orgasm, time and money, and anal conditions. Pagliarani ransacks all of this materials focusing on the commercialization of language and the media; art, commodities and exchange value; capital, nuclear armament, and world poverty; labour, money, and gold production. The result is an hallucinated, somewhat grotesque, and satiric account of all systems of communication and of our social structures at large. Here are a few lines from ('Dittico della merce: I. La merce esclusa') (Diptych of Goods: I. The excluded goods) and from 'Dittico del fecaloro: I. fecaloro' (Diptych of fecalgold: I. fecalgold):

Uso e scambi linguistici b) L'equazione di valore linguistico Conside-
   riamo l'equazione x merce A =
y merce B
            e applichiamola al linguaggio
                        Dio è l'essere onnipotente
Qui la quantità (x, y) per entrambi i termini è ridotta a uno
c'è un solo Dio ed egli e l'unico essere onnipotente (55)

Linguistic use and exchanges b) The equation of linguistic value Let us consider the equation x goods A = / y goods B / and let us apply it to language / God is an omnipotent being / Here the quality (x, y) for both terms is reduced to one / there is only God and he is the only omnipotent being

l'elemento feci appare rimosso: nell'esperienza individuale
vengono concesse o negate nell'ambito di una struttura primordiale di
   lotta-scambio

che ci sembra l'essenziale della situazione anale
        tirare i remi in barca
le cosiddette costipazioni vent'anni di pausa intestinale
si possono sbloccare se si esamina il complesso del denaro nel soggetto
    (69)

the feces element appears repressed: in the individual experience / they are allowed or denied within the context of a primordial struggle-exchange structure / that seems to us the core of an anal situation / to draw the oars back in the boat / the so-called constipations of twenty years of intestinal pause / can be unblocked if one examines the subject's money complex

Fundamental structures of our present civilization are associated with acts of defecation or urination to such an extent that not only our dominant socio-economic values and systems (revolving around money and gold) but also the private sphere of love are related to feces ('Fecalgold,' 'Fecaloro'; 'Fecallove,' 'Fecamore' [70, 72]. Dominated by this social structures ('what is left / to the Western world / if you eliminate the faith / in the possession / of gold' ['che rimane / all'Occidente / se togliete la fede / nel possesso / dell'oro' (75)]), the individual, as indicated by the closing poem on love, is caught in a 'desert of emotions,' a state of 'emotional pestilence' (deserto emozionale; peste emozionale' [74]) from which no easy escape is in sight. The brutal critique and provocation indicate a desire for otherness that is not yet realizable.

5 Edoardo Sanguineti and the Labyrinth of Poetry

A rather precocious writer with an intellectual background in European art and aesthetics, Edoardo Sanguineti made a vital contribution to the innovations and the deprovincialization of Italian literature. Indeed, his poetry in particular represents a decisive turning-point for post-war Italian letters.[1]

The formal revolt and linguistic disorder pursued by the new avant-garde manifests itself in Sanguineti's poetry as an alienated language with semantic incongruities arranged through a shattered and lacerated syntax. This language is not to be interpreted simply as a transcription of a personal nervous breakdown, but as an objective representation of a historical and social alienation (the pathological language is the counterpart of a pathological reality) relived from the inside, on the page.[2] In this perspective, the alienated language can be viewed in a clinical sense and as an artistic concept, without excluding literary techniques tied to Victor Shklovsky's notion of defamiliarization (*ostranenie*) or Bertolt Brecht's alienation-effect (*Verfremdungseffekt*). For Sanguineti, such a strategy stems from the urgency to plunge into the 'Palus Putredinis,' into the fetid historical swamp of collective chaos, irrationality, and alienation, with the hope of coming out of it somewhat cleansed.

Sanguineti's first collection, a poem entitled *Laborintus* (Varese: Magenta, 1956), which is divided in twenty-seven sections, should be read within this context. Written between 1951 and 1954, when Sanguineti was in his early twenties, *Laborintus* represents one of the most radical breaks from the tradition of Hermetic and neorealistic literary models. It undoubtedly opened the road to the poetic experimentation of the 1960s and beyond. The title, taken from a thirteenth-century treatise on rhetoric by Everardus Alemannus and from an anonymous epigraph to this same text ('quasi laborem habens intus'), suggests, through the symbol of the labyrinth, the difficulty if not the impossibility of escape and (in combination with the epigraph) a condition of psychological strain (labour) and distress.[3] *Laborintus* portrays the descent into a historical hell ('a living Hell' ['Infernum viventes,' sec. 8]) – the swamp of capitalist alienation in which the conscience is lost in the falsity and contradictions of bourgeois ideologies. In addition, the apocalyptic climate of the poem can be related to the tensions generated by the Cold War and the traumas and insecurities brought about by the atomic age. In fact, the 'long, smoky mushrooms' ('lunghi funghi fumosi,' sec. 2) is a clear description of an atomic explosion as is the reference to the 'Valles Mortis' ('Death Valley') (sec. 3).

Through a Dantean journey into the psychological and social chaos of contemporary reality, Sanguineti transcribes a delirious mental collapse ('naufragio mentale,' sec. 3) with the intent of resolving it ('but complication like alienation like bitter alienation corollary' [*I Nov*, 207] ['ma complicazione come alienazione come aspra alienazione corollario,' sec. 15]) into a liberating, therapeutic process. Social and psychological fractures produced by capitalist-bourgeois realities (their disabling effects are portrayed by a crippled character satirically named 'Moneybags,' sec. 18) find a correspondence in the linguistic chaos of the text. What makes this poem a contemporary epic of the alienated and neurotic state of mind is the fact that such a condition is represented by form itself, an abnormal and quasi-aphasic use of language.

Laborintus is constructed as a plurilinguistic, babelic text in which fragments of sentences, quotations from foreign languages (English, French, German, Greek, Latin), neologisms, scientific terms, and segments of banal conversations are assembled in a montage that indiscriminately combines the language of erudition with that of the colloquial:

ancora καὶ τὰ τῶν ποιητῶν and CAPITAL LETTERS
et ce mélange de comique ah sono avvilito adesso et de pathétique
una tristezza ah in me contengo qui devoit plaire
sono dimesso et devoit même sono dimesso, non umile
surprendre! ma distratto da futilità ma immerso in qualche cosa
and CREATURES gli amori OF THE MIND di spiacevole realmente
très-intéressant mi è accaduto dans le pathétique un incidente
che dans le comique mi autorizza très-agréable
a sottrire!
    e qui convien ricordarsi che Aristotile

sì c'è la tristezza mi dice c'è anche questo ma non questo
soltanto, io ho capito and REPRESENTATIONS non si vale mai
OF THE THINGS delle parole passioni o patetico per significar
le perturbazioni and SEMINAL PRINCIPLES dell'animo; et πάθη
tragicam scaenam fecit πάθημα e L ma leggi lambda ... (sec. 23)

again καὶ τὰ τῶν ποιητῶν and CAPITAL LETTERS / et ce mélange de comique
ah I'm disheartened now et de pathétique / a sadness ah in me qui devoit
plaire / I'm raggedly et devoit même I'm raggedly, not humble / surprendre! yet distracted by futility yet immersed in something / and CREATURES
the loves OF THE MIND actually unpleasant / très intéressant an accident
happened to me dans le pathétique / that dans le comique authorizes me
très agréable / to suffer! / and here we ought to remember that Aristotle /
yes there is sadness he tells me there's this too but not this / only I understood and REPRESENTATIONS never takes advantage / OF THE THINGS of
passion words or pathetic to signify / the perturbations and SEMINAL
PRINCIPLES of the soul; et πάθη / tragicam scaenam fecit πάθημα and L
read lambda ... (*I Nov*, 223, 225)

The traditional stylistic resources employed for creating unity and
harmony are displaced by a hybridization and contamination of styles
that indiscriminately joins the tragic with the comic or the melodra-
matic. (Clearly the impression of randomness is the result of a calculated construction. So much so that, in its self-reflexive moments, the
text often makes direct references to its conflicting stylistic modes. This
effect is reached also by adopting a technique of quotationism that
assembles cut-ups of medieval and modern texts, from Nicholas of
Cusa to Ugo Foscolo and Stalin.) The objective is to create formal dissonances and discontinuities that, on the one hand, perform the function
of reconstructing the mental state of a nervous breakdown, and, on the
other, play a subversive role by contesting the appeasing effects of a
balanced and graceful poetic language. Formal order and harmony are
perceived as a means to conceal the alienation and the conflicts present
within bourgeois society ('the terrifying / experience of conflicts' [*I
Nov*, 201] ['esperienza / terrificante dei conflitti,' sec. 10]). Section six
of the poem makes direct reference to order as a form of 'limitation'
and 'simplification' against which 'complication' must be opposed.
The formal disorder of *Laborintus*, then, reflects an attempt to bring to
the surface (to consciousness) an actual state of social and individual
alienation and to subvert literary models and practices that serve the

purpose of disguising it. It is in this respect that poetic forms can serve as a strategy of negative dialectics.

The absence of time sequences or of syntactic links causes the poem to follow an accidental narrative flow, featuring casual juxtapositions of linguistic segments and discontinuous progressions of storyline. The use of paratactic and elliptical clauses, the obsessive tendency to adopt parenthetic constructions, the pleonastic use of conjunctions, and spasmodic recurrences of punctuation marks (or their total absence) and exclamatory syntagms all contribute to create an oneiric and hallucinatory form of writing:

> ah il mio sonno; e ah? e involuzione? e ah e oh? devoluzione? (eh uh?)
> e volizione! e nel tuo aspetto e infinito e generantur!
> ex putrefactione; complesse terre; ex superfluitate;
>> livida Palus
> livida nascitur bene strutturata Palus; lividissima (lividissima terra)
> (lividissima): cuius aqua est livida; (aqua) nascitur! (aqua) lividissima!
>> (sec. 26)

> ah my slumber; and ah? and involution? and ah and oh? devolution? (and uh?) / and volition and in your appearance and infinite and generantur! / ex putrefactione; complex soils; ex superfluitate; / livida Palus / livida nascitur well arranged Palus; very livid (very livid soil) / (very livid): cuius aqua est livida; (aqua) nascitur! (aqua) lividissima! (*I Nov*, 227)

Such linguistic disorder and turbulence aims to reconnect poetry with the project of the historical avant-garde and, at the same time, to radicalize its practices by moving close to coeval experiments in the field of painting and music. It seems as if Sanguineti, with *Laborintus*, is attempting to uproot the lyrical tradition of Italian poetry by assimilating stylistic modes that were developing outside the confines of literature. One of Sanguineti's goals is thus that of bridging the aesthetic gap between the traditional and exhausted language of Italian poetry and innovative means of expressions from other art forms. The atonality of *Laborintus* – together with its semantic dissonances, agitated rhythms, and lack of hierarchical coordinations of discourse – is a poetic equivalent of the conflicting and disharmonizing elements present in serial music or Action Painting (see chapters, 1 and 2).

The main recurrent themes of *Laborintus* are tied to the archetypal symbols of Jungian psychology: the process of individuation, the search for the totality of one's self, the unity of private and collective, the integration of conscious and unconscious (this latter aspect is confirmed by a direct reference to the realization of the shadow: 'in the shadow mecum' ['nell'ombra mecum,' sec. 24']). The female character, Ellie, who appears at the outset of the poem, is first described as one's body but soon assumes the function of the Jungian *anima* which the male protagonist, Laszo, attempts to rejoin ('I want the mystic unity' [*I Nov*, 199] ['voglio l'unità mistica,' sec. 10]). This archetype, associated with the figure of the circle as a symbol of the totality of the psyche ('Ellie within a circle' [*I Nov*, 215] ['Ellie dentro un cerchio,' sec. 16]), acquires also the role of a life-giving Great Mother ('lividissima mater,' sec. 26) who is identified with the swamp itself ('livida Palus,' 'lividissima terra,' sec. 26). The 'livid' soil of the 'Palus Putredinis' is putrefaction and birth at the same time. In fact, the link with an event of birth is clearly established by the recurrent Latin terms 'nascitur' and 'generantur' – to be born and to generate – present in the same section, together with 'fetus' in the subsequent and closing part of the poem. The Palus, the inescapable labyrinth ('labyrinth un mécanisme impossible thing' [*I Nov*, 211] ['labirinto un mécanisme impossibile cosa, sec. 15]), the landscape of historical chaos, becomes a 'miraculous mire,' ('miracolosa melma,' sec. 25). The desire for transformation – underscored in the opening section by the repetition of the Latin verb 'desiderantur' – both of the matter (swamp) and of the psyche – are tied to Jungian concepts of alchemy. The structuring of the 'I,' in fact, is delineated through magic and alchemic allusions (cf. secs. 13, 17). However, unity and totality ('totality construction of a vision' ['totalità costruzione di visione,' sec. 17]) are not directly experienced. Order, both formal and psychological, is not re-established, allowing the poem to maintain a vital tension up to the end. It is worth noting that the image of the valley, connected in the opening sections with the motif of death and destruction portrayed by the swamp – the 'Valles Mortis,' the valley of death, sec. 3 – is contemporaneously an archetypal image and a Dantean reference. Dante's dark valley of the *Inferno* becomes a 'Paradise Valley' (sec. 10) but with a difference. For the Christian medieval poet, paradise and totality – the latter encompassing both the consciousness of the human condition and the experience of the divine light – represent an achievement. For Sanguineti, as a secular poet of a modern epic, they are a utopia, the object of an unresolved struggle. As a historical materialist, Sanguineti is well aware that self-consciousness does not dissolve the material conditions and social contradictions that form the basis of the self and of identity. Harmony and 'paradise' as expressions of totality can be achieved only through the radical subversion of social relations.

The linguistic fragmentation of *Laborintus* corresponds to the fragmentation of the subject. The 'I' emerges either as a splintered presence ('the fracture of a personality' [*I Nov*, 189] ['la rottura di una personalità, sec. 2]) or as a multitude of voices ('I am I am a multitude' [*I Nov*, 191] ['io sono io sono una moltitudine,' sec. 2]). To be sure, this is not a poem in which the 'I' performs the function of extracting the personal and the autobiographical. The 'reduction of the I' takes place in *Laborintus* not only through its fractured condition but also through its treatment as a social portrait. The 'I' is more of an allegorical figure of the historical collective than a private entity. Furthermore, it must be clear that the fragmentation of the 'I' does not entail the abdication of the subject. Fragmentation is adopted neither as an end in itself (a joyous collapse of 'strong' or circumscribed identities) nor as an ontological dimension of human existence. *Laborintus* displays the condition of the 'I' *before* the revolution; it is living the Marxian pre-history, enduring all the alienating effects of a state of degradation. The impossibility of monoglossia – adopting here Bakhtinian notions – stems in *Laborintus* from the impossibility of a unified poetic self. The reader is faced with a sort of dialogized heteroglossia that, with its polyglottism and conflicting linguistic registers, denounces at once both the impossibility of a univocal lyric voice and the impossibility of the sublime. Subjected to an overdose of alienation, the 'I' reaches the realization of its condition and it elects anarchy as a way of adopting a critical distance from its historical realities and, thus, as a form of dissent combined with utopian perspectives.

However, in *Laborintus* the *complicatio* (complication) does not reach a *complexio oppositorum*, a 'coniunctio' (sec. 16) capable of offering a unified reality ('ut duo unum fiant,' sec. 15) where the opposites become one. Denying any possible synthesis, *Laborintus* represents the *bolgia* (pit) of historical contradictions, with no hope of immediate redemption or salvation. Through constant irony, parody, and demystification, Sanguineti is relentlessly set on demolishing any myth which aims at providing a resolution within the bourgeois Inferno. The only possible strategy is to subvert the system by practising 'anarchy as a radical complication' ('anarchia come complicazione radicale,' sec. 6), as a manifestation of an anomalous and deviant consciousness, a 'heteroclite conscience' ('coscienza eteroclita,' sec. 6) that has explored all the negativity of the alienated existence and has set in motion possibilities of change ('in permutation permanent alienation' [*I Nov*, 207] [in permutazione permanente alienazione,' sec. 15]).

The fractured and deranged language of *Laborintus* is retained in many ways in Sanguineti's second volume of verse, entitled *Erotopaegnia* (Erotic Games [Milan: Rusconi and Paolazzi, 1961]), a collection of erotic poems divided into seventeen sections. The apocalyptic vision, however, finds a liberating outlet in the verbal excitement of *Erotopaegnia*. The playful, often bizarre and grotesque eroticism of the love games is mirrored by constant linguistic and philological wordplay. The orgasms and the sexual pleasures envisioned in the poem establish a parallel with the pleasure principle associated with the playfulness of the language. Although the linguistic frolicking cannot be detached altogether from the tragic perception of reality expressed in *Laborintus* (the historical chaos of that collection is replaced by the natural chaos of instincts and passions), the corporality and sexuality of *Erotopaegnia* promote something of an orgiastic catharsis, a strong indication of a possible constructive contact with reality. As well, the comic style, rather pronounced in the description of acts of coitus and sexual organs ('consistent tail! frigid whip! oh muscle! oh fist! penetrating / ... / how you whinnied, / my spade; how, my pyramid, you wept!' [*I Nov*, 249] ['consitente coda! frigida frusta! oh muscolo! oh pugno! penetrante / ... / come nitristi, / mia vanga; come, mia piramide, lacrimasti!, sec. 11]), serves to temper the dramatic and tragic overtones. The general impression, however, is that the comic is not employed in Sanguineti's poetry as a device for counterbalancing the tragic and thus providing humour as a form of relief. It is a stylistic strategy that, with its low linguistic register, aims to exclude pathos and lofty language. Indeed, these linguistic tensions constitute a distinctive feature of the new avant-garde.

The central episodes of the collection portray orgies, taking place in a university swimming pool (sec. 9) or around a racing track (sec. 10). Students have intercourse in toilet stalls, parade their testicles, engage in homosexual games, and are represented as animal-like creatures – horses, vipers, crocodiles (sec. 11). Here are the closing lines of section 9:

e lucidissima; e vibrante, allora, ardente, l'acqua; e in calde coppe,
copulati; in stridenti vasche, voltolati; urlando, bollenti:

in questo ventre (così allora urlando!) premendo! pressi, allora, gemendo;
colando, impressi: oh, frangibili (dissi);
      e vidi lei, innescata, grondando, oh!
(praesentibus testibus vidi); lei vibrata vidi; vibrante lei appunto; pressa.

and most shiny; and vibrant, then, burning, the water; and in hot cups, /
copulated; in shrieking basins, rolled about; screaming, boiling: / in this
belly (so shouting then!) pressing! pressed, then moaning; / dripping,
impressed: oh, breakable (I said); / and I saw her, primed, dripping wet,
oh! / (praesentibus testibus vidi); I saw her vibrated; vibrating; / precisely
her; pressed. (*I Nov*, 243)

The orgiastic language, combined with the predominantly oneiric
narration, has a rhetorical and ideological energy which indicates that
Sanguineti is beginning to move away from the anarchic solutions of
his initial project towards a counter-ideology as an alternative to bourgeois values and models. For instance, the dream images acquire the
function of revealing possible truths concealed behind alienated bourgeois existence. In fact, the collection that immediately follows *Erotopaegnia*, *Purgatorio de l'Inferno* (Purgatory of Hell), comprising texts
written between 1960 and 1963 and published, together with the two
previous volumes, in the trilogy *Triperuno* (Three to One; Milan: Feltrinelli, 1964), presents on a linguistic level the recovery of a more linear discourse and, on a thematic level, a more articulated and rational
criticism of dominant ideologies.[4] In other words, if *Laborintus* represents the impossibility of communication within the social hell and the
immersion in the irrational, *Purgatorio de l'Inferno* displays the necessity of transforming poetry into a medium capable of communicating
alternative ideologies. This new perspective exhibits, if not the absolute certainty of a social and political paradise, at least a hope, a utopian dream expressed from the vantage point of purgatory. As the
poems addressed to his infant son, Alessandro, demonstrate, Sanguineti's shift towards a poetry of content often takes on the form of a
direct attack on the negative values of bourgeois society:

piangi piangi, che ti compero una lunga spada blu di plastica, un frigori-
    fero
Bosch in miniatura, un salvadanaio di terra cotta, un quaderno
con tredici righe, un'azione della Montecatini:
            piangi piangi, che ti compero

una piccola maschera antigas, un flacone di sciroppo ricostituente,
un robot, un catechismo con illustrazioni a colori, una carta geografica
con bandierine vittoriose. (sec. 9)

cry cry, I'll buy you a long blue plastic sword, / a miniature Bosch refrig-
erator, a clay piggy bank, a notebook / with thirteen lines, a Montecatini
share: / cry cry, I'll buy you / a little gas mask, a bottle of revitalizing
syrup, / a robot, a catechism book with colour illustrations, a / map /
with victorious little flags.

Behind the history of bourgeois civilization, with its greed and violence, there lies only a sense of nothingness that needs to surface as
political consciousness:

questo è il gatto con gli stivali, questa è la pace di Barcellona
fra Carlo V e Clemente VII, è la locomotiva, è il pesco
fiorito, è il cavalluccio marino: ma se volti il foglio, Alessandro,
ci vedi il denaro: ...
                        e questo è il denaro,
e questi sono i generali con le loro mitragliatrici, e sono i cimiteri
con le loro tombe, e sono le casse di risparmio con le loro cassette
di sicurezza, e sono i libri di storia con le loro storie:
ma se volti il foglio, Alessandro, non ci vedi niente. (sec. 10)

this is Puss 'n Boots, this is the peace of Barcelona / between Charles V
and Clement VII, this is the locomotive, this is the blossomed / peach tree,
this is the sea-horse, but if you turn the page, Alessandro, / you see
money: ... / and this is money, / and these are the generals with their
machine guns, and the cemeteries / with their tombs, and these are the
savings banks with their safety / deposit boxes, and these are the history
books with their stories: / but if you turn the page, Alessandro, you see
nothing.

The only possible redemption from the negativity of bourgeois history (constant reference are made to nazism, to fascism in its various
social and political expressions, and to the oppressive state of Italian
politics and society) is offered by Marxist ideology, the advent of communism, and the family as a centre of resistance ('we are redeemed
(I said to my wife): in this marriage; ah / in this (I said), (we) are
redeemed, ah we (also) / had to / recover this consciousness (this polit-

ical consciousness) this biting / (this indépassable: le marxisme) ['siamo redenti (a mia moglie dissi): in questo matriminio; ah / in questa (dissi), (noi) siamo redenti, ah questa dovevamo (anche) / coscienza (questa coscienza politica) ritrovare: mordente, questa / (indépassable, questo: le marxisme) [sec. 3]). The communist project, with its utopian perspective and promise of liberation, represents the antithesis to the dehumanizing 'pre-history' of capitalist society. In fact, the closing section of the poem makes direct reference to a future redemption through light, dreams, and children:

(ma nel night, a Palermo, li ho sentiti davvero, io, che dicevano: perché
vivi tu? e dicevano: come ti giustifichi?
                          dicevano: ma ti giustifichi, tu?)
ma adesso, vedi: ma adesso, quale stanchezza? e quale (in questa nostra
preistoria), quale tranquillità?
                 ma vedi il fango che ci sta alle spalle,
e il sole in mezzo agli alberi, e i bambini che dormono:
                          i bambini
che sognano (che parlano sognando); (ma i bambini, li vedi, cosi inquieti);
(dormendo, i bambini); (sognando, adesso).
(sec. 17)

(but at the nightclub, in Palermo, I, indeed, heard them that they were saying: why / do you live? and they were saying: how do you justify yourself? / they were saying: but do you justify yourself, you?) / but now, you see: but now, what tiredness? and what (in this prehistory of ours / what tranquillity? / but you see the mire left behind, / and the sun in the midst of trees, and the children sleeping: / the children / dreaming (they talk dreaming); (but the children, you see them, so restless); / (the children, sleeping); (dreaming, now).

In 1968 Sanguineti's small collection *T.A.T.* was published together with 'Reisebilder' (it would be reprinted in 1972 under the title of *Wirrwarr*, a German term meaning disorder).[5] The volume is divided in two distinct, antithetical sections and only the first part reflects the chaos suggested by the title. With *T.A.T.*, which stands for 'Testo di Appercezione Tematica' (Thematic Apperception Test), Sanguineti abandons the communicative project initiated with *Purgatorio de l'Inferno* and reverts to a linguistic derangement that, in many ways, is even more radical than the disorder expressed in *Laborintus*. In

T.A.T., the linguistic sign often undergoes total desemantization, effecting an irreconcilable split between signifier and signified. The dismemberment of normal language is carried out not only on a syntagmatic level but also within words which are often shredded into phonemes or assembled on the page in a cluster of solitary and silent fragments:

e sopra: nel caso che LUI fosse (e: nel caso che LUI); e sotto: nel
caso (e: nel; e: ne; e: n);
                              e: in tormento; (e per incutere
terrore: (disgusto, forse); nelle ragazze, anche);
                                          e il 24
febbraio scrisse: je ne pense plus ...
(sec. 1)

and above: in case HE were (and: in case that HE); and under: in / case
(and: in; and: e; and: n); / and: in torment; (and to arouse / terror: (disgust,
perhaps); in the young ladies, also); / and the 24th of / February he wrote:
je ne pense plus ...

This reduction of language to a signification that constantly annihilates itself not only represents the insurmountable division between word and reality but declares the inability of poetry, and of all literature, to make sense of the intricate manifestations of history and consciousness. Tragically nihilistic, *T.A.T.*, with its aphasic gibberish, communicates the impossibility of communication and denies literature any redeeming function.

At the opposite pole, and as a dialectical antithesis, is the second part of the volume, 'Reisebilder' (in German, travel illustrations), which, like Heinrich Heine's homonymous works (1824), is structured as a medley of travel notes recounting a trip Sanguineti took through Belgium, Holland, and Germany. The most pronounced feature of this collection is the recovery of a linguistic normality that repeatedly aims at approximating colloquial language. The poems reveal both a narrative breadth absent in all preceding poetry and the emergence of a subjectivity that seems to enwrap the 'I' in a totally private dimension. These elements, however, should not be interpreted as a simple return to traditional intimate forms of poetry, or as the fatal collapse of a political engagement resulting from disillusionment with the post-1968 social realities. On the contrary, with 'Reisebilder,' the political dimension of literature is shifted exclusively towards the personal and the private, with the intent to interpret them from a Marxist perspective. Indeed, Marxism, becomes – in Sanguineti's own words – 'a general anthropology: which explains the entire existence' ('un'antropologia generale: che spiega tutta la vita,' sec. 17). This is not to say that 'Reisebilder' does not express disappointment or convey a sense of existential and intellectual crisis. Closed within the bourgeois limits (section 23 addresses the question of intellectual alienation and the social division of labour), life in its everyday manifestations cannot but exude – according to Sanguineti – 'a mortal moral malady' ('una mortale malattia morale') that degrades and deforms all experiences. These prose poems ('petite proses en poème,' sec. 5), reminiscent of the lowbrow and anti-lyrical language of the Crepuscular poets, are laced with heavy doses of irony typical of the works of Guido Gozzano, a poet to whom Sanguineti devoted various critical studies.[6] This is particularly apparent in a series of disenchanted self-portraits ('I dreamt of being like Hoffmann/in a state of delirium: and I am almost a look-alike of a mediocre English comedian'; 'a man of little relevance as Mao would say' ['mi sognavo simile a un Hoffmann/ in delirio: e sono quasi il sosia di un mediocre comico inglese' (sec. 29); 'un uomo di picolo cabotaggio come direbbe Mao' (sec. 33)]). Nonetheless, these portraits do not represent so much a self-victimizing and defeatist attitude as a demystifying view of the poet's figure in a capitalist society. Having dissolved the traditional aura that surrounded poetry, bourgeois society has also transformed the poet into a 'wage-earner' ('dipendente salariato' [sec. 19]). In 'Reisebilder,' utopia gives way to the uneventful actions of everyday reality and, corresponding to its anti-sublime perception of existence, features a lowbrow diction and a prosaic style. 'Reisebilder,' with its diary-like monologues, its self-irony and parodic use of poetic language, marks another stage of Sanguineti's writing, a stage that continues and is expanded in other collections, such as *Postkarten* (Postcards) and *Stracciafoglio* (Scribbling Pad), published long after Gruppo 63 was disbanded.

These collections continue the trend set by 'Reisebilder' in the use of a colloquial, domestic lexicon and in the epistolary, epigrammatic style centred upon irony and parody. The dejected tone of 'Reisebilder' is still present in *Postkarten* (Milan: Feltrinelli, 1978), enveloping more and more not only the poet but also poetry and literature as a whole ('I leave you with five words, and good-bye: / I never believed in anything' ['vi lascio cinque parole, e addio: / non ho creduto in niente' (sec. 50)]). All possible styles are refused ('today my style is not to have a style' ['oggi il mio stile è non avere stile' (sec. 62)]) and poetry sinks to such a level of domesticity as to be equated with a banal cooking recipe (sec. 49).

With the exception of the second part of the volume, 'Fuori catalogo' (Unlisted) which groups together a series of heterogeneous poems written between 1957 and 1979, including the diatribe against Pier Paolo Pasolini, 'Una polemica in prosa' (A Polemic in Prose), *Stracciafoglio* (Milan: Feltrinelli, 1980) is the diary of a poet who, in the guise of an anti-hero wandering among the ruins of ideological utopias, can offer only one heroic act: self-parody. Poetry becomes a medium of derision and self-derision, a language of destruction and self-destruction. Sanguineti is inevitably confronted with an unsurmountable paradox: as a bourgeois superstructure, poetry (and literature as a whole) must be sabotaged, but the task of sabotage is assigned to literature itself. Examined from such a metalinguistic perspective, this stage of Sanguineti's poetry must be interpreted not as a simple return to earlier traditions of Italian twentieth-century poetry but as a renewed transgression of literary models.

In other collections, including *Novissimum testamentum* (The Newest Will; Lecce: Manni, 1986) and *Bisbidis* (Whispering)[7] [Milan: Feltrinelli, 1987]), Sanguineti proceeds in two opposite directions. At one extreme, he presents poetry as a medium stylistically impoverished, a 'haemorrhage of words' ('emorragia di parole,' *Scartabello* [Notebook], sec. 31)[8] that often points to a state of aphasia or to the decaying and enfeebling processes of the body – the motif of the body incarnated in the text and of the body as a text is a recurrent one. This perspective – summarized by a verse in *Bisbidis*, 'to know well how to write badly' ('sapere bene come scrivere male,' 'Rebus,' sec. 18) – expresses Sanguineti's attack on literature and the urgent need to demystify a bourgeois institution. Literature must question itself and its ways of ordering the world – such is Sanguineti's paradoxical struggle. At the other extreme, Sanguineti's linguistic vigour and extraordinarily rich poetic erudition transform his writing into pleasure and eroticism. Poems such as 'Mimus albus' (*Novissimum testamentum*) and the series 'Alfabeto apocalittico' (Apocalyptic Alphabet) in *Bisbidis*, generate a high degree of semantic energy through homophonic combinations and semantic variations and permutations – anagrams are occasionally used as well as acrostics – that reach a level of Baroque virtuosity. Here is the 'tautogram' 'B' of the latter series, which comprises a poem for each letter of the Italian alphabet:

balza bolsa la bestia babilonica,
bruto bruco di bubbola bubbonica:
blocca le bocche alle bambe bambine,
bruca le brume brivida le brine:
butta alla bionda più brutta la bava,
borra di burro alla bruma più brava:
belva balzana non beve alla briglia,
bocca baciata non buca bottiglia. (*Bisbidis*, 82)

bounding breathless the babylonian beast, / brute grub of bubonic bilge: /
block up the beaks of the babysh bimbas, / browse on the broom-mists &
bear-beat blanched bristle / boot and bawd to the best bad-looking blond, /
bespunk with butter the brunette of the best: / band-socked beast won't
buzzle at the bridle, / beak bussed doesn't bore through the bottle. (Trans.
Howard Rodger MacLean, in Barilli, *Voyage to the End of the Word*, 57)

Texts such as this exploit all sort of linguistic nuances and, with capricious combinations, reveal the ideological urgency of freeing poetic discourse from any form of inhibition, thus opening it to the manifestations of the libido. (Lines from 'La philosophie dans le théâtre,' included in *Novissimum testamentum*, read: 'stimulate true mouths to ejaculate thoughts as thick fluid / of words, and the words become flesh' ['stimolando vere bocche a eiaculare pensieri in un liquame / di parole, e le parole a farsi carne' (39)]). At the same time, these poems indicate that Sanguineti is a materialist poet inasmuch as he works with the materiality of language. He is guided by the conviction that tinkering with the signifiers can eventually effect changes in the signifieds.

The adventure inside the materiality of the signifier does not suggest the absence of reference in the linguistic sign or the impossibility of the writer acting as the agent of his/her own signification. Sanguineti's poetry proclaims neither the death of the author nor the reduction of poetry to an infinite labyrinth of tropes produced by a rhetorical machine without any connection to history and reality. Unquestionably, Sanguineti has abandoned all pre-Freudian conceptions rooted in the principle of an autonomous self above language or outside it. Indeed, the weakening of the subject is a constant feature of Sanguineti's works from the 1980s to the present (see, for example, poems such as 'Codicillo' [Codicil], 'Rebus,' and 'L'ultima passeggiata' [The Last Walk] in *Bisbidis*). However, he has always remained committed to the principle that poetry, as a metalinguistic production of ideologies, is inseparable from a signification that finds its origin inside historical and social boundaries. The materiality of the signifier emerges from a dialectical and materialistic conception; the autonomy of the signifier is not detached from its heteronomous nature, namely, the relationship it establishes with social structures. Signification is born of the dialectical encounter between the materiality of language and linguistic activity, the work performed by a subject who inhabits history and its ideologies.

Tragic and comic, grotesque and oneiric, parodic and clownish, Sanguineti's *pastiches* are not evasive, formal exercises stemming from superfluous refinements of literary culture. Literature is never conceived by Sanguineti as a metahistorical system. Writing is always a mirror of an ideology and, as such, is the locus in which the poet carries out his social and intellectual struggles. Sanguineti's poetry, with its innovative and provocative language, constantly places the reader in a conflict not only with literary models but also with reality.

6 The Poetic Nomadism of Antonio Porta

Antonio Porta's poetic production is guided by a nomadic conception of writing that advocates a constant pursuit of new forms.[1] In his works, writing becomes a linguistic and existential journey marked by tension and restlessness. Literature is conceived as an open and endless project, a work in progress in which the exploration of language and the inquisitive gaze on the world always coincide.

Influenced by the general philosophical orientation provided by phenomenology and existentialism, particularly the writings of Karl Jaspers and Maurice Merleau-Ponty, Porta believes that experiences of reality and acts of cognition are never definitive or totalizing. For him, subjectivity as an expression of being-in-the-world is under constant revision. The subject is not a pre-given entity but the result of an ever-changing dialogue with language and externality. Existence is marked by undisclosure and transcendence, and consequently the desire for authenticity becomes an incessant quest. The invisible lies behind both the human and the natural worlds.

Porta's initial experiments, *La palpebra rovesciata* (The Overturned Eyelid [Milan: Azimuth, 1960]) and *Aprire* (To Open [Milan: Scheiwiller, 1964]), feature a visual approach to reality and an adherence to external events as strategies for bracketing the 'I' and its inner concerns.[2] He constructs an apparently impassive and casual montage of traumatic events taken from daily chronicles, juxtaposed to absurd banalities or often splintered by the defamiliarizing effects of decontextualized quotations. The broken and jittery narration proceeds through short syntactic segments dominated by a slow and strenuous rhythmic patterns.

Most of these poems are populated by hallucinating and schizoid characters and nightmarish and sado-masochistic encounters that verge on the surreal. Reminiscent of Samuel Beckett's theatre or Max Beckmann's and Francis Bacon's Expressionist paintings, Porta's texts are marked by a fragmented narration and a psychological tension that produce a state of suffocating alienation, a tragic vision of existence inevitably dominated by killings, death, anatomical horrors, lacerated matter in a state of decay, cruelty, and social atrocities. Cases in point are poems such as 'Europa cavalca un toro nero' (Europe Rides a Black Bull) and 'Aprire'[3]:

> Cani azzannano i passanti, uomini
> raccomandabili guidano l'assassino,
> fuori, presto, scivoli ...
>
> Gli occhi crepano come uova.
> Afferra la doppietta e spara
> nella casa della madre. Gli occhi
> sono funghi presi a pedate.
> Mani affumicate e testa
> grattugiata corre alla polveriera,
> inciampa, nel cielo lentamente
> s'innalza l'esplosione e i vetri
> bruciano infranti d'un fuoco
> giallo; abitanti immobili
> il capo basso, contano le formiche. ('Europa cavalca un toro nero,
>   IR, 35–6)

Dogs snap at passersby, trustworthy / men guide the assassin, / outside, soon, you slip ... / The eyes crack like eggs. / He grabs the double-barrel and fires / into his mother's house. / The eyes are mushrooms kicked to pieces. / Smoked hands and grated / head he runs to the magazine, / stumbles, slowly the explosion / ascends to the sky and the windows / burn shattered with a yellow blaze; motionless inhabitants / head down, counting ants. (*I Nov*, 322, 325, 327)

> sul pavimento gocce di sudore, alzandosi,
> la macchia non scompare, dietro la tenda,
> la seta nera del fazzoletto, luccica sul soffitto,
> la mano si appoggia, il fuoco nella mano,
> sulla poltrona un nodo di seta, luccica,
> ferita, ora il sangue sulla parete,
> la seta del fazzoletto agita una mano. ('Aprire,' IR, 87)

on the floor drops of sweat, rising, / the strain won't rub out behind the curtain, / the black silk of the handkerchief, shines on the ceiling, / the hand comes to rest, the fire in the hand, / a silk knot on the armchair, it shines, / wounded, now the blood on the wall, / the handkerchief's silk waves a hand. (*I Nov*, 369)

The first poem reveals the ethical and civil dimension of Porta's poetry. In her wandering across the land on a black bull – the colour black becomes a clear emblem of mourning – the mythological figure of Europe (the young woman kidnapped by Jupiter who had metamorphosed into a white bull) witnesses a railroad disaster, a labourer's death in the workplace, a political murder, social oppression and racial persecution, prostitution, suicide, and a nuclear explosion. The poem is built with short and dry segments that give an account of social realities in a documentary-like fashion, without any direct intervention of the narrative voice.

However, this impression can often be deceptive. The seemingly detached and cold gaze on traumatic, everyday realities turns into an investigation of objects and events, as if they were enigmas to be deciphered. Indeed, Porta attempts to transcend them in search of some meaning concealed behind their phenomenical appearance. This results in a poetry permeated by a cognitive tension charged with emotional and existential agitation.

In dealing with the relationship of the individual with oneself, with others, or with nature, Porta is obsessed with the presence of an evil that inevitably emerges in every human expression and to which nature also succumbs. 'Vegetali, animali' (Plants, Animals) and 'La pelliccia del castoro' (The Beaver Skin) are perhaps the poems that most forcefully convey this tragic aspect of his poetry. Here are a few lines from the latter text:

In gola penetra scuotendo
le anche l'animale impellicciato,
dilata la bocca dell'esofago,
lo stomaco si distende, in attesa
d'essere venduto e lavorato
come pelle per guanti. (*IR*, 56)

The furry animal penetrates / the throat shaking the haunches, / the esophagus' mouth dilates, / the stomach distends, waiting / to be sold and worked / as skin for gloves. (*I Nov*, 333)

Violence and evil are not only the result of human actions but are embedded in the natural world, in the same act of living. In its materiality, life is constantly being corroded and subjected to a state of disintegration. In 'La palpebra rovesciata,' (The Eyelid Insideout) which also serves as the title of one of Porta's collections, life is in fact exposed to a form of cancer that destroys it just as a bunch of caterpillars reduces a leaf to skeleton.

As a form of knowledge, poetry assumes the task of penetrating these and other distressing realities as a way of searching for some forms of truth. In the poem 'Dialogo con Herz' (Dialogue with Herz), one of the characters explains:

> '... scoprire un cunicolo,
> giungere al fondamento.' 'Toccare le radici
> e assaggiare le sostanze nutritive.' ...
>   'Stizzito solleva
> la maschera dall'asfalto, ricade nell'incertezza
> di un universo in furioso divenire.'
> 'Scivolo nuotando tra alghe pericolose.
> Penetro in una fogna. Affondo
> in fitte vegetazioni, mi riempio
> di formiche e di foglie. Mastico piume,
> è quasi la conoscenza ...' (*IR*, 49–50)

> ['... find a tunnel, / reach the ground.' 'To touch the roots / and taste nourishing substances.' ... / 'Irritated he takes / the mask off the pavement and again tumbles into the / uncertainty / of a universe in furious becoming.' 'I slip swimming through dangerous seaweed. / I push through a sewer, I sink / in thick vegetation, I fill up / with ants and leaves. I chew on feathers, / it's almost like knowing ...' (*I Nov*, 363, 365)

As the last lines clearly reveal, any act of cognition, for Porta, is destined to be fragile and transient. The desire of knowledge never eradicates human uncertainties. The poem 'Aprire' displays the search for a cognitive opening of reality. The insistent presence of the preposition 'behind' ('dietro') and the constant use of the asyndeton give the poem an obsessive and hammering-like movement that phonetically and semantically suggests an obstacle to be demolished ('Nothing behind the door, behind the curtain, / the fingerprint stuck on the wall, under it, / the car, the window, it stops, behind the curtain' [*I Nov*, 369]

['Dietro la porta nulla, dietro la tenda, / l'impronta impressa sulla parete, sotto, l'auto, la finestra, si ferma, dietro la tenda' (*IR*, 87)]).

However, the obstacle is impenetrable and all the tension accumulated in the attempt to break through it is never released, since the truth behind a mysterious crime, alluded in the entire poem, remains unresolved: the reader never comes to know either the victim or the killer. The numerous antinomic constructs and paradoxes present throughout the entire poem suggest an unsurmountable ambiguity of the real from which definitive truths cannot be extrapolated.

This general outlook, however, does not lead to a passive acceptance of the existing state of things. The poem 'Di fronte alla luna' (In Front of the Moon) displays a direct attack on social inequities and oppressions ('Go up in an helicopter and watch, don't / remember anything. Come down and throw punches / ... / Or rent a plane, / the explosive falls violently' [*I Nov*, 339, 341] ['Sali in elicottero e osserva, non / ricordare nulla. Scendi e fai a pugni / ... / O si affitti un aereo, / l'esplosivo precipita con violenza' (*IR*, 40–1)]). However, the urge to revolt is countered by the awareness that a poet's social antagonism is easily absorbed and rendered innocuous by that same society against which the attacks are conducted:

Avvertimento utile: la società
materasso, gommapiuma, carta
assorbente. Pedate con rabbia e macchie
d'inchiostro: il poeta scatta
di forza, approda tra i nemici,
annega nel cocktail, senza saperlo. (*IR*, 41)

Warning, useful: the mattress / society, foam rubber, blotting / paper. Angry kicks and ink / spots: the poet snaps / hard, lands among enemies, / drowns in the cocktail, without knowing. (*I Nov*, 341)

In this poem, too, the figure of the antithesis and the tension it generates is dominant. On the one hand, poetry's role is associated with an act of self-mutilation (in the final stanza, the poet's vocal chords are pulled out and swallowed) that can produce only a condition of impotence and, on the other, the validity of its cognitive function is resolutely reaffirmed ('But the end of art is, at least, to discover / the image of / man / us' [*I Nov*, 347] ['Ma scoprire, almeno, è il fine dell'arte, / l'immagine di / uomo, noi' (*IR*, 45)]). Escape from society is not contemplated as a possible solution. For the protagonist of the poem 'Meridiani e paralleli' (Meridians and Parallels), departure from society ends in madness and desolation in a remote island. As well, cognition does not offer absolute deliverance. Indeed, knowledge becomes, in Porta's world-view, the source of a traumatic and tragic rapport with reality.

In the series of poems entitled 'Rapporti umani' (Human Relationships), a fragmented and agitated narration discloses characters trapped in nightmarish physical violence. Their brutal actions often acquire animal attributes. Porta carefully avoids the thrilling traits of the horror story – many poems include vicious manifestations of eroticism – by appropriately counterbalancing his dehumanized and horrific images of existence with anticlimatic effects, often obtained through references to actions of ordinary, everyday experience:

I due stanno abbracciati, con un mazzo di crisantemi
bevono alla loro tazza, le unghie nella schiena, la
candela gli brucia le mani, continua a camminare in
ginocchio, tenero pallone, curva del ventre, partorirà
un gatto ... (*IR*, sec. XV, 108)

The two are embraced, with a bunch of chrysanthemums / they drink from their cup, nails in the back, the / candle burns the hands, he continues walking on his / knees, tender balloon, a curve of the belly, she will bear / a cat ...

Con la punta ammazza formiche, lo spillo infilza-ragni,
annoda le bacche nel fazzoletto di lino, lo bacia lungamente
gli recide le dita, una mano, i piedi e il membro ... (*IR*, sec. XX, 113)

With the tip kills ants, the spider-piercing pin, / ties the berries in a linen handkerchief, she kisses him at length / cuts off his fingers, one hand, his feet and penis ...

This series documents a condition of historical alienation in which the individual is dissociated from himself/herself and from others. In Porta's world, there are no relationships but exchanges of bodies and things, a world in which even intercourse is displayed as a reified relation. The alienation is linguistically objectified in incongruous syntactic constructs and discrepant spatio-temporal sequences. Only occasionally does the language become more restrained and linear, coinciding with possible projections of the 'I,' as in the following lines:

... sulla via di casa, il
gocciolìo del sudore: entrando qualcosa
accadde, non ricordo; dietro il portone,
immobile tra i cristalli, l'ostilità di
mia moglie e mi chiesi chi era.
Per togliere la polvere, chinato, si recidevano
le stringhe, la fronte mi sanguinava, tra i
cristalli spezzati, le stringhe tra i capelli,
e premevo, frugando tra le schegge, scrivendo
nella polvere, la lingua mi si tagliava,
lambendo, il sangue colava dagli occhi, sulle tempie,
i figli non sanno nulla ... (*IR*, sec. XI, 104)

towards home, the / dripping of the sweat: entering something / happened, I don't remember; behind the door, / motionless amongst the crystals, my wife's / hostility and I asked myself who she was. / To get rid of the dust, bent forward, the shoelaces / were breaking, my forehead bleeding, amongst / the shattered crystals, the / shoelaces in the hair, / and I pressed rummaging through the fragments, writing / in the dust, my tongue being cut, / gliding over, my blood running down from the / eyes, on the temples, / my children know nothing ...

In one of the most radical moments of this first stage of his career, Porta arrives at the conception of poetry as a discourse reduced to zero: the reduction of language to zero corresponding to the negation of the world. A case in point is the experiment in concrete poetry titled *Zero*, in which the verbal signs, freed from syntactic constrains and rhythmic recurrences, bring to life a montage of disconnected perceptions, forming a discourse that destroys the pseudorational order of daily communication and forces the reader to experience a signification that constantly annihilates itself.[4] However, Porta is always far from advocating absolutist solutions.

Events without order or perspective, syntagms clashing in antithetical or conflicting constructions, mutilated and solitary signs – these are the recurring elements that create the disquieting and crumbling reality of *Zero*. The result is a poetic world that opposes all forms of communication, as expressed by the dominant culture, and experiences a semantic collapse that exposes a reified and alienating language and, at the same time, creates a tension awaiting new and liberating conditions of existence:

> tante agita la sua coda, gli occhi fissi nell'ipnosi, roteando le gambe
> tato, dilatati e richiusi, franato con un muro di mattoni, sotto le finestre di
> per salire gli scalini, riprese a scavare sotto la torre, le ossa ripulite gli av
> schizzò nella pianura, con una coda di scintille, annottando, gola palpi
> (*IR*, sec. 4, 74)

> [many he wags his tail, eyes in a hypnotic stare, swinging the legs / ted, dilated and closed up, collapsed with a brick wall, under the windows of / in order to walk up the stairs, he started to dig under the tower again, the cleaned up bones, the adv / he sketched on the plain, with a tail of sparks, growing dark, you touch throat (Trans. Lawrence R. Smith, *The New Italian Poetry*, 447)

In his subsequent collection, *Cara* (Dear [Milan: Feltrinelli, 1969]), Porta drastically changes his stylistic register and accentuates a poetics of provocation and subversion. *Cara* pursues a metaliterary operation centred on the mechanisms and the primary structures of poetic language, involving concurrently a critique of the formal institutions of tradition. With *Cara* – the title seems to refer with affection and irony to poetry itself – the signifieds undergo a drastic atomization that blocks the emergence of substantial and organic semantic nuclei. Essentially, Porta recycles materials present in his previous collections, restructuring them in a new formal organization, as if he wanted to assign to poetic forms the function of finding different ways of dealing with specific contents. The interpretation of reality is delegated, in a radical fashion, to poetry's linguistic space, especially its rhythmic and syntactic structures. The most elementary organization of the texts that make up this collection is constituted by a catalogue of narrative microsegments, divided graphically, which undergo modulations and permutations of their rhythm and syntax totally devoid of any semantic articulation (in many instances, texts are constructed with two or three separate columns, making possible different horizontal and vertical readings). Each segment is semantically autonomous and is not inserted in any sequence tied to principles of continuity or subordination. The impression is like viewing a film without a plot, blocked in the synchronic fixedness of each individual frame. Here is the initial sequence of a poem entitled 'Come se fosse un ritmo' (As If It Were a Rhythm):

si servono di uncini
chiedono dei fagioli
amano la musica
ballano in cerchio
escono dalle finestre
aprono la botola
cambiano posizione
controllano l'orario
pieni di medicine
si appendono al soffitto
si servono di forbici
(*Cara*, 39)

si alzano dalle sedie
azzannano i bambini
si tolgono le scarpe
seguono lo spartito
vanno a fare il bagno
rientrano dalla finestra
si chinano sul water
escono di chiesa
cadono dalle sedie
colano con lentezza
li prendono a pedate

they use hooks
they order beans
they love music
they dance in a circle
they leave through the windows
they open the trap door
they change position
they change the schedule
full of medicine
they hang from the ceiling
they use scissors

they rise from the chairs
they sink their teeth into the children
they take off their shoes
they follow the score
they go take a bath
they come back through the window
they bend over the toilet
they leave the church
they fall out of chairs
they pour slowly
they kick others around

(Trans. Paul Vangelisti, *Invasions & Other Poems* [San Francisco: Red Hill Press, 1986], 13)

Porta reduces to the bone the syntactic figure and his lexicon is surprisingly elementary and impoverished for a poetic context. Indeed, his poetry pursues a process of total flattening of the rhetorical procedures tied to traditional poetic forms. It is an act of provocation in that it refuses to manage the institution of poetry as a privileged space made up of a highbrow, aestheticized, and seductive language.

The non-hierarchical and essentially asynchronic syntactic organization of this poetry atomizes the perception of reality and freezes the events in the instant of their occurrence. All prospects of narrative progression are completely blocked, and, for the reader, there is no possibility of engaging with the symbolic or metaphoric plane of language. The chilling literality of *Cara*'s language, the intransitivity of its verbal signs, together with the syntactic and rhythmic construction that is obsessively forced to return upon itself, seem to hypothesize that language represents only the material presence of itself. Poetry is its inner structure, the rhythmic space in which it moves. Even though the signifiers refer to repetitive and absurd acts of daily experience, to gestures and behaviours of others observed through a lens of estrangement and inauthenticity, they underline primarily their own construction: the poetic devices that regulate and organize them. These features make *Cara* an extremely daring experiment in metapoetry.

The metapoetic dimension of this collection is underscored in texts like 'Sonetto' (Sonnet), 'Lirica' (Lyric), and 'Rima' (Rhyme), which are constructed exclusively with the intent of evidentiating mechanisms of literariness and linguistic strategies associated with poetry. The persistent use of anaphora, epanados, epanalepsis, and phonetic devices like alliteration, paronomasia, and assonance are another clear indication that the objective of these poems is to exhibit their own internal structure. Here is the last section of 'Lirica':

> non il ricordo dei ricordi dimenticati
>> oppure lo sgradevole luogo della dimenticanza
> non gli alberi seppelliscono sotto le strade
>> oppure crescono in luoghi stretti d'assedio
> non si vedono né ascoltano il canto perfetto
>> oppure camminano con sicurezza decrescente
>>> cresce con la peluria l'animale sognato (*Cara*, 97)

not the remembrance of forgotten remembrances / or the unpleasant place of oblivion / not the trees they bury under the streets / or they grow in places under siege / not seeing each other nor they listen to the perfect singing / or they walk with decreasing certainty / the fancied animal grows with fuzz

The self-reflexivity of this project represents a radical rejection of literature as a vehicle for administering discourses conceived outside its domain. Poetry wants to speak of itself, it wants to reclaim the specificity of its language. This is why texts like 'Come è scomparso Mallarmé' (The Way Mallarmé Has Disappeared) and 'Critica della poesia' (Criticism of Poetry) are centred on a form of poetry that investigates its present condition. The latter text, together with 'Agente in pubblico' (Agent in Public), seems to express a desire to overcome traditional poetic boundaries in search of new visual and spatial possibilities, reminiscent of works related to Op and Kinetic Art.

Whenever we witness, in some rare texts of this collection, the surfacing of the 'I' or a direct attempt to ideologize poetic discourse, neither reassuring statements nor definite conclusions are offered. In 'Le fonti dell'inganno' (The Sources of Deception), the line 'stand up at once to sit down again stand up' ('alzati subito per sederti di nuovo alzati') reveals a state of anxiety, a contradictory existential condition for which there are no solutions (102). (Inner tensions emerge also in verses like 'one rolls in the courtyard / Walnuts get eaten head bent over the plate / ... / the first phalanxes deboned by the throat / of domestic mice / in every part of the body' ['si rotala nel cortile / Si mangiano le noci e si china il capo sul piatto / ... / le prime falangi disossate dalla gola / di topolini domestici / in ogni parte del corpo' (101)]).

Perhaps owing to the profound socio-political changes that affected Italian society beginning in 1968, Porta's poetry also embarks in a decisive new direction: poetic interventions in the linguistic code develop into direct attacks on an automatized and massified social language. The first confirmation of this new tendency is *Metropolis* (Milan: Feltrinelli, 1971), a collection that contains texts written between 1969 and 1970. *Metropolis* presents two complementary operations: a contentious and demystifying inquiry into the reified linguistic repertory of contemporary culture, juxtaposed to proposals for therapeutic-language models. Poetry is engaged on a double front: on the one hand, it is called to provide a critical examination of socio-linguistic historical conditions, and, on the other, it is set on an exploration of its own spaces of communication.

In the first half of this collection, Porta denounces a closed, anti-critical, and anti-dialectical language always ready to manufacture its messages in a rigid, banal, and flatly dogmatic fashion for rapid and automatic consumption by passive consumers. In 'Quello che tutti pensano' (What Everyone Thinks), catalogues of commonplaces, linguistic stereotypes, and defining *topoi* that range from politics to religion, sex to psychology, sociology to art, are compiled in a seemingly casual montage. The conflicting combinations cancel meanings, demystify them, and reveal all sorts of falsehood. Here are some segments:

che la libertà è prima di tutto un dovere
che la libertà sta nell'aderire alla legge
che il destino dell'uomo è segnato fin dalla nascita
che l'amore è destinato a diminuire col tempo
che si vede dalla faccia che uno è un porco
che bisogna dire di sì il più tardi possibile
che bisogna dire di no per farsi rispettare
che vivere insieme ai cinesi è impensabile ...
che le bombe possono metterle solo i figli dei ricchi
che gli studenti non pensano a fare l'amore
che gli studenti occupano le università solo per accoppiarsi
che le lettere d'amore di Marx non esistono
che le lettere d'amore di Rosa Lux ci fanno bene sperare
che i coiti a gruppi sono passati di moda
che i vescovi sono diventati tolleranti
che la polizia sa chi è il capo ma non può dirlo
l'omossessualità è o non è una vergogna
non c'è altro da fare che attendere
(sec. 2, 11–12)

that freedom is first and foremost a duty / that freedom depends on obeying laws / that man's destiny is decided from birth / that love grows weak with time / that one can tell from a man's face that he is a pig / that one must hold off as long as possible before saying yes / that in order to be respected one must say no / that to coexist with the Chinese in unthinkable / ... / that only the sons of the rich can plant bombs / that students don't think of sex / that students go to the university just to find a mate / that Marx's love letters do not exist / that Rosa Lux's love letters give us hope / that group sex is out of style / that bishops have become tolerant / that the police know who the leader is but cannot tell / is or isn't homosexuality shameful / there is nothing else to do but wait (Trans. Pasquale Verdicchio, *Metropolis* [Copenhagen and Los Angeles: Green Integer, 1999], 17–19)

This destructive process demonstrates the degradation of language to an object of consumerism, to an authoritarian and alienating instrument that adopts prevaricating definitions as a form of manipulation. In the 'metropolis' of mass society, there is a need to ingest trivial, simplified, and shallow forms of information dissociated from all complexities. The 'metropolis' is indeed the space in which one is constantly confronted by an endless inventory of banalities and stupidities. It suffices to note how Freudian and psychoanalytic theories are reduced to cliches ('sexuality is the driving force of everything'; 'civilization is founded on death'; 'orgasm is a return to the womb') or how Marx's notions are turned into a trite statement ('economics is the basic determining fact for everything') ('che la sessualita è il motore di tutto'; 'che la civiltà si fonda sulla morte'; 'che l'orgasmo è il ritorno alla madre'; 'che alla base ci sta il fatto economico che tutto determina' [secs. V, VI, VIII, V respectively]). The people of the modern metropolis speak in a robot-like language made up of slogans mechanically assimilated – indeed, the title of this collection can be seen as a direct reference to the homonymous film by Fritz Lang which features machine-like beings who have lost their humanity.

A distant model for this collection could be Gustave Flaubert's *Dictionnaire des idées reçues* (1847). Porta, however, rather differently from the French novelist, does not catalogue the idiotic commonplaces of his times with dispassionate and neutral impartiality. 'What everyone thinks' is an ironic and parodic poetic operation for which some affinities can be drawn with Pop Art. Like that art movement, Porta's poems adopt procedures of decontextualization, serialization, and iteration of materials with the objective of making a social commentary. The stereotype of the 'ready-made' image of Pop Art, extracted from the consumer culture, becomes Porta's linguistic stereotype of the 'already-spoken.'

If the objective of this first section of *Metropolis* is that of overcoming the anonymity of social language, the second section, titled 'La rose,' is an attempt at recovering a healthy linguistic ambiguity through the force of poetry. The poems of this section represent an experiment dictated by the necessity of rescuing the creativity of language in a time in which it is threatened by the automatism and the fossilization of its collective usage. 'La rose,' then, is an act of poetic freedom that demonstrates a total indifference towards the organization of its contents in a focused and specific discourse. The result is the creation of a series of surreal images that, in their unusual associations, display all the resourcefulness and inventive potentialities of language:

l'interno al riparo la bocca con foglie
sbucciano il corpo nei giardini domenicali
fiorita la pelle tra le pareti mobili
i pavoni del cuore scendono dalla neve ...

gabbie presenti pareti non visibili
il seme galleggia senza luogo
incitano le mosche i cavalli alla rivolta
spine riempite di fazzoletti ombrosi (31, 37)

interior under repair[5] the mouth with leaves / the body peeled in domin-
ical gardens / skin flowered through mobile walls / the heart's peacocks
come down from the snow / ... / present cages invisible walls / sperm
floats aimlessly / flies incite horses into revolution / thorns full of shad-
owy kerchiefs. (Trans. Pasquale Verdicchio, 55, 67)

The rose becomes an ambivalent image connected both to the traditional motif of beauty and love and to poetry itself. It represents a passionate reality, a vital space invaded by an amorous tension that
cannot be contained by any definitive and uncomplicated resolutions
('I know how to enter I know it is forbidden / I know how to run away
I know I won't / how to call you I won't open my mouth / how to
come closer I won't touch you' [trans. Verdicchio, 63] ['come entrare so
che non si entra / so come fuggire so che non fuggirò / come chiamarti
so che non aprirò bocca / come avvicinarti che non ti toccherò' (Metropolis, 35)]).

Besides 'La rose,' the second half of Metropolis, moving in the opposite
direction and yet complementary to the destructive tension of the opening section, uses defalsifying language models as an hypothesis for a
recovery of communication. The first series of poems, 'Modello di bambini per linguaggio' (Children's Model for Language), presents a regression to infantile linguistic procedures aimed at regaining an elementary
and primordial expressiveness. The simplification of both the syntactic
organization and of the semantic fields coincides with an uncomplicated interaction with the world. This series denotes simple sensory
actions that are directed towards the encounter with a microuniverse of
objects that are made familiar through basic tactile, visual, tasting, and
hearing perceptions ('eats salt / burns finger / beard burns / ... / wall
hard / sings cat / blackbird screams / pigeon flies / leaf green / bell
sounds / ... / hot pasta / foot hurt / eye full' [trans. Verdicchio, 73,
75] [mangia sale / scotta dito / barba scotta / ... / muro duro / canta
gatto / merlo grida / piccio vola / foglia verde / campa suona / ...
calda pasta / piede male / occhio pieno' (Metropolis, 41–2)]).

The second model, devoted to the working couples of the modern
metropolis, offers a possible catharsis for their frustrating lack of com-

munication. The closing poem is a desublimating model for self-portraits. With its repetitive and fluid rhythm, similar to that of nursery rhymes, 'Modello per autoritratti' (Model for Self-Portraits) suggests a process for dislodging outmoded conceptions of the 'I' and of subjectivity. This poetry, however, does not uphold a nihilistic effacement of the subject. Following phenomenological perspectives, it refuses to encapsule the 'I' in any definitive and paralysing version. There is no pre-constituted and immobile subject. As it encounters the world, the 'I' is in a constant state of changes and modulations:

io non sono non c'è non chi è
non abito non credo non ho
cinquantanni ventuno dodici che c'è
quando bevo nell'acqua nuotare non so
con la penna che danza la polvere che avanza
non credo non vedo se esco né tocco
mangiare se fame digerire non do
prima corpo poi mente poi dico poi niente
è un'altra chissà se alla fine cadrà
né una vita né due né un pianeta né un altro
le lingue non capisco le grida annichilisco (*Metropolis*, 53)

I am not there is not who is / I do not live do not believe do not have / fifty years twenty twelve what is it / when I drink in the water swimming I cannot / with the pen dancing the leftover dust / I do not believe do not see if I go out or touch / eating if hunger digest I don't give / first body then mind then say then nothing / it's another if in the end it will fall / neither one life nor two neither one planet nor another / languages I do not understand and annihilate screams (Trans. Pasquale Verdicchio, 97, 99)

Following the demise of Gruppo 63, Porta's poetry shifts towards a more direct investigation of socio-historical realities and reaches transparent ideological positions. A case in point is the collection *Week-end* (Rome: Cooperativa Scrittori, 1974), in which capitalist society is portrayed as a total debasement of life. This ideological clarification is accompanied, as an immediate expressive correlative, by the recovery of a narrative flow that has abandoned the lacerated and magmatic linguistic constructs of earlier works. This poetry denounces the depersonalizing effects of automation, the anonymity of the individual, the atrophy and suffocation brought on by organized and alienating labour. Critical awareness of the squalid conditions of the industrial, capitalist reality – a 'plundered land' populated by 'boneless men,' wandering through the 'Rich ... Chemical Cathedral' ('terra predata'; 'uomini disossati'; 'Ricca ... Cattedrale Chimica') – generates, as an antithetical yearning, the vision of a utopian city which will subsist not as a fossilized and immobile structure but as a flexible 'point of protection' ('punto di protezione') in which people, possessing a purified linguistic code ('the thoughts language that is to be taken literally' ['il pensiero linguaggio che va preso alla lettera']), will meet others and leave them according only to their own desires. The motif of the journey, interpretable as a metaphor of knowledge and liberation, is tied to that of labour restored to a non-alienating condition, strictly connected to the autonomous survival of the nomad, in a world where 'land ownership doesn't exist' ('non esiste proprietà del suolo').[6]

The constant metamorphosis of Porta's poetry indicates its obstinate commitment to explore language and to pierce its opacity in search of transparency. The poet-nomad with his project of transforming the world is continuously anxious to set out on the endless journey of language. A clear indication of a new poetic direction comes in 'Brevi lettere' (Brief Letters), a series of texts that opens the collection *Passi Passaggi* (Steps Passages) [Milan: Mondadori, 1980]).[7] The epistolary style of these poems reveals a project of communication, one aimed at opening a more direct dialogue with the reader. The poet sends out messages that stem from news reports, occurrences in his own life, or simply daily events transfigured into signals emitting hidden pulsations of existence. Examined from an ideological perspective, *Passi Passaggi* is rooted in the realization that poetry must regain its voice, must undergo a shift towards messages aimed at transforming the world and leaving behind its horrors. However, Porta's project does not regress to an easy, rigid signification. His adherence to a poetics in progress has its correlation in a signification in progress. It does not have any claim to transcendental truths. With its 'thin passages that the wind keeps open' ('passaggi sottili che il vento tiene aperti' [78]), poetry is a 'bridge oscillating between an indefinite point and another undefinable, distant and mutable' ('ponte oscillante tra un punto indefinito verso un altro punto indefinibile, distante e mutevole').[8] This is the case with 'La scelta della voce' (Choosing a Voice), which is comprised of texts originally written for the theatre. Metamorphic manifestations of the body, cannibalistic acts, sexual desire, birth, rebirth, and love are the emblems of regeneration and transformation. Porta, however, carefully avoids any form of seductive and reassuring lyricism: the mythical and fabulous dimension is in fact frequently undercut by the presence of a familiar, everyday language and by continuous outbursts of self-irony. The literary references, the problematic affirmations on writing ('writing / writing itself wants to erase itself' [*Passenger*, 48] ['la scrittura / scrivendosi vuole cancellarsi' (sec. IV)]), together with the tension between silence and voice, display a poetic space far from sentimental effusions and definitive solutions.

The communicative form present in the last stages of Porta's poetry results in a less traumatic rapport with reality. In other words, the recovery of a simpler, more linear formal organization of the texts interacts with a new perception of the world. The dimension of the tragic, which was the recurrent trait of the first collections, is replaced in *Invasioni* (Invasions [Milan: Mondadori, 1984]) by the luminosity and the transparency produced by the lightness of images. With this series of poems, Porta's new language tends to transfigure reality into an adventure of surreal, dream-like perceptions ('locked away in the cupboard / the kite / flies in my mind'; 'butterflies made of light / fly down the mountainside / the scorpions crouch' [trans. Anthony Baldry, *Invasions & Other Poems*]) ('rinchiuso nell'armadio / l'aquilone / vola nella mia mente'; 'farfalle di luce volano giù dalla montagna / gli scorpioni si acquattano' [*Invasioni*, 59, 66]).

Porta's recovery of the communicative force of language, together with its possibilities of penetrating reality, is born out of complexity; it is the outcome of a long, tense relationship with language. His constructive project represents a form of opposition and resistance to any theory which claims that language is a fictive, illusory medium and affirms the collapse of all cognitive possibilities. Porta does not accept the apocalyptic claims of the absence of reality in language. For him, reality does not vanish behind the displacing movement of language. Poetic language, Porta maintains in the introduction to his anthology *Nel fare poesia* (Making Poetry), 'is "within" the *langue*, as man's history hands it to us, not fixed forever but in a continuous transformation because the *langue* in turn is "within" the prelinguistic ocean, the immediate experience, the sentiment that derives from it, and even the ecstasy of being-in-the-world' ('sta "dentro" la lingua, come la storia degli uomini ce la consegna, non fissata per sempre ma in continua trasformazione perché la lingua a sua volta sta "dentro" l'oceano prelinguistico, l'esperienza immediata, il sentimento che ne scaturisce, e perfino l'estasi dell'esserci' [5]).

Porta's constructive project, with its linguistic and political ramifications, is also at the basis of his last poetic collection, *Il giardiniere contro il becchino* (The Gardener against the Grave-digger [Milan: Mondadori, 1988]). The opening section with its triumph of life over death, announces a narrative and mythical dimension that constantly communicates the necessity of struggle, of not laying down arms, of planting, as the gardener of the book's title, the seed of life:

Che cosa fai, giardiniere?
Hai gettato le armi?
Sei impaurito dalla neve, dal gelo?
Prendi una delle vanghe da trincea,
lo sai che scavando un poco
sotto la neve non va sottozero,
tu conosci l'invisibile materiale
l'utero di ogni seme. (18)

What are you doing, gardener? / Have you surrendered your arms? / Are you frightened by the snow, by the frost? / Take one of the hoes used for trenches, / you know that digging a little / beneath the snow it doesn't reach below zero, / you know the invisible material / the uterus of every seed.

The closing poems, in the section 'Airone' (Heron), convey a sense of liberation and of regained vitality. Poetry is ready to re-establish its role of mediation with reality. Words are no longer estranging and reified entities but revealing links between the 'I' and the world. In 'Airone,' words are liberating, vital messages:

quello che è rimasto,
quello che resiste,
là sotto, tu lo vedi,
airone, sotto le montagne di macerie,
dentro i crateri delle bombe,
sotto le colline d'immondizia.
lì dove resiste, continua,
rinasce la semplice vita,
ultima, dimenticata, dileggiata
rimossa, ridotta a poltiglia
nella mente degli uomini,

la semplice vita,
il nascere e morire,
rinascere e volare via,
aprirsi, amare,
quello che è vivo, amore,
sotto la semina dell'odio. (sec. 4, 80–1)

that which has remained, / that which resists, / under there, you see it, / heron, under the mountains of rubble, / inside the craters made by the bombs, / under the hills of dirt, / there where it resists, continues, / the simple life is reborn, / last, forgotten, sneered, / removed, reduced to pulp / in the mind of men, / the simple life, / birth and death, / born again and flying away, / opening up, loving, / that which is alive, love, / under the sowing of hate.

In Porta's poetry, language can suddenly explode and venture on new and unexpected itineraries. The constant verbal tension and the continuous revision of the cognitive canons of reality confer on his poetry a rare and fertile quality. Tragically, this poetic vitality was cut short. Porta died in 1989 after a massive heart attack.

7 Nanni Balestrini and the Invisibility of the Poetic 'I'

Nanni Balestrini takes the revolt of the Novissimi against conventional forms of poetry and the commodification of the linguistic code to extreme limits.[1] His experimentation can in fact be recognized as one of the group's most radical attempts to break down literary practices tied to principles of subjectivity or to representational canons. In Balestrini's poetic space, there is no possibility either of a subjective use of language or of formulating a narration of the life-world. This is a poetry in which the authorial voice is essentially pulverized and made invisible. Writing, conventionally intended as an individual expression of style and imagination, practically comes to an end, as does language's ability to conceptualize the status of reality. Faced by an alienated and reified language as a social system of communication and by an equally alienated and fossilized literary speech, Balestrini finds it mystifying and self-defeating to search for any form of poetry as an authentic expression of the 'I.' Poetry's goal can no longer be identified with the disclosure of sentiments or with the intuition of transhistorical properties of a universal spirit, as claimed by the idealist aesthetic model of Benedetto Croce, whose influence was deeply felt within the dominant literary and artistic movements in Italy. Accordingly, Balestrini's poetic activity cannot be associated with the creation of a figural language in search of a private symbolic space or with the construction of an allegorical system of meanings. Indeed, in some ways, this poetry can be seen as a parody both of daily social communication and of conventional poetic language.

Balestrini's poetic production, dating from the late 1950s to the late 1960s – essentially all his production associated with the Novissimi and with Gruppo 63 – performs two interrelated and complementary functions. On the one hand, it mocks existing modes of communication by simulating texts totally devoid of messages (a commodified and automatized linguistic code becomes incapable of producing real communication), and, on the other, it strives to revitalize language by making it the subject of poetic activity. In other words, Balestrini's poetry is an act of destruction and provocation inasmuch as it creates an aesthetic experience of the loss of meaning to which a commercialized, robotized, and trivialized linguistic code is subjected within the context of capitalism and consumer society. But, at the same time, it tries to resematicize language by providing the reader with poetic materials that manifest all the fecundity of linguistic ambiguity and unpredictability. Indeed, it can be said that the poet tries to rediscover life in the midst of the linguistic ruins of our contemporariness. In this sense, as will be discussed, Balestrini's texts are a perfect demonstration of the poetics of the open work and there is no doubt that they feel the effects of the cultural climate created in that period by the initial spread of formalism, structuralism, information theory, and linguistics at large.

Balestrini published his first poems in journals such as *Il Gesto, Azimuth, Mac espace* (edited by the artists and art critics like Enrico Baj, Piero Manzoni, and Gillo Dorfles), and, starting at its foundation in 1956, *Il Verri*, of which he became a member of the editorial board. These early poems, written between 1954 and 1956, were collected by Balestrini many years later in the volume *Osservazioni sul volo degli uccelli* (Observations on the Flight of Birds [Milan: Scheiwiller, 1988]). The dominant feature of the collection (in particular 'Fuso orario' [Time Zone], 'I testimoni' [The Witnesses], and 'Mattino d'ebbrezza' [Morning of Inebriation]) is the attention given to the concreteness of the objects and to the immediacy of images, a trait that recalls Pound's concept of 'presentation.' In fact, Pound's ideogrammatic method is well absorbed by Balestrini. The juxtaposition of objects and events follows paratactic or asyndetic constructions that try to capture the simultaneity of perceptions and discard discursive and descriptive modes of writing. These early poems were excluded from the anthology of the Novissimi. Even though they display advanced aesthetic qualities, they have not yet achieved the level of linguistic provocation and disarray to be found in the collection *Il sasso appeso* (The Dangling Rock [Milan: Scheiwiller, 1961]), the work that anticipates the major traits of Balestrini's entire poetic project.

Here, possibilities of narration are continuously frustrated by the presence of semantic oppositions, antitheses, and antinomies that not only cause a state of tension but also create a linguistic and mental suspension that opens the texts to a multiplicity of meanings. The following are segments of the introductory section:

> non c'è pericolo che non arriviamo, pazienti godiamoci il viaggio
> godiamoci, non c'è pericolo se ci perdiamo, tanto non si viaggia
> (il profilo di un paziente su un carrello attraversando la carestia),
> tanto non si arriva, arriveremo: all'ameba, alla mecca, alla mela,
> dietro gli uccelli in fuga bassi dalla città minata, dal maltempo ...
> Gonfio di miele il fazzoletto sul sedile posteriore vuoto
> e dopo un'ora ne avevamo abbastanza e continua (non ne usciremo)
>
> fumando e raccontando *quand'ero tossicomane* può continuare
> *con queste mani sempre pulite seppellivo diseppellivo I [vivi* ... (sec. 1)

> We'll get there, don't worry, relax, let's enjoy the ride, / let's make the
> most of it, don't worry if we get lost, we are not really travelling / (profile
> of a patient on a rollaway crossing the famine), / anyway we're not get-
> ting there, we'll get there: amoeba, to Mecca, to apple, / behind the birds
> fleeing low from the mined city, from bad weather /...// Bloated with
> honey the handkerchief on the empty back seat / and after an hour we'd
> had enough and he goes on (we'll never make it through this) // smoking
> and telling of *when I was an addict* he can go on / *with these always clean
> hands I buried and unburied the living* ... (*I Nov* 273, 275)

The menacing presence of a dangling rock attached to a fragile string functions as a unifying element for the five sections that form the first part of this short collection. The threat of this rather bizarre and baffling image is juxtaposed to the recurrent theme of an escape that is presented either as an actual possibility or as a purely fictional concept. The escape has to take place from a 'mined city' ('città minata,' [sec. 1]), from 'swollen walls' ('muri gonfi' [sec. 3]), from a 'decayed Europe' ('Europa cariata' [sec. 5]), or from earth itself (earth is represented as a howling planet whose gravitational force must be eluded – 'the scarf that defies / gravity' ['la sciarpa che sfugge / la gravità' (sec. 5)]). The escape from these perilous spatial settings (made even more precarious by the presence of a storm and a landslide that 'swallows' everything [secs. 1 and 3, respectively]) corresponds to the need to flee from the negativity of a temporal condition if survival is to be assured. The 'wounded season' ('stagione piagata' [sec. 5]) takes on all the meaning of a historical predicament. Although the action of cutting the string from the dangling rock indicates the possibility of liberation ('if the rope holds out / we'll manage to get out if we use the blade' ['se la corda terrà / dunque riusciremo a uscire se useremo la lama'] (sec. 3)]), references to spatial movements or to a journey, which are found in every section, do not actually portray any advancement or progression. The reader, in fact, is confronted by a 'motionless' state of mobility, or by antithetic actions and gestures that cancel each other out. Indeed, in the closing section, any allusion to externality is set against a metapoetic space in which all deliberations shift towards the action of writing and to fictitious circumstances:

> ... (ma lasciami parlare) ... a perdita d'uomo un'altra ... strofa:
> Abbondanti cespugli di ginestre fanno tutto giallo e non ne vale
> la pena, né quel sasso maledetto col suo spago che dondola teso,
> e noi senza partire dunque l'intero pomeriggio fissando i corvi alti,
> ogni parola con convinzione, e una nuvola, una tragica finzione, la cosa
> appesa (lasciatemi finire), o un'altra cosa, fino a averne abbastanza.
> (sec. 5)

> ... (please let me speak) ... as far as the walking can see ... another stanza: /
> Lush broom bushes glow all yellow and it's not worth / the trouble nor is
> that damned dangling rock with its string hanging taut / while we with-
> out ever leaving therefore staring the whole afternoon at ravens high
> above, / each word with conviction, and a cloud, a tragic put-on, the
> hanging / thing (let me finish), or something else, until we've had enough.
> (*I Nov* 281, 283)

There is no doubt that the poem sends signals of discontent with socio-historical conditions and stirs up a spirit of dissent. Nonetheless, definitive messages are not there and readers are forced to deal with the semantic suspension and uncertainty of the poem by establishing a dialogue and constructing their own possible meanings. Indeed, the texts that form the second and closing section of the collection, titled 'Frammenti del sasso appeso' (Fragments of the Dangling Rock), are organized in a structure similar to a chessboard in which horizontal, vertical, or diagonal readings are possible either within each single text or through combinations with another. Balestrini aims at liberating readers from the oppressive constrictions imposed by the authorial voice, transforming them into active agents responsible for the production of textual meaning. (It is worth noting that the suppression of syntactic and grammatical connections is often replaced by recurrent white spaces that, in many ways, are meant to be filled by the reader.) The semantic ruptures, indeterminacy, and aleatory combinations of these texts would become the distinctive trait of Balestrini's entire production during the 1960s. Here is one of the 'fragments' (titled 'A2'):

> e con queste parole (in primo piano
> taceva il mondo intorno   a lui taceva il mondo
> per renderlo amorfo
> manipolandolo il mosaico e
> la stesura)
> *rossa e spessa* (viste dal basso)   gli spettatori non videro altro
> nel ventre riempito dalla neve
> tutte si accesero le luci

and with these words (in the foreground / the surrounding world was silent for him the world was silent / to render it formless / manipulating the mosaic / the draft) / *red and thick* (seen from below) / the spectators saw nothing else / in the snow-filled belly / all lights came on (*I Nov* 285)

When in 1963 Balestrini published his first major collection *Come si agisce* (How to Act [Milan: Feltrinelli]), which includes *Il sasso appeso*, his objectives were more transparent but still very much in line with his previous work: poetry appears as an autonomous verbal organism, a rational construction essentially stripped of any emotion, whose linguistic disorder is the result of a cold and calculated procedure that makes chance and randomness an integral part of its strategy. Undoubtedly, Balestrini's revolt against all forms of poetic conventions can be connected to the Dadaists' blasphemous violation of all genres. More specifically, Balestrini assimilates the Dadaist technique of ready-mades or of cut-and-paste montages. In fact, *Come si agisce* is constructed exclusively with pre-existing written and oral fragments, defying all rules of syntactic and semantic expectations. (For his materials, Balestrini ransacks newspapers, magazines, journals, linguistic stereotypes, and literary texts. Regarding the latter procedure, cases in point are 'De cultu virginis' (The Cult of the Virgin), which utilizes fragments and allusions derived from works by authors such as Giordano Bruno, Foscolo, and Stendhal; and 'De magnalibus urbis M.' (The Marvels of the City of M.), an ironic denunciation of Milan assembled through references to a text by the medieval poet Bonvesin da la Riva, who, like Balestrini, was born in that city.) At the same time, however, Balestrini's procedures are not dominated solely by accidental combinations, as is the case with Dadaist poetic experiments, but follow a well-planned scheme, a rigorous system of disorder. From this perspective, it is apparent that his poetry is mediated by a linguistic awareness brought about by a structuralist view of art and of poetry in particular.

Come si agisce exemplifies a purely linguistic approach to poetry that, in many ways, embodies attitudes and poetics close to structuralism. In this collection, poetry is exclusively identified with a verbal activity that foregrounds, as its principal discourse, the linguistic sign itself. As is the case with structuralist poetics and theoretical reflections, Balestrini's texts find meaning in their internal organization and in their non-instrumental use of the linguistic medium. This implies that, by refusing to adopt linguistic signs in their representational function and accepted natural relationship with an object or an external reality, Balestrini underscores their arbitrariness and meaninglessness outside a system of internal structures. By focusing on the autonomy of the text and its internal and material construction, poetry becomes a speech aimed at displaying the modes of its own operation: the formal elements that condition meaning or trigger constellations of meanings, the virtuality of signs that produce signification, and the general procedures veiled behind the text.

The linguistic self-awareness of the texts as well as their formal organization address the readers' linguistic consciousness and the semiotic practices through which we try to apprehend reality. As a consequence, this metalinguistic poetic orientation entails a radical strategy of cultural subversion. By exposing the linguistic alienation produced by bourgeois society, Balestrini's poetry attempts to dismantle both the mythologies and the artificial consciousness concealed behind its system of communication. The reader is asked to endure a heavy dose of linguistic alienation as a way to break through the veil of a seemingly natural social language. At the same time, the pervasive disorder of the texts, immersed in a relentless process of uncertainty and randomness, frees the signifier from any fixed signified and allows the reader to experience endless possibilities of associations and meanings. A good example is the series of poems titled 'Corpi in moto e corpi in equilibrio' (Bodies in Motion and Bodies in Equilibrium), which present constant semantic shifts and incongruities, involving discordant morphological and syntactic constructs, that generate absurd and totally unpredictable actions and gestures:

> Quante volte me lo
> al cavallo che si era avvicinato
> al rumore del muro crollato
>
> e afferrò la maniglia scricchiolante
> col pacco sotto il braccio – e posarlo
> dove l'aveva preso e nessuno
>
> (ci sono tante sedie) lì c'era
> a ricevere, controllare, a dire.
> Che cosa. (Ma lo disse: rimani?)

> [How many times did / at the horse that had come near / at the sound of the crumbled wall // and he grabbed the creaking handle / with the package under his arm – and to put it / back where he had got it and nobody // (there are so many chairs) he was there / to welcome, supervise, to say. / What. (But he said it: Will you stay?) (*I Nov* 293)

The only elements that produce links within the text are the recurrent appearances of animals (horses, birds, and sharks) that are juxtaposed to syntagms like 'to drop the bomb' ('sganciare la bomba') or 'the blue hole of the soul' ('buca azzurra dell'anima'). The daring ambiguities and incongruities produced by the text frustrate symbolic or allegorical constrictions and leave the reader with ample interpretative possibilities. What counts is the semantic vitality produced by the connections and juxtapositions of syntagms. In a note to 'Apologo dell'evaso' (Apologue of the Fugitive), included in the anthology of the Novissimi (*IN*, 138; *I Nov*, 267), Giuliani rightly points out that Balestrini's montages move like the components of Calder's mobiles – constantly shifting the process of signification. Here are the opening lines of the poem:

> La massima della mia azione difforme,
> infausto al popolo il fiume
> che al cinema videro spopolare
>
> il delta, i fertilissimi campi

e i più nocivi insetti (chiara
minaccia ai vizi dei governanti!).

Fra i pampini ovunque liberi
galleggiavano, gonfi – e si fa vano
l'ufficio dello storico. (*IN*, 137)

The maxim for my contrary action, / ill-fated for the people, the river / the movie showed devastating // the delta, the most fertile fields / and insects of the worst sort (a clear / threat to the vices of our leaders!). // Amid the vine leaves everywhere / they floated free, bloated – and the historian's / task becomes pointless. (*I Nov*, 263)

There is no doubt that Balestrini assimilates the concepts of information theory.[2] The deliberate disorder of the poems, their programmed entropy, is born out of the conviction that the higher the degree of uncertainty, ambiguity, or improbability of a message, the higher the degree of information produced. This is not to say, however, that the open-ended construction can be dissociated from a specific intention of the author. Although the reader is exposed to a textual organization that has the possibility of creating an unlimited semiosis, the revolutionary and subversive design of the author cannot be annulled by the reader's hermeneutic action. Balestrini's texts defy traditional concepts associated with the task of a reader (identify themes, unwrap prepackaged messages), but, at the same time, they are inscribed by a literary and social intention that necessarily steers their responses and their cultural evaluations in particular interpretative directions. To be sure, Balestrini definitively desecrates the traditional role of the author and decentres poetry from sentimental and inner concerns of the self to a language-focused activity. Indeed, Balestrini does not write his own personal words; rather, he employs existing verbal materials. Nevertheless, the *intentio auctoris* is impressed in the texts and it inevitably invades the reader's hermeneutic space.

There are recurrent fragments in the collections that clearly evidence Balestrini's critique of the socio-political system and his revolutionary objectives.[3] Here are a few examples: 'a revolution of the globe is mature it is everywhere' ('una rivoluzione del globo è matura è dappertutto' [79]); 'enslaved by the economic interests of a minority' ('asserviti agli interessi economici di una minoranza' [81]); 'the executioner's / shadow ... corrupters of words' ('l'ombra / del boia ... corruttori di parole' [86]); 'another history is possible' ('un'altra storia è possibile' [172]); 'the problem is not solved with a substitution of principles' ('il problema non si risolve con una sostituzione di principi' [173]); 'there is no dialectics' (non c'è nessuna dialettica' [178]); 'it imposes the intimate fascism of all historicisms' ('impone l'intimo fascismo di tutti gli storicismi' [179]); 'today every structure of values is a false structure it is a falsifying structure' ('ogni struttura di valori oggi è una struttura falsa è una struttura falsificante' [180]). The titles given to a series of poems, such as 'La critica del linguaggio' (The Critique of Language) or 'Lo sventramento della storia' (The Disembowelment of History) contribute to directing some of the reader's interpretative movements.

The collection contains concrete poems and two examples of 'poesia elettronica' ('electronic poetry'). The cut-and-paste technique must have automatically suggested to Balestrini the possibility of working with concrete poems – the series is entitled 'Cronogrammi' (Chronograms). The diverse newspaper typographic characters are preserved, providing the poet with the possibility of working almost exclusively with the physical properties of the written word (in many ways, they recall Kurt Schwitters's collage-poems). By reducing semantic objectives and highlighting the visual qualities of the words, Balestrini makes the aesthetic expectation coincide with the materiality of the sign.

Cronogramma 2. 'È tutto pronto' (All Is Ready), in *Come si agisce*, 199

Even though this was a rather defiant aesthetic statement, it already had, by that time, its own tradition. This was not the case with electronic poetry, which perhaps represents Balestrini's most sacrilegious experiment, one that provocatively demolishes both the traditional concept of authorship (the author as the centre of production of meanings and inspiration) and the sacred aura associated with poetry.

In 1961, using an IBM 7070 computer, Balestrini produced the first poem written with the collaboration of a machine,'Tape Mark I' (together with 'Tape Mark II,' it is included in *Come si agisce;* the former was originally published in *Almanacco Bompiani* [Milan: Bompiani, 1962]). The computer is fed with short passages from Michito Hachiya's *Hiroshima Diary*, Laotse's *Tao te ching*, and Paul Goldwin's *The Mystery of the Elevator*. It is programmed to select material randomly by following a number of syntactic possibilities and avoiding repetitions or contiguous elements taken from the same passage. The results are extraordinary. Here is a stanza centred on the devastating vision of the first atomic bomb:

> I capelli tra le labbra, esse tornano tutte
> alla loro radice, nell'accecante globo di fuoco
> io contemplo il loro ritorno, finché non muove le dita
> lentamente, e malgrado che le cose fioriscano
> assume la ben nota forma di fungo cercando
> di afferrare mentre la moltitudine delle cose accade.

> Hair between the lips, they all return / to their roots, in the blinding fireball / I observe their return, until he moves his fingers / slowly, and even though things blossom / it assumes the well-known form of the mushroom attempting / to grab while the multitude of things occur.

The second poem, 'Tape Mark II,' is generated by the computer utilizing a number of syntagms taken from the entire collection, *Come si agisce*, and performing a series of combinations, variations, and permutations. The ninety stanzas (each composed of five lines) created by the computer achieve the highest degree possible of poetic impersonality and refute the humanistic concept of the subject as the centre of signification. Language and its internal properties become the source for the production of meaning. Without doubt, these experiments are a clear indication that Balestrini was at the forefront of a view of literature that, from the 1960s onward, revolved around the concept of the 'death of the author' and the rebirth of the reader – as demonstrated by post-structuralist theories and reader-response criticism. As has been argued, however, Balestrini's poetic operation is animated by a spirit of critique and dissent. The bracketing of the 'I' discloses an aesthetic strategy that cannot be separated from an ideological project that aims to confront both the social system and its production of meanings. In this sense, even though Balestrini's techniques seem to be in tune with postmodernist writing, he cannot be aligned with a nihilistic and anti-foundational postmodern view of the world. Poetry, in his case, is firmly linked to a modernist project of opposition.

In 1965 Balestrini published a short collection, *Altri procedimenti* (Other Procedures [Milan, Scheiwiller]), which was later included in a larger work entitled *Ma noi facciamone un'altra* (But Let's Make Another [Milan: Feltrinelli, 1968]). An examination of all of Balestrini's poetry from 1964 to 1968 (thus encompassing both collections) clearly shows that his poetic project has been driven towards a substantial radicalization. Indeed, these collections represent his most extreme challenge to conventional notions of literariness and of the functions associated with a poetic text. (After this period, following the breakdown of Gruppo 63, Balestrini's formal anarchism is greatly attenuated, favouring more overtly political attacks on the system.)[4] This radicalization is evidenced by two major elements: the hostility to syntactic linearity, present in the previous works, is now turned on the word itself and even on the syllable; and the referential attributes connected with ordinary communication are annulled in such a way as to foreground exclusively the physical substance of language.

In the opening poem of the collection, 'Istruzioni' (Instructions), Balestrini introduces his project by making references not only to the relationship between language and revolution (the poetic work on language envisioned as a possibility of transformation and creation of a new future) but also to the condition of 'disease' afflicting language ('malattia del linguaggio'). Indeed, in most poems, words are mutilated and dismembered, as if showing tangible physical lacerations. The catastrophe of signification, pursued in the earlier collections by demolishing syntactic solidarity between syntagms (a formal construct to communicate the negation of language as an instrument of social communication), has an impact now on the micro elements of the linguistic articulation, namely, both on the phonemes and on the monemes. In the series 'Perimetri' (Perimeters), the process of disarticulation reaches such extreme limits that the linguistic fractures can be experienced either as a manifestation of aphasia or as embryonic elements of a system struggling to generate a signifying whole. (It could actually be seen as a sort of pre-semiotic construct whose potential for meaning requires that the reader fills its many gaps of signification.) Here is a section of one of the poems belonging to this series:

> ha mostrato
> tti di quest
> che trovand
>
> si riuniscon
> dei singoli
>
> no in corris
> problema da fronteggiare
> e quale appartenere ed e
> orrispondenz
>
> questa zona
>
> e come si ve
> appartenenza
> l'altro cer
>
> ortandi dife
> nea di separ
> uno dei piú osi nelle im
> o uno in questo non è tu
> è solo il pu   gnuno termin
> per quelli
>
> no decidere
> numero di st
>
> disposti dis
> ile stabilir   de nella fig
> all'uno o a

Ha shown / ll of thes / that findin / is gathere / of individuals / no in corres / problem of confront / what belongs to and e / orrespond / this zone / and how is seen / belonging the other reas // ordant dife nea of separ / one of the most ous in the im / or one in this isn't you / it's only the fi stone term / for those / or limit a / not decide / number of st / disposed dis / yle to establish of in the fig / to one or at. (Trans. Enzo Minarelli, in R. Barilli, *Voyage to the End of the Word*, 63–4)

.

The treatment of the poetic text as a self-sufficient organism, an object in its own right ('to make of language an object' ('fare del linguaggio un oggetto' ['Istruzioni']), triggers in this collection the tendency to place emphasis on the materiality of language and its graphic properties. The resulting visual and spatial traits of a large number of poems testify to Balestrini's significant move towards formal devices close to concrete poetry. In these poems, discursive syntax, conventional articulation, and expected phonetic units as means of communication are replaced by a spatial syntax that underscores geometric and graphic patterns. If traditional poetry is essentially grounded in metric, phonetic, or syntactic equivalences, they are here replaced by the recurrence of visual and spatial units. A case in point is the series 'Istruzioni' (Instructions), 'Perimetri' (Perimeters), 'Tre volte al giorno la vomita' (He Vomits It Three Times a Day), and 'Una brutta storia' (An Ugly Story), where the poems take on the shape of rectangles, squares, hexagons, and other configurations. These texts acquire a plurisemiotic dimension inasmuch as they can be experienced as the result of intersemiotic procedures. In fact, they display the integration of a plurality of aesthetic domains (visual, spatial, graphic, phonetic, semantic) that the reader has to activate, putting in motion their interrelationships. This syncretic orientation, however, does not produce ordered and unified correlations of the constitutive elements of the text. Indeed, these texts can be seen as works in progress rather than finished products. The adoption of language not as a medium of referentiality but as a physical object does not reduce the polysemic valency of the texts. On the contrary, while the poem communicates its own material structure, its materiality is charged with a high degree of ambiguity and plurisignification. In the first section of a group of poems entitled 'Ma noi' (But We), it is stated rather explicitly:

> non la riproduzione
> con gli occhi del linguaggio
> da qualsiasi parte ti metti
> non mima niente
> un varco incolmabile
> un mare di ambiguità

> not the reproduction / with the eyes of language / wherever you may stand / mimes nothing / an unfulfillable gap / a sea of ambiguity

Privileging the potentialities of visibility or iconicity of verbal signs (it is significant that, in a series of poems entitled 'A colori' [In Colour], direct references are made to the visual experience of painting or of advertising images) does not annul the arbitrary relationship between signifier and signified. Balestrini launches his attacks against any attempt to crystallize signs in immanent meanings. In fact, in the opening section of the series just mentioned, we read:

> *albero / quadro per l'autunno*
> l'albero cioè un albero
> verbale cioè un albero
> il verde è un albero
> l'albero della pubblicità
> albero sensibile
> l'albero dell'albero
> e ci sono altri alberi

> *tree / picture for the fall* / the tree that is a verbal / tree that is a tree / the green is a tree / the tree of advertising / sensible tree / the tree of the tree / and there are other trees

It is significant that the poem ends with a reference to a 'picture for the spring' ('*quadro per la primavera*') and transformation, as attested by the very last line, 'but the future can be invented' ('*ma il futuro può essere inventato*').

The formal ambiguity and polysemy of the texts cannot allow for narrative packages easily unwrapped by the reader and offering definitive directions to follow in order to reach the desired changes of the life-world. This fundamental trait, on which Balestrini's poetic procedures firmly rest, is made apparent in the poem 'Invece della rivoluzione' (Instead of the Revolution). In this text, formed by twenty- seven stanzas of seven lines each, the syntagm 'invece della rivoluzione' becomes like a recurrent and obsessive beat of a drum, whose only variations are represented by the difference with which words are arbitrarily amputated at the beginning or at the end of a line. The remaining syntagms reveal a lexicon associated with the activities of a science lab (beakers, cultures of organisms, processes of sterilization, tubes, cotton-balls), but the results of the experiment are not provided. The only revolution that the reader is provided with is that pertaining to language and to the conventional notions of poetry. Here is the opening stanza:

invece della rivoluzione invece della
a rivoluzione invece della rivoluzione
e invece della rivoluzione invece dell
lla rivoluzione invece della rivoluzion
one invece della rivoluzione invece de
ella rivoluzione invece della rivoluzio
ione invece della rivoluzione invece d

instead of the revolution instead of the / th revolution instead of the revolution / on instead of the revolution instead of th / f the revolution instead of the revolut / tion instead of the revolution instead of / f the revolution instead of the revolu / lution instead of the revolution instead o

The rejection of an all-encompassing narration, namely, the refusal to supply the reader with ready-made solutions for social problems, finds its formal expression particularly in the use of a writing mode that seems to be governed by the figure of the synecdoche. Balestrini's deliberate omission of the whole and the resulting attention to the particular – be it an object or an event – is a key formal and conceptual strategy of this entire collection. Perhaps the use of the synecdoche as a narrative mode is best illustrated by the poem 'I funerali di Togliatti' (Togliatti's Funeral). The title triggers in the mind of the reader a number of expectations that are completely frustrated. A poem on the death, in 1964, of Palmiro Togliatti, leader of the Italian Communist Party and a legendary figure tied to anti-fascism and to the hopes of a new society, contains the promise of a eulogy or, at least, the possibility of transfiguring the event into an occasion for nourishing the Marxist spirit of revolution. Nothing of this sort is delivered by the poem. The text is constructed by twenty stanzas (made of quatrains, tercets, and one couplet) that minutely describe the flowers of a wreath which is never pictured in its entirety:

peluria rossa forma disegni irregola
on minore accentuazione di vermiglio
con grande croce vermiglia al centro
segna il contorno è coperta di peluria argentea

red fuzz forms irregul designs / ith minor accentuation of vermilion / with a large vermilion cross at the centre / marks the outline its covered with silver fuzz

The recurrent presence of the colour red is anchored to a floral materiality and never departs from the denotative level of speech. In other words, even though the reader may associate the colour with communism, the text does not take any measure to make allusions to even the most basic aspects of a revolutionary ideal. The synecdoche defeats both metaphoric and symbolic meanings, leaving the reader with the task of imagining the whole. Balestrini's verbal revolution cannot be separated from the invisibility of the authorial voice and from the rejection of patronizing messages. If poetry has to take on the role of a radical alternative to the dominant linguistic practices, it must radicalize the role of the reader. For poetry, the only real revolution is the revolution of its language.

8 Other Poets, Other Subversions

The five Novissimi represent the poetic core of Gruppo 63. However, they were not alone. A number of poets joined the group and actively participated in its various gatherings. Indeed, even at the time of the publication of the anthology edited by Giuliani, rumours circulated that Edoardo Cacciatore[1] had been considered for inclusion in the group but his 'candidature' was firmly opposed by Sanguineti. Cacciatore never participated to the activities of Gruppo 63 or associated with any literary circles, remaining essentially a loner throughout his entire poetic career. There is no question, however, that Cacciatore's poetry displays traits of a linguistic experimentation that can be situated within the general area of the new avant-garde. From his initial publication in the mid-1950s, *La restituzione* (The Restitution [Florence, Vallecchi, 1955]) to his central collections of the 1960s, *Lo specchio e la trottola* (The Mirror and the Top [Florence: Vallecchi, 1960]) and *Tutti i poteri* (All the Powers [Milan: Feltrinelli, 1969]), Cacciatore demonstrated an hallucinatory and provocative poetic language that inevitably follows the urges of the signifiers. Homophonic orchestrations, often based on obsessive alliterative constructs, create a sort of neo-Baroque poetry that, with its philosophical questioning, frequently accentuates the absurdity and nonsense of the world.

Beside the five Novissimi, the other main poets who took part in the various gatherings of Gruppo 63 with readings of their texts were Amelia Rosselli, Giuseppe Guglielmi, Adriano Spatola, Giorgio Celli, Corrado Costa, and Patrizia Vicinelli (to these names can be added that of Giulia Niccolai, who, although she did not read her texts at the group's gatherings, was associated with the new avant-garde in many different ways).

While Rosselli was an active participant in the group, the inclusion of her poetry within the project of the neoavant-garde poses a number of issues.[2] Indeed, her allegiance to the group was somewhat problematic. Following its first gathering, in 1963, Rosselli wrote a series of ironic poems addressed to members of the new avant-garde (Enrico Filippini, Adriano Spatola, Giuseppe Guglielmi, and others), in which she distanced herself from the literary and ideological conflicts provoked by the Palermo debate and dismissed the group's attacks on Pasolini and lyrical poetry.[3] It should be noted that Rosselli's poetry had aroused Pasolini's interest before her involvement with Gruppo 63. In fact, he introduced a series of her poems in an article entitled 'Notizia su Amelia Rosselli' (Il Menabò 6 [1963]: 66–9). In an interview with Giacinto Spagnoletti, Rosselli described the controversy between Pasolini and Gruppo 63 as an 'absurd war' ('assurda guerra') and stated that, out of the entire group, she felt only Porta's influence.[4] Rosselli reaffirmed her critical view of the group in another interview with Elio Pecora. Asked to comment on her relationship with Gruppo 63, she declared:

Usano tecniche superatissime. È necessario passare per molte tecniche, ma è obbligatorio, prima di pubblicare i propri versi, conoscere quel che è stato detto e scritto nel passato prossimo e remoto. Il surrealismo è consunto. È bene aggiornarsi viaggiando e leggendo gli stranieri in lingua originale. Di quel gruppo apprezzo Porta per la serietà della ricerca e Pagliarani de 'La ragazza Carla,' anteriore alla nascita della neoavanguardia. (E. Pecora, 'Un incontro con Amelia Rosselli,' Galleria, January–August 1997, 153)

They employ outmoded techniques. It is necessary to go through many techniques, but before publishing, it is imperative to know what has been said and written both in the immediate and remote past. Surrealism is worn out. It is worthwhile to be updated by travelling and reading foreign writers in their original language. Of the group, I value Porta for the seriousness of his research and Pagliarani's 'La ragazza Carla,' anterior to the birth of the new avant-garde.

The fundamental issues surrounding Rosselli poetry can be posed as follows: Is her poetic language autonomous in relation to the aesthetic models championed by the new avant-garde? Is her magmatic and traumatized language the result of a mental illness (Rosselli suffered most of her life from serious psychological problems and she committed suicide in 1996) or of the literary climate engendered by Gruppo 63?

Rosselli's first major publication, *Variazioni belliche* (War Variations [Milan: Garzanti, 1964]), comprising poems written between 1959 and 1962, exhibits a sharp contrast between the regularity and uniformity of the metric organization and the linguistic turmoil created by a fractured syntax and a heterogeneous lexicon. This poetry seems to carry traces of Rosselli's linguistic upbringing (as a child and adolescent, she spoke Italian, English, and French at home), both on the level of syntactic constructs and in the lexical presence of the latter two languages. Her plurilinguism and unsettling formal structures can thus be seen as the embodiment of a personal linguistic and emotional condition. This private linguistic background, however, merges with traces of a literary memory that combines Dante and medieval Italian locutions with those of Tasso, Donne, Leopardi, Rimbaud, Campana, and Montale. Rosselli's agitated language mirrors an inner struggle that revolves around the impossibility of experiencing an identity without dichotomies and conflicts. She is torn between absence and desire, emptiness and longing for plenitude, the limitations of human existence and the search for an absolute. Many poems of this collection reveal a religious and metaphysical unrest that leaves unanswered questions on love and death, God, and life's ordeals, both individual and social.

The general impression is that, if, for the Novissimi and Gruppo 63 at large, poetry is mediated by a cultural project and a search for new poetics, in Rosselli's case the lyrical attributes of her poetry (indeed, not in sync with the Novissimi's reduction of the 'I') reveal that it is born of a psychological compulsion. The shattered language of the new avant-garde generally results from a calculated construction, whereas Rosselli seems to pursue the goal of liberating hidden areas of the psyche through a more immediate and spontaneous linguistic externalization. As a result, her poetry often embarks on a voyage in the unconscious (entrusting the sequence of words to phonetic associations engendered primarily by the play of the signifiers) and acquires the opaqueness of oracular and visionary speech. Accordingly, whereas the Novissimi construct a poetry of madness starting from the awareness of a social and literary alienation of language, Rosselli gives voice to a linguistic delirium that is generated above all by an emotional distress. However, it must be pointed out that Rosselli's subsequent collections (*Serie ospedaliera* [Hospital Series (Milan: Il Saggiatore, 1969)]) and *Documento 1966–1973* (Document 1966–1973 [Milan: Garzanti, 1976]), written during her involvement with Gruppo 63, occasionally exhibit an accentuation of linguistic disorder. The cultural climate generated by Gruppo 63 offered Rosselli an encounter with alternative modes of writing in which she must have recognized her own rejection of the logic and linearity of traditional linguistic forms. However, her departures from the group are substantial. Rosselli pursues an alternative lyric poetry based on the exploration of unusual images and metaphors that does not coincide with the new avant-garde's major objectives. Her poetry transcribes the lacerations of a psyche that desperately attempts to establish a dialogue with the other but is inevitably divided between the urge for communication and the mistrust of the word. Here are a few lines from *Variazioni belliche*:

Cos'ha il mio cuore che batte sì soavemente
ed egli fa disperato, ei
più duri sondaggi? tu Quelle
scolanze che vi imprissi pr'ia ch'eo
si turmintussi sì
fieramente, tutti gli sono dispariti! O sei muiei
conigli correnti per nervu ei per
brimosi canali dei la mia linfa (o vita!)
non stoppano, allora sì, c'io, my
iavvicyno allae mortae! In tutta schiellezze mia anima
tu ponigli rimedio, t'imbraccio, tu, –
trova queia Parola Soave, tu ritorna
alla compressa favella che fa sì che l'amore resta.

What's with my heart that beats so tenderly / and desperately makes, maketh / the hardest testings? you Those / xtures that I imprinted on before he / tormented himself so / fiercely, and are vanished for him! O mye six / rabbits coursing throughte nervies he for / musty canals of this here lymph (o life!) / they don't stop, then yes, tha'I, me / getso close to this death! In all sinceauity my soul / may you remedy it, I ambrace you, you, – / may you find dat Tender Word, may you return / to the clear tongue that lets love here to stay. (*PL*, 415; trans. by Lucia Re and Paul Vangelisti)

And here is a text from *Serie ospedaliera*:

Ti vendo i miei fornelli, poi li sgraffi
e ti siedi impreparato sulla scrivania
se ti vendo il leggiero giogo della

mia inferma mente, meno roba ho, più
contenta sono. Disfatta dalla pioggia
e dai dolori incommensurabile mestruazione
senilità che s'avvicina, petrolifera
immaginazione.

I sell you my cooking stove, then you scratch it / and sit unprepared on
the desk / if I sell you the light yoke of / my diseased mind, the less stuff
I have, the / happier I am. Undone by the rain / and by sorrows immea-
surable menstruation / senility approaching, gaslight / imagination. (*PL*,
415; trans. by Lucia Re and Paul Vangelisti)

Giuseppe Guglielmi (brother of Angelo, another member of Gruppo
63) was attuned both to the linguistic practices of the new avant-garde
and, in general, to the ideological orientation of its Marxist wing.[5] His
first collection, *Essere e non avere* (Being and Not Having [Varese: Editrice Magenta, 1955]), was published in the same series 'Oggetto e simbolo' (Object and Symbol), edited by Luciano Anceschi, in which
Sanguineti's *Laborintus* appeared the following year. This collection,
however, does not share the iconoclastic formal disposition of the latter. At this early stage, Guglielmi's poetic language relies heavily on
the use of symbolic objects and on a linear and communicative speech
that lacks the alienating effects of the works produced by the new
avant-garde. The poems included in *Essere e non avere* revolve primarily around the condition of the 'I.' Guglielmi presents a restless subject distressed by the overwhelming passage of time and by the
senselessness of its existential options. The feeling of being exiled from
life that pervades the entire collection is not yet investigated – as it will
be in the subsequent collection – from a social or ideological perspective. Nonetheless, this initial emotional tension allows Guglielmi to
experiment with an agitated language that will erupt in *Panglosse* (Pan-
glosses [Milan: Feltrinelli, 1967]), a publication undoubtedly affected
by the poetic climate aroused by Gruppo 63.[6]
    This collection combines an investigation of the dreary individual
and social conditions under capitalism with a reflection on language
and its functions within the literary domain – the title itself, with its
Greek prefix 'pan,' makes a strong reference to an all-encompassing
linguistic operation. Guglielmi's philosophical disposition tends to create a conceptual and theoretical discourse, drawing its lexicon princi-
pally from Hegel, Marx, Husserl, and Freud. However, the language of

these poetic 'glosses' displays a constant clash of stylistic registers and occasional code-mixing (expressions, terms, and sentences in Latin, German, and French). The philosophical and psychoanalytic language constantly collides with colloquial or archaic Italian, creating a mixture of high and low style that incorporates tragic discourse and comic locution.

The linguistic fragmentation corresponds to a view of a mutilated and alienated subject incapable of reconstructing a unity, a centre of identity, and thus condemned to experience all manifestations of the world (work, sexuality, the other) through an 'unhappy consciousness.' The Hegelian reference present in one of the most significant poems of the entire collection, 'La coscienza infelice' (The Unhappy Conscience), underscores the view of a consciousness that contains differences and contradictions – a divided and doubled consciousness torn between presence and absence, desire of freedom and the weight of history, hope and despair. The conflicts and lacerations that dominate the subjects's life-world are linked to a devastating 'social hell' ('inferi sociali') produced by captalism with its exploitation, division of labour, and alienation ('The evil all the universal evil / is mostly contained in Capital') ('Il male tutto il male universale / in gran parte contiene il Capitale' ['Proverbi romani' (Roman Proverbs) 30]). Guglielmi's critique of capitalism, however, does not engender rhetorical attitudes of redemption or utopian assurances of a future without turmoil and chaos ('we speak of utopia with a large outlet into entropy') ('parliamo d'utopia con largo sbocco nell'entropia') (['La coscienza infelice'] 45). Human reality is perceived as a history of oppression, repression, and sublimation that poetic language and ideology (the former seen also as a potential access to the unconscious through the unrestricted connections of its signifiers) attempt to unmask. Guglielmi acknowledges the commodified condition of language within the structures of capitalism and literature's inability to find solutions (The Stolen Language) ('La lingua rubata' [21–2]). Writing oscillates between the hope of having a grip on reality and the awareness of being an activity without promises and definite goals ('Writing is nothing but pure gesture. / Excrement and urination') ('La scrittura non è che puro gesto. / Sterco e minzioni' ['La vera teodicea' (The True Theodicy) 34]). On the one hand, Guglielmi espouses a modern outlook by privileging a language of social critique and searching for a state of authenticity concealed behind the wall of alienation. On the other, he displays an unsettling tension that undermines those same possibilities and opens his poetry to differ-

ences and conflicts that revolve around the desire of subversion and a
dystopic vision that threatens to erode all meanings:

> la vera realtà di ciò che è
> è
> ci è nascosta
> le scienze restano divise non c'è utraquismo ancora
> scienze della natura e scienze della storia divise
> questa divisione non ditemi che non è alienante
> ditemi piuttosto i vostri benefici enumeratemeli tutti
> il danaro il possesso la merda il sublime
> il fango le nostre lacrime d'amore
> i vostri coiti per coniugî non tutti uguali
> che potete ogni giorno inventare per inventarvi:
> l'industria è il reale e noi non rimaniamo
> nel fango nella merda nel danaro e perciò siamo
> non naturali,
> spirito nostro denaturato leggermente di rosso colorato
> ('La coscienza infelice,' 44–5)

the true reality of that which is / is / it is hidden from us / the sciences
remain divided utraquism isn't here yet / the sciences of nature and the
sciences of history are divided / don't tell me this division is not alienating / rather tell me what your benefits are list them all / money possession shit the sublime / mud our tears of love / your copulations for mar-
riages not all the same / that every day you can invent for inventing
yourselves: industry is the real and we don't remain in the mud in the shit
in the money and that's why we are / not natural / our unnatured spirit
slightly coloured of red

One of the youngest poets to take part in the activities of Gruppo 63
was Adriano Spatola.[7] He read his poems at the group's gatherings in
1963 and 1966. Indeed, Spatola's literary background was formed
entirely within the cultural climate of the new avant-garde. He was first
involved with *Il Verri* (Spatola was a student of its editor, Luciano Anceschi, at the University of Bologna) and later became one of the associate
editors of *Quindici*. In 1968 he founded a small publishing house
devoted to poetry, Edizioni Geiger, and, in 1972, following the demise
of the group, he and Giulia Niccolai gave life to a highly regarded
poetry review, *Tam Tam*. At the end of the 1970s, he launched an audio-
cassette magazine specifically aimed at promoting sound poetry.

Spatola's commitment to all forms of experimentation, including sound, concrete, and visual poetry (for this latter feature of his poetic production, see chapter 9), was constant and forceful. Spatola's poetic orientation was based on the tenet that there exists a historical necessity for incessant change in aesthetic language. In the cultural situation of the 1960s, he saw the urgent need for poetry to cross its traditional boundaries and depart from the written page. This is the principal premise behind Spatola's notion of 'total poetry' ('poesia totale'), set out in his most ambitious theoretical publication, *Verso la poesia totale* (Towards Total Poetry; Salerno: Rumma, 1969).

In his view, poetry must pursue the recovery of its vocal and visual properties, or the invention of a gestural language that fuses the word with the performance. For Spatola, poetry is a self-sufficient creation that, at the same time, takes on the role of a 'conscience of communication.' In the editorial that introduces the second issue of *Tam Tam*, Spatola stresses the importance of a form of 'poetry which constructs itself as an objective metamorphosis, not as a metaphorical paraphrase of reality, ('poesia che si costruisca come metamorfosi oggettiva, non come parafrasi metaforica della realtà').[8]

Indeed, the most striking feature of Spatola's works during the years of the new avant-garde, *L'ebreo negro* (The Nigger Jew) [Milan: Scheiwiller, 1966]) and *Majakovskiiiiiiij* (Turin: Geiger, 1971; containing texts written in the late 1960s), is the search for a state of verbal self-sufficiency that rejects any subordination to social or emotional issues (both collections are later included in *La composizione del testo* [Rome: Cooperativa Scrittori, 1978]). Spatola's main ambition is to revitalize poetry's language, working on the potentialities of the signifiers and the specific devices offered by poetry. The result is an imaginative and surreal form of poetry that reclaims its verbal space and creates an unsettling relationship with the world:

girare la nave su se stessa gettarsi nel buco nell'acqua
e pesci a scalare gli scogli pinne che cercano appigli
il vecchio senza figli l'ultimo dei vivi che si masturba e guarda
rossa striata e palpitante la specie che si estingue
nudo pingue canuto senza pelle lambito dalle onde si masturba
alghe meduse plancton sulla lingua fra i denti sugli occhiali
e cicli mestruali delle orbite vuote flaccide dietro le lenti
    ('Catalogopoema,' 2, *L'ebreo negro*)

·   the boat turning on itself diving into the hole in the water / and fish climb-

ing the cliffs fins searching for footholds / the old one without sons the
last of the living masturbates watches / red stripped and palpitating the
species becoming extinct / naked obese white-haired without skin lapped
by the waves he masturbates / seaweed jelly fish plankton on the tongue
between the teeth on his glasses / and the menstrual cycles of empty orbs
flabby behind the lenses (Trans. Paul Vangelisti, *Various Devices* [Los
Angeles: Red Hill Press, 1978])

As an autonomous verbal experience ('the text is a living object sup-
plied with keys') ('Il testo è un oggetto vivente fornito di chiavi' ['La
composizione del testo,' 'The Composition of the Text,' *Majakovskiiiiii-
ijjjj*]), poetry creates its own world, but, at the same time, it does not
renounce a discourse that rebounds on the perception of things present
and expresses the desire for things to be. Indeed, Spatola's poetry is
underscored by agitated and provoking images that cannot but turn the
reader's attention to the world's state of affairs. Here is a powerful section of the poem that provides the title to the collection *L'ebreo negro*:

sigillatemi il naso, mettetemi i piombi alle orecchie, chiudetemi il
buco del culo, cemento dentro la bocca

portatemi ad occhi aperti attraverso la città illuminata

(alberi intorno, nessuno per strada)
poi, súbito, a destra: violento carnevale

questi che corrono zoppi incontro ai vuoti tassì dimenando le banconote

scivolando via vuoti i tassì senza fermarsi

questi che dalle nicchie tolgono gli imbalsamati amorini

fogne in continua vomitazione, liquido nero dentro le scarpe (sec. 4)

seal my nose, shut my ears with wax, plug my / asshole, cement inside my
mouth // carry me with eyes wide open through the bright lit city //
(trees all around, nobody in the street) // then suddenly, to the right: a
violent carnival // those who lurch cripple in front of empty taxis wag-
ging dollar bills // taxis sliding away empty without slowing down //
those who tear embalmed cupids from their niches // sewers continually
vomiting, black liquid in the shoes (trans. P. Vangelisti, *Various Devices*)

As mentioned, Giulia Niccolai – Spatola's companion for many years – never read her works at the gatherings organized by Gruppo 63, but she did contribute to *Quindici* and was greatly affected by its aesthetic orientation and spirit of experimentation.[9] Beginning in the late 1960s, she became a proponent of the poetry of nonsense, reconnecting her work to old masters such as Edward Lear and Lewis Carroll (she was inspired by the latter to write, in English, a series of concrete poems entitled *Humpty Dumpty* [Turin: Geiger, 1969]), mediated by Joyce's polyglotism, Aldo Palazzeschi's ironic linguistic amusements, and Dadaism's transgressive practices. Niccolai's poetry is a constant eruption of puns, clever phonetic associations, lexical conflations of different languages, and semantic and etymological wordplay. The results are whimsical and polysemic creations that, on the one hand, liberate language from fossilized forms, and, on the other, put in motion a process that invites the reader to revisit the world through unusually imaginative lenses. One of Niccolai's most daring and ingenious collections is *Greenwich* (Turin: Geiger, 1971), whose period of gestation and composition coincides with the demise of Gruppo 63. Here, drawing on 'the language of territories' ('il linguaggio dei territori'), as it is defined in the introductory note to the collection (*Greenwich*, reprinted in *Harry's Bar e altre poesie 1969–1980* [Milan: Feltrinelli, 1981, 73]), Niccolai constructs texts in various languages (Latin, Italian, Spanish, English, French), using only place names taken from the *World Atlas* of the *Encyclopedia Britannica*. These are highly allusive poems that suggest vestiges of meaning. It is a sort of linguistic voyage through the names of geographic places arranged in sequences that mimic syntactic units. Here is a text that makes use of place names in English, entitled 'Hell gates':

> Kincardine guam and glasgow masbate la vandee.
> Gomorah lambeth – york cape, york town and yorkshire
> to tibet –
> Lockport missouri gehenna mobile the jebel levant states
> Stockholm, hot springs, south shields, hell canyon
>   and
> hell gates.
> (*Harry's Bar*, 85)

And here is one that combines names of Italian cities and towns with an ironic allusion to a popular song by Charles Aznavour:

> Igea travagliato

trento treviso e trieste
di disgrazia in disgrazia
fino pomezia.
Como è trieste Venezia ...
('Como è trieste Venezia,' *Harry's Bar*, 95)

This playful and comic mode of writing, adopted as a strategy for prodding language to produce fresh and adventurous meanings, is central to all Niccolai's production, including her more recent works. An exception are two groups of poems, 'Dai Novissimi' (From the Novissimi) and 'Sostituzione' (Substitution), which are constructed using cut-ups of works related to literary theory and criticism. Indeed, for the first series, Niccolai employs fragments taken from Giuliani's introduction and notes to the anthology of the Novissimi. It results in a theoretically dense poetry that engages the reader in a reflection on the aesthetic and philosophical dimensions of literature and writing:

La capacità delle contraddizioni:
l'uso subito soffocato
e il punto di passaggio,
il mutamento.
La scelta di questi scontri finali:
liberando l'andamento
e il particolare procedimento
aperto. (*Harry's Bar*, sec. 8, 59)

The capacity of contradiction, / the habit immediately suffocated / and the point of crossing, / the change. / The choice of this final collision: / setting loose the motion / and the particular passage / wide open
(Trans. G. Niccolai and Paul Vangelisti, *Substitution*, [Los Angeles: Red Hill Press, 1975])

Aligned with some of the key positions of the Novissimi and Gruppo 63, Niccolai's views as expressed in 'Il soggetto è il linguaggio' (The Subject Is the Language), from the series 'Sostituzione,' (Substitution), is that poetry can find its vital essence only in the subversion of ordinary speech:

Le cose esistono per essere dette
e la lingua racconta. Oltraggia a sua volta

in un linguaggio già violato da altri
avere il linguaggio è un modo di essere.

Il soggetto è dunque il linguaggio
con cui perpretare una personale violazione.
(*Harry's Bar*, 65)

Things exist to be said / and language narrates. It outrages in turn / a language already violated by others / to possess language is a way of being. // The subject is therefore the language / with which to commit a capital offence. (*Substitution*)

Another woman poet associated with Gruppo 63 – her involvement began in 1966, at the La Spezia gathering – was Patrizia Vicinelli.[10] She was particularly active within the context of sound poetry and, together with Emilio Villa and Aldo Braibanti, worked for some years in the area of experimental theatre. In the 1960s she published one poetry collection *à, a. A,* (Milan: Lerici, 1967), in which numerous texts are primarily centred on sound as their main communicative medium. This is a short but quite radical publication. Vicinelli achieves an alienation-effect not only by fragmenting the syntactic and semantic levels of ordinary language but also by disjoining single letters. Particularly in the first half of the collection, she approaches language essentially from the perspective of its materiality. In these texts we witness an explosion of words, shattered and randomly scattered on the page. Letters are inverted or mutilated in various segments; graphic conventions are totally undermined by superimposing different words or letters; the printed letters – constantly changing their characters – are mixed with handwritten sequences and erasures; words are tied together without allowing for the appropriate breaks; the Italian is interrupted by the frequent sequences in French, English, or Latin. This is a collection that exhibits a strong tension between a state of aphasia and the search for meaning, the reduction of language to primeval, arbitrary sounds and the need for the subject to construct possible identities through poetic discourse. Awareness of the impossibility of rebuilding a transparency of meanings from personal and collective linguistic ruins forces the subject to adopt numerous masks (a motif that emerges particularly in the closing poem, 'Alla fine' [At the End]), which can yield neither emotive securities nor comforting models of existence.

Two other poets who were active within Gruppo 63 were Giorgio Celli and Corrado Costa. Both, together with Porta and Spatola, were involved, as editors, with *Malebolge*, a literature review published between 1964 and 1967. They formed the 'Gruppo parasurrealista,' whose aim was to reconnect with Surrealism, emphasizing a language of imagination without any compromise with conventional forms of communication. Generally, however, they elude the irrational tendencies and psychic automatism associated with the Surrealist movement by adopting calculated linguistic constructs and cogitated images.

Celli, an entomologist at the University of Bologna, underlines the exhaustion of codified and institutionalized literary forms and the necessity for poetry to adopt other linguistic registers, in particular the language of science.[11] For Celli, by metabolizing scientific and extraliterary speeches, poetry dilates conventional notions of reality and opens up an ideological dialogue with the world of science. Indeed, Celli advocates a true synergy of poetic and scientific language. This is not to say, however, that he favours a linear and functional language associated with scientific discourse. In his view, biological evolution is the 'unconscious of history' ('l'inconscio della storia') and dreams are the 'language of phylogenesis' ('il linguaggio della filogenesi').[12] This implies that poetry must reject pragmatic forms of discourse in order to recover a sort of primordial language, in sync with the biological, animal memory inscribed in all our cells and organs:

perquisivano la tipografia clandestina della memoria esaminando
chimicamente i metaboliti ideologici dell'osmosi familiare
voltando la rossa enfiagione dei miei organi come dita di un guanto
ricostruendo
l'intricata filiazione ideologica del mio patrimonio cromosomico
(*Pesce gotico* [Gothic Fish], sec. 10)

they were searching the clandestine printing of the memory chemically / examining the ideological metabolites of the familiar osmosis / turning inside out the red tumescence of my organs as glove's fingers / reconstructing / the intricate ideological filiation of my chromosome inheritance

From this perspective, Celli urges a return to the objectives pursued by Surrealism but without deserting the logic of science. In a note to the long poem *Morte di un biologo* (Death of a Biologist [Bologna: Centro Duchamp, 1970]) – the text narrates, in graphic scientific detail, the death of a biologist and the process of decomposition of the body – he declares that 'metaphors are born of the violent and systematic collision of numerous and converging logical propositions' ('metafore nascono dalla violenta sistematica collisione di numerose proposizioni logiche convergenti,' unpaginated). The result is a form of poetry in which the language of science provides access into the fantastic. The fantastic-surrealist procedures are an attempt at disclosing unexplored versions of the world and offering a passageway to the multiplicity of its states of being, as in the following verses from *Il pesce gotico*:

> forse la storia è un ciclo biologico
> tutto questo non è che un protoplasma
> dove le babilonie e gli zuccheri si consumano bruciando
> ... stratificazioni di felci d'antrace di scapole di mutamenti
> planetari che devi rivivere in chiave di galassia
> il tuo cervello perforato da stupri di satelliti
> (sec. 13, 23–6)

perhaps history is a biological cycle / all of this is nothing but a protoplasm / where babelisms and sugars are consumed by burning / ... stratification of ferns of anthrax of scapulae of planetary / mutations that you must relive in the perspective of a galaxy / your brain perforated by satellites' rapes

Here is a short poem from the same collection in which biology, surreal images, and a vision of astonishment in the face of the phenomena of the world, all fuse together:

> frattanto io miracolo filogenetico vertebrato verticale
> metabolizzando assiduamente in metafisica le mie proteine
> sul cavallo senz'ombra di favola
> con una vescica urinaria d'incoparabile fattura (sec. 9)

meanwhile I a phylogenetic miracle vertical vertebrate / assiduously metabolizing my proteins in metaphysics / on the horse without a shadow of a fable / with a urinary bladder of incomparable make

Corrado Costa favours a poetry located at the margins of all conventions.[13] As disclosed by a collection of essays titled *Inferno provvisorio* (Provisional Hell [Milan: Feltrinelli, 1970]), he links literature with phobias, perversion, desecration, and eroticism. In his exploration of forms of literature whose project is to cross linguistic and social boundaries, he encounters the works of Baudelaire, the Marquis De Sade, George Bataille, and Jacques Lacan. Indeed, the topic of boundaries re-emerges in a short collection of poems, *Le nostre posizioni* (Our Positions [Turin: Edizioni Geiger, 1972]), in which Costa openly disputes, as in 'Collocazioni dei nomi' (Classification of Names), all Naturalistic restrictions imposed on poetry and literature in general. Here is a poem, 'Appena dentro il complemento di luogo' (Barely Inside the Complement of Place), on the theme of the margins and the 'position' of the subject in relation to the life-world:

> passa vicino al margine
> vicino a un pesce dentro una bottiglia
> il fiume passa
> il pesce è fermo
> solidamente trattenuto in disparte
> al margine dell'acqua
> segna con il capo
> l'orlo esterno del fiume

> passes near the edge / near a fish in a bottle / the river passes / the fish doesn't move / held firmly apart / at the edge of the water / indicates with the head / the external boundary of the river (*Our Positions* [trans. by Paul Vangelisti (Los Angeles: Red Hill Press, 1975)])

Costa's most significant poetry collection is *Pseudobaudelaire* (Milan: Scheiwiller, 1964). Here he engages the reader with visions, insights, and images that relentlessly defy ordinary perceptions of the world and advocate a move 'towards an unknown direction' ('verso una ignota direzione'), as declared in the closing line of 'Lode a Francis Bacon' (16) (In Praise of Francis Bacon). This poetry is an exploration of passions and neuroses, sentiments of fear and guilt, love and violence, through figures of hostages, victims, and executioners. The prison house of this social and psychological condition cannot generate any life ('installed in the ideological uterus – he will not be born' ['istallato nell'utero ideologico – non nascerà'] (Text on a Prison Wall) ('Testo sul muro di un carcere,' 41), since it is a place of repression and subjugation ('cold / foxes, bloodhounds of affliction / masters of conscience hunting for contrition / game-bag filled with grief') ('volpi / fredde, segugi d'afflizione / direttori di coscienza in caccia di contrizione / fanno carniere di dolore' ['Ballata di buona dottrina,' 25] [Ballad of Good Doctrine]). Costa's mapping of conditioning and coercion takes on political connotations, as in 'Agiografia: atti dei voltagabbana' (Hagiography: Acts of Volte-Faces):

nell'orribile nevicata pro e contro il branco
è uscito a caccia il lupo – nell'orribile nevicata
capitalismo – han fuso sottoterra il sangue delle viti
pro e contro la vendemmia hanno reciso la gola della vigna
han dato fuoco al vento – circondato
pro e contro il campo hanno falciato i falciatori
in nome della storia – pro e contro – ha lavorato il mercenario (19)

in the horrible snowfall pro and against the herd / the wolf went out hunting – in the horrible snowfall / capitalism – they've fused underground the vine's blood / pro and against vintage they've cut off the vine's throat / they've set ablaze the wind – they've surrounded / pro and against the field they've mowed down the mowers / in the name of history – pro and against – the mercenary has worked

The last two poems of the collection, 'Angelus Novus' (The New Angel) and 'Ancora sulla possibilità per vivere' (Still on the Possibility of Living), on the one hand announce liberating events capable of transforming our human reality ('angelus domini of the reality about to arrive' ['angelus domini della realtà in arrivo']), and, on the other, undermine the legitimacy of the motivations concealed behind them. There are no certainties or guarantees living in freedom outside rules and systems. Freedom demands that everything be contested and constantly reinvented:

come se dio nascesse preghiera per preghiera
come se ogni ostaggio impugnasse la storia
come se ogni sillaba contestasse il poema
('Ancora sulla possibilità del vivere,' 45)

as if god were born prayer after prayer / as if every hostage seized history / as if every syllable contested the poem

9 Crossing the Boundaries of the Word: The Visual Poets

An aesthetics of transgression both of the linguistic code and of conventional literary models animated the principal objectives pursued by the Novissimi and Gruppo 63. It must be underscored, however, that although the group was guided by the view that traditional poetic canons had reached a point of exhaustion and non-communication, it never envisaged crossing the boundaries of language, still regarded as poetry's exclusive medium. Indeed, even the most daring experiments, like those by Balestrini and Porta carried out with collage techniques inspired by concretism, accentuate the visibility of the poem without abandoning the linguistic sign. This was not the case with various other small groups of poets that emerged during the same time-frame as Gruppo 63. As will be discussed, some groups dated back to the late 1950s while others launched their activities between the early 1960s and the beginning of the 1970s.

Although their techniques and aesthetic orientation varied widely, they all shared the desire to overcome the limits of poetry as a strictly verbal form of communication, transforming it through a multiplicity of iconographic and figurative materials. Soon the term 'visual poetry' ('poesia visiva') was coined to designate these new poetic experiences, and particularly to define the works produced by the so-called technological poets who, in 1963, formed Gruppo 70 with its base in Florence. This group made one of the most radical breaks with conventional poetry. It adopted a variety of extralinguistic materials that put in place a process of contamination that shifted poetry from a verbal genre towards a semiotic area that could not be accurately described as literary since it leaned heavily on the visual arts. Members of this group, like Lamberto Pignotti and Eugenio Miccini, had participated in the early gatherings of Gruppo 63, but, in founding Gruppo 70, they staked out a distinct and autonomous position. In fact, this was the only other group that is typically associated with the project of the new avant-garde. However, in order to present a comprehensive outline of the research in the area of visual poetry, a number of groups will be briefly analysed here.

The attempt to transcend the semantic boundaries of the linguistic sign is not an entirely new phenomenon. Indeed, the earliest visual experimentations with words date back to antiquity. Various types of iconographic experiments using the letters of the alphabet can be traced to Greek bucolic poetry (600 BC) or to the *carmina figurata* by Simmias of Rhodes (300 BC) and other Alexandrine poets. The combination of writing and figurative compositions was particularly popular in the medieval and Baroque periods but appeared in other eras as well, examples being the Rabelais poem shaped like a bottle or the poem in the form of mouse's tail in Lewis Carroll's *Alice's Adventures in Wonderland*. By the end of the nineteenth century and the turn of the twentieth, Stéphane Mallarmé (*Un coup de dés*) and Guillaume Apollinaire (*Calligrammes*) had revitalized this tradition by foregrounding the text as an iconic object and a spatial configuration.

As a whole, the historical avant-garde expanded significantly the work in this area. With its typographical revolution (*parole in libertà, tavole parolibere*), Futurism expressed a clear desire to reach a fusion of different arts. The typographical and *zaum* experimentation of Russian Cubo-Futurism or the collages created by the Dadaists (Kurt Schwitters's *i-Gedicht* or Tristan Tzara's and Francis Picabia's graphic experiments) can be placed in a similar context. Surrealism also contributed to the exploration of new possibilities for visual poetry. The *poème-objet*, a combination of words and symbolic objects, was a Surrealist creation.

In the 1940s, continuing the experimentation initiated by Futurism, Carlo Belloli wrote a number of poems (*Testi-poemi murali, Tavole visuali*) that heralded the concretism of the 1950s. This area is represented by the Brazilian group 'Noigandres' (the name, taken from a word that Ezra Pound derived from the Provençal poet Daniel Arnaut and used in his *Canto XX*, seems to indicate an homage to the American poet and his interest in ideogrammatic writing), Eugen Gomringer (*Konstellationen*), Helmut Heissenbüttel (*Kombinationen*), Diter Rot (*Bok*), and many others. (Lettrisme, a movement that emerged immediately after the Second World War, can also be situated in this general area of visual writing.)

The visual experimentation pursued in Italy starting in the 1960s was undoubtedly rooted in these general poetic perspectives. However, it displayed significant new features that stem from the social, aesthetic, and cultural context of the times. The electronic media (television in particular was the most desired of the consumer goods in the Italy of the early 1960s) started to eclipse the centrality of traditional book culture, opening the doors to the so-called 'age of images' ('civiltà delle immagini'). It is not a coincidence that the poets of Gruppo 70 paid much attention to Marshall McLuhan's theories on mass media and their effects on human consciousness. Visual poets became fully aware of the fact that the 'Gutenberg Galaxy,' with its logic and linear structure, had started to be pushed towards the periphery by the immediacy and sensorial force of the image-centred media. In many instances, this awareness was coupled with the ideological orientation of the counterculture of the times, which had not relinquished the belief that the arts can serve as a countervailing force to an alienating mass culture by producing messages of revolt and social critique. At the same time, subversive ideas and visionary activism converged with theories of structural linguistics, semiotics, information theory, and Gestalt psychology. In so doing, they assimilated into their poetic practices a critical awareness of the processes that regulate the various codes of communication and of the way they shape the perception of ourselves and of the world.

The terms adopted to categorize this body of experimentation are numerous: 'visual poetry' ('poesia visuale'), 'visual writing' ('scrittura visuale'), 'new writing' ('nuova scrittura'), 'verbal-visual poetry' ('poesia verbo-visiva'), 'symbiotic writing' ('scrittura simbiotica'), and others. However, the term 'poesia visiva' (as already mentioned, it emerged within the context of Gruppo 70) became the predominant one not only to describe the works of this particular group but also to designate the general area of poetic practice that arose after the experience of concrete poetry. The work of most groups centred on journals such as *Ana etcetera*, founded in 1958 by Martino and Anna Oberto, whose cultural background was particularly tied to Wittgenstein's philosophy of language and Pound's ideogrammatic principles; *Documento-Sud*, established in the same year in Naples by Luigi Castellano, Stelio Maria Martini, and Luciano Caruso, which explored possible integrations of poetry and visual arts (later, in 1964, members of the group founded *Linea-Sud*); *Ex*, published between 1963 and 1968 by Mario Diacono and Emilio Villa, who practised a form of writing that embraced visual poetry and conceptual art; *Tool*, founded in 1965 by Vincenzo Accame and Ugo Carrega, which presented as its main objectives the exploration of symbiotic possibilities between linguistic signs and other codes of communication; *Tèchne*, founded in 1969 by Eugenio Miccini, which underlined the links between art and technology; and *Lotta poetica*, founded by Sarenco (pseudonym of Isaia Mabellini) and Paul De Vree in 1971, which aimed at tying visual poetry to Marxism and political activism.

Even though it is possible to isolate particular and distinctive features that characterize the work of each of the numerous groups involved in the experimentation with visual poetry, for the purposes of a general analysis, three dominant trends can be identified: concrete, symbiotic, and technological poetry.

Concrete poetry, represented by poets such as Arrigo Lora Totino, Mirella Bentivoglio, and Adriano Spatola, explores the material base of language and the graphic possibilities it can produce. In their work, the optic resources of the linguistic sign interact with its the semantic component, creating an amplification of the message or subtle shifts of meaning. Generally, this poetry communicates its own formal structure, establishing an homological relation between form and content. For Arrigo Lora-Totino, concrete poetry must display the immediacy of an ideogram; it is an anti-discursive form of communication aimed at opposing the grandiloquence of traditional literature and other verbal practices. In his view, concretism produces essential, 'crystalline' structures that are similar to an architectural construction. To describe this concept, he has coined the term 'verbotectonincs' ('verbotetture'), which signifies the art and the logic of construction lying behind a concrete poem. This, in fact, is seen as a structured field of functions which relate to one another in all their parts – graphic, spatial, oral, semantic.[1] Lora-Totino expands Belloli's basic intuitions towards more elaborate and complex abstractions. In his texts he employs spatial arrangements of single words, serial structures, iterations, and permutations that confer on the linguistic sign all sorts of conceptual associations.

Mariella Bentivoglio[2] searches for primary communicative structures by isolating single letters and words. However, she often combines the visual resources of the linguistic sign with other graphic elements. Indeed, her works present an apparent cross-pollination of concretism, design, and conceptual art. Her experience with concretism leads her towards the 'object-poems' ('poemi oggetti') which, though not renouncing in most cases the presence of the linguistic sign, belong to an aesthetic environment that is closer to Duchamp than to concretism.

Adriano Spatola experiments with concrete poetry, adopting as materials printed letters and words from which semantic possibilities have been practically erased. In fact, contrary to the dominant practices of concrete poetry, Spatola's objective is not that of recovering a non-alienated meaning of the word or of broadening its semantic reverberations through graphic elaborations. Essentially, he eradicates any possible meaning associated with the word by working exclusively on its materiality and figurative properties. A case in point is constituted by the series *Zeroglifici* (Bologna: Sampietro, 1966), in which letters are segmented and blown up, fragmented or inverted, creating sequences that are virtually unreadable. The American edition, titled *Zerogliphics* (Los Angeles: The Red Hill Press, 1977), presents new texts in which letters and words are totally dismembered. Indeed, they often seem to explode, leaving behind only undecipherable debris. Even when words, occasionally derived from advertisements of well-known consumer products, can be barely reconstructed, the emphasis is on their objectification as floating rabbles and not on their semantic properties.

This metalinguistic operation, on the one hand, desemanticizes the verbal sign, and, on the other, semanticizes it at an iconographic level. As a process of semantic destruction, Spatola's work is definitely charged with ideological overtones that contest the reified condition of contemporary language and place it in tune with the tendencies tied to the linguistic project of Gruppo 63. (A highly conceptual experimentation aimed at obliterating the linguistic sign is also conducted by Emilio Isgrò, particularly with a series of texts titled 'Cancellature' [Erasures], in which words are blotted out with black ink, leaving only occasional syllables unable to construct signifying semantic units.)[3]

The merging of the territories of poetic writing and those pertaining to visual codes is also pursued with different materials and techniques by the poets who can be grouped in the area of symbiotic writing, in which various elements (phonetic, graphic, spatial, figurative, chromatic) interact, conditioning and modifying their ordinary meanings. The aim of poets such as Ugo Carrega and Vincenzo Accame is to produce a unified aesthetic act that fuses together visual (printed or handwritten letters and words), phonetic, and semantic resources of the linguistic sign. These poets gradually develop poetic objects that create an area of abstract and conceptual communication that seems to bridge writing and painting. In fact, in the late 1960s, Carrega, in particular, employed a multitude of materials such as wood, plastic, rocks, canvas, and oil colours in combination with the written word. On the other hand, Accame accentuates the material and graphic properties of handwriting, shaping some of his texts in geometrical forms – the circle is a recurrent figure. Often, words become microscopic scribbles flowing in different directions and the legibility of letters practically disappears. Carrega claims that 'everything is language' ('tutto è linguaggio'); and Accame, in a statement of poetics, declares:

Il mio lavoro tende a produrre comunicazione. Prima di essere parola o grafismo, la traccia che lascio sulla carta è *segno* ... senza mediazioni metaforiche o metafisiche, leggibile per quello che è, nella sua oggettualità visuale.

My work aims at producing an act of communication. Before being a word or a graphic presence, the mark I impress on the paper is a *sign* ... without metaphoric or metaphysical mediation, readable for what it is, a visual objectification.[4]

The major and most innovative tendency of visual poetry is linked to the work of poets belonging to Gruppo 70. The theoretical orientation of the group emerged from the conference 'Arte e comunucazione' (Art and Communication) held in Florence in 1963 and organized by a group of poets and artists that included Antonio Bueno, Giuseppe Chiari, Marcello Guasti, Eugenio Miccini, and Lamberto Pignotti. A second conference devoted to art and technology was held in 1964, followed by an exhibition organized at Forte Belvedere (in Florence) on the same subject, with the participation of painters, musicians, and poets. Starting in this period, Gruppo 70 included, besides the two principal figures, Lamberto Pignotti and Eugenio Miccini, such poets as Lucia Marcucci, Ketty La Rocca, Emilio Isgrò, Sarenco, Luciano Ori, and Michele Perfetti.

These poets make extensive use of extralinguistic materials selected from images produced by mass media (commercial photographs, advertisements, comic strips, photo romances, and so on). Their primary goal is to establish a connection between poetry, technology, and the products of consumer society. As a result, poetry shifts from an exclusively verbal practice towards a general art of the sign. This poetry displays an encounter, a convergence of different codes of communication that, by interacting with each other, offer new possibilities of signification. At the conference 'Arte e tecnologia' (Art and Technology), Miccini stated:

> La letteratura di oggi deve operare il riscatto estetico, anzichè utilitario, dei simboli dell'attuale civiltà; utilizzare i ricalchi semantici di tutti i materiali, verbali e non, che la civiltà tecnologica disperde per inserirli in un diverso contesto a livello di comunicazione ... L'arte della parola, ma ache la parola *tout cort*, veramente rischia di perdere il suo posto preminente e forse anche un ruolo d'ancella, nella scala dei valori della socialità, della vita di relazione, per cederlo all'immagine, al segnale ottico. All'istituto letterario non rimane che l'intelligenza col nemico (l'immagine) o perire. ('Arte e tecnologia,' *Marcatré*, 11–12–13, 1964, 26)

> Literature today must pursue an aesthetic redemption, as opposed to a utilitarian objective, of the symbols related to our present civilization; it has to utilize the semantic procedures of all materials, both verbal and non-verbal, that the technological civilization scatters around, by inserting them in a different context and level of communication ... The art of the word, indeed the word itself, truly risks losing its pre-eminent position and perhaps its ancillary role, in the scale of social values and human relations, surrendering it to the image, the optical signal. Literature as an institution has to deal intelligently with the enemy (the image) or perish.

The intent, however, is not that of confronting the crisis of the written word with a simple infusion of images. Undoubtedly, one of the objectives of these visual poets is to supplant the linearity and temporal deferrals (connected to the act of reading) of the written text with the rapid communicative possibilities of the image, generally relegating words to a bare minimum. Images and words have to create a sort of synergy that makes them function in sync.

La Rocca even employs road signs whose original denotation is completely transformed when 'read' in conjunction with the words that accompany them.[5] In her case, familiar visual images assume a completely new signification through the unexpected connotations triggered by their relationship with verbal messages. Ori creates visual concerts by substituting, on the conventional five-line music score, notes with images and words.[6] A 'street sonata' is made with images of cars and road signals, combined with fabricated musical directions such as 'Accelerating' ('Accelerando'), 'Without Slowing Down' ('Senza rallentare'); a 'bidet concert' is constructed with recurrent images of the washing vessel, accompanied by directions such as 'Allegro molto moderato,' 'Allegretto con brio,' and 'Adagio (alla Chopin)'; a 'labour symphony' is produced with images of nuts and bolts and a series of instructions. On the one hand, Ori explores possibilities of expanding the verbo-visual experimentation by linking it to the realm of music, and, on the other, he breaks the sacred halo surrounding classical music with a mocking attitude. On the correlation between verbal and visual codes, Pignotti explains:

> La poesia visiva, per essere tale, pretente un effettivo rapporto, una vera interazione, fra parole e immagini visive in un unico contesto (che in genere assume l'aspetto del collage e più raramente si affida a elementi dipinti o disegnati), e non la semplice convivenza. Le componenti verbali e quelle visive non dovrebbero essere proposte né dovrebbero essere fruite separatamente, a meno di fraintendere, o voler fraintendere il senso di una tale esperienza. ('Poesia concreta e visiva,' *I problemi di Ulisse*, XI, 1972, 104)

> To be defined as such, visual poetry requires an effective relationship, a true interaction between words and visual images in a single context, and not their simple co-existence (generally it adopts the aspect of a collage and rarely makes use of painted or drawn elements). The verbal and visual components should not be proposed and neither should they be viewed separately, unless one misunderstands or wishes to distort the sense of this experience.

Indeed, it seems that visual poetry espouses a sort of synaesthetic process through which it involves simultaneously a number of senses, thus attempting to widen the territory of isolated aesthetic domains. Nevertheless, these principles cover only in part the objectives of the poetic project undertaken by Gruppo 70.

In their general direction, the practices of Gruppo 70 cannot be separated from political and ideological strategies. The movement is engaged in exposing the rhetorics and the conditioning power of our everyday iconographies. The materials of mass communication are constantly subjected to processes of irony, parody, sarcasm, and defamiliarazation that aim at displacing their banal and stereotypical representations. As with Gruppo 63, its poetic project is thus one of social critique and subversion. These poets generally see their activity as a struggle against the oppression and alienation of reified social products and the cultural values they create. Their objective is to subvert these modes of communication while attempting, at the same time, to reactivate the aesthetic potentialities of the visual images exploited by the media.

In aestheticizing popular images, kitsch, and assorted objects and stereotypes of our everyday experience, visual poetry displays some resemblances to the coeval movement of Pop Art. However, although in both trends it is possible to see a collapse of the divergence between popular culture and high art, their traits do not always coincide. Pop Art, like visual poetry, generally shows a good dosage of irony towards the material it employs, but it does not develop the political orientation present in the latter. Some of the nihilistic postures of Andy Warhol (clear signs of a postmodern paradigm) do not seem to find any place with members of Gruppo 70.

There exists no possibility of accord between poets of Gruppo 70 and the civilization responsible for generating models of communication and values based on the language of advertisement, fashion, romance novels, horoscopes, and other jargons of the culture industry.[7] Miccini and Perfetti, guided by the model of the poet as an iconoclast and social dissenter, write:

> Qual'è, quindi, il rapporto tra la poesia visiva e la società? Di fronte al fenomeno vistoso del cancro comunicativo costituito dai mass media ... si è formata come una specie di interlingua massificata ... che corrisponde perfettamente ad analoghi atteggiamenti massificati. La lingua è così ridotta a feticcio e, come tale, a merce; quindi, interamente alienata. La poesia visiva è una trasfigurazione semiologica di tutti gli accadimenti antropologici del nostro tempo. Non ignora la propria civiltà, ma la nega.[8]

> What is, then, the relationship between visual poetry and society? The conspicuous phenomenon of the communication cancer produced by the mass media ... resulted in the formation of a sort of mass interlanguage ... to which analogous mass attitudes correspond perfectly. Language is thus reduced to a fetish and, as such, to a commodity; hence, completely alienated. Visual poetry is a semiological transfiguration of all anthropological events of our times. It does not ignore its own civilization, it rejects it.

The material of mass culture is constantly decontextualized and demystified through the use of desecrating and provocative collages.

In some instances, particularly in the case of Pignotti and Marcucci, advertisements or segments of comic strips and photo romances are transformed, through additional images or words, into political messages of dissension and revolt.[9] The happiness promised by the consumer goods, values, and lifestyles associated with the so-called affluent society ('società del benessere') are opposed by messages that expose the negativity of this new human condition, at both a national and an international level (occasionally, references are made to events such as the Vietnam War and the use of napalm bombs, police brutality, and political repression around the world). The objective is to create a critical social awareness capable of unmasking the mythologies, the superficiality, the emptiness, and the oppressive nature of modern society. Indeed, visual poets perceive their activity as a form of terrorism, a 'semiological warfare' ('guerriglia semiologica') – an expression used by, among others, Marcucci, Miccini, Pignotti) against the alienating messages of consumer society, messages manfactured, in their view, to produce standard reactions and control social desires. In the words of Pignotti, those messages are 'commands, instructions, orders given by the voice of the master' ('comandi, istruzioni, ordini impartiti dalla "voce del padrone"' ['Poesia visiva: verso una guerriglia semiologica?' P/P, 49]).

With its aim of uncovering the rhetorical mechanisms and emotional and subliminal effects concealed behind words and images, Gruppo 70 assigns to poetry the role of cultural and political struggle. Its project is that of contributing toward the rise of a cultural revolution charged with liberating effects. In his protest against social institutions and values, Miccini even makes use of games like rebus and crossword puzzles.[10] Some of his more direct political works utilize city maps to mark those public buildings that are to be put to flames in the event of a revolutionary uprising. A member of the group who most explicitly defines the political objectives of visual poetry is Sarenco.[11] Many of his works are made of photographs and defiant written comments documenting political violence and repression. He writes:

> ciò che noi esigiamo e l'unità di politica e arte, l'unità di contenuto e forma, l'unità di contenuto politico rivoluzionario e forma artistica il più possibile perfetta ... la nostra posizione 'poetica' d'avanguardia non può non essere una posizione fondamentalmente 'politica' d'avanguardia: la coscienza del valore assoluto della lotta di classe per il trionfo della dittatura del proletariato. ('Editoriali,' P/P, 25)

what we demand is the unity between politics and art, the unity of content and form, the unity of a political revolutionary content and artistic
form as perfect as possible ... our avant-garde 'poetic' position cannot but
be a fundamentally avant-garde 'political' position: the awareness of the
absolute value of class struggle for the triumph of the dictatorship of the
proletariat.

The correlation between visual poetry and class struggle is evidenced
also by Marcucci. She sees the task of the visual poet similar to that of a
guerrilla fighter, ready to attack and destroy the 'false culture' ('cultura falsa'). She adds:

Questa necessità gli viene dalla causa stessa per cui egli agisce: ossia dalla
lotta di classe. La lotta di classe è un aspetto della 'lotta per la vita' ... una
specie di guerra continua che tutto travolge. L'intellettuale, o meglio,
l'operatore di cultura, non deve essere solamente uno scontento inquieto,
ma un guerrigliere pronto al compito della lotta senza quartiere. ('La
posizione dell'operatore di poesia visiva nella lotta di classe e nella guerriglia,' *P/P*, 11, 12)

This necessity arises from the same cause for which he acts: namely, the
class struggle. Class struggle is an aspect of the 'struggle for life' ... a sort
of continuous war that sweeps away everything. The intellectual, or better said, the cultural operator, should not simply be a restless and discon-
tented individual, but a guerrilla fighter ready to take on the task of a
struggle without boundaries.

Even when the political tones are not so pronounced, the model of
struggle and counter-culture emerges all the same. For Pignotti, the
main task of the technological poet is to return to the sender – consumer society – its own products, shattered and desecrated, imbued
with all the signs of a culture of opposition. In his works, Pignotti
draws from a variety of materials that include not only advertisements, fashion magazines, photo romances, and postcards but also
comic strips and even stamps. Particularly for these last two materials,
he adopts the 'balloon' technique to offer biting or ironic handwritten
social messages. He writes:

I pezzi del mondo tecnologico vengono smontati, classificati, ricostruiti,
rovesciati; essenziale è capire le regole del funzionamento ... Dunque:

poesia-fumetto, poesia rotocalco. O meglio: poesia-controfumetto, poesia-contropubblicità, poesia controrotocalco. I moduli e i veicoli delle odierne comunicazioni di massa sono infatti assunti e contestati a un tempo. (*Istruzioni per l'uso degli ultimi modelli di poesia*, 126)

Pieces of our technological world are taken apart, classified, reassembled, or turned upside down; it is essential to understand the mechanisms which regulate them ... The result is comic-strip poetry, tabloid-poetry. Or, better said: counter comic-strip poetry, counter advertisement-poetry, counter tabloid-poetry. Forms and means of present-day mass communication are utilized and contested at the same time.

In its social and cultural struggle, Gruppo 70 longs for a democratization of art by envisaging poems in stadiums, on billboards, or boxes of matches, with the intent of subduing the elitism connected to the aesthetic experience and displacing its customary spaces – the book, the library, or the museum. However, this utopian aspiration never became a reality. Indeed, as the group gradually left underground culture behind and organized exhibits of visual poetry in important art centres such as Amsterdam, New York, and Tokyo, the elitism of printed poetry was substituted for the elitism of the art gallery. Some pieces of visual poetry eventually found their way onto the walls of bourgeois living-rooms. Nonetheless, this contradiction was lived with full awareness. In one of Sarenco's poems, entitled 'Museo', (Museum), we read: 'everyone / sooner / or later / ends up / in the / art / gallery / with a / piece / (gift / of the / author)' ('tutti / prima / o poi / finiamo / alla / galleria / d'arte / moderna / con un / pezzo / (dono / dell'autore').[12]

10 Closing Remarks

The phenomenon of the Italian neoavant-garde reveals both the complexity and the contradictions that accompany projects of artistic and literary innovation within the economic and cultural structures of late capitalism. Literature is not an innocent activity and it cannot nourish the illusion of easily escaping the power and control of economic and ideological forces. Indeed, the relationship between literature and hegemonic social discourses, or between literary language and the social system of communication, was a central preoccupation of the neoavant-garde. Even though it did not abandon the transgressive fury that characterized the historical avant-garde, it deeply problematicized and undermined literature's antagonistic thrust and its ability to stand outside prevailing social conditions. In spite of its Marxist wing's aspiration to ideologize literature's formal activity by linking it to a project of subversion and revolution, its potential impact on praxis was radically questioned by the group as a whole or forcefully dismissed by its postmodern bloc. Indeed, the *neoavanguardia* represents the abandonment of an illusion, namely, literature's ability to overturn social and political conditions. However, it should be underscored that, if, on the one hand, the experience of the *neoavanguardia* exhibits the traumatic signs and the crisis affecting all aesthetic activities in our age, on the other, it demonstrates that literary language possesses powerful internal resources that still have a significant role to play.

As a whole, the neoavant-garde did not assign to literature an autonomous status destined to turn it into a diversion cut off from the life-world. Clearly, while the Italian new avant-garde has rejected stale and naive canons of representation, it accorded great relevance to literature's work on language. This activity is connected not only to literature's own internal dynamics (more specifically, to the conflicting relationships that take place among its various tendencies) but also to language as a social code of communication. The common ground that joins the two major camps of the neoavant-garde is founded on the premise that, in literature, reality occurs first and foremost in the form of linguistic modalities. In this postulate resides the specificity of literature and the social space in which it operates. The displacement of dominant literary sites and norms of social communication coincides with the displacement of established grammars of the world. A subversive use of language implies a subversion of the linguistic modalities through which we construct reality.

It can be submitted that, for the neoavant-garde, literature behaves like an ecosystem. Like any other environment, it is affected by all sorts of pollutants and waste. Worn-out and rotting materials are dumped daily into its territory, making it sterile and unproductive. As the literary word reaches a state of obsolescence and tumescence, it is turned into a reified and alienating presence, its power of communication and imagination inevitably lost. The linguistic otherness pursued by the *neoavanguardia* represents an attempt to revitalize the word by revolting against any sign of decay both within literature's environment and within that larger environment of communication, namely, language as a social system. Ultimately, for both camps of the neoavant-garde, dislodging atrophied and conventional forms of writing meant abandoning ossified and alienated forms of thought. In exposing the negativity of an alienated human existence, the new avant-garde recognized literature's liberating function. On the one hand, it relinquished the vision of literature as a tool for subverting social and political structures, but, on the other, it did not banish the literary word to a separateness fatally dissociated from social life.

There is no doubt that the neoavant-garde identified and addressed issues that continue to be at the centre of any significant investigation into the status of literature in present-day culture. How is it possible to legitimize any form of antagonism within the current political economy of the sign? Given the social mechanism of commodification and the instant cannibalization of innovative forms on behalf of the hegemonic institutions, how is it possible to devise a literary project of counter-culture? How can a bourgeois institution be sabotaged and kept alive at the same time? If transgression is immediately codified, how can literature perform a role of critique and subversion? How can signs of difference exist if they are destined to become almost immediately signs of sameness? If techniques of shock are rapidly absorbed and normalized, does it imply that avant-gardism has reached a point of exhaustion? If all linguistic and aesthetic boundaries have been crossed, is the result an inevitable implosion, an irreversible collapse of any avant-gardist project?

Unquestionably, the postmodern wing of the neoavant-garde proclaimed the end of ideologies, the end of knowledge, the end of history, the end of dialectics, the end of the real, the end of the avant-garde. These theoretical postures gave voice to that ontology of the catastrophe which gained enormous ground from the 1960s on, and particularly towards the end of the millennium. Nevertheless, it should be stressed that the *neoavanguardia*, even in Guglielmi's most extreme postmodern positions, did not renounce the possibility of a critical stance on language and the world. It never admitted a sameness that would block any form of tension. A critique of traditional language turns inevitably into a critique of dominant historical paradigms.

The neoavant-garde's denunciation of conventional forms of representation and mimesis, together with its condemnation of the post-war trend of reducing the literary activity to social commitment, discloses a daring attempt at shifting literature towards other tasks and possibilities. This is not a declaration of literature's impotence as a social medium of communication. Rather, it is a forceful attempt to free the language of literature from tautological, decorative, and subordinate roles. The neoavant-garde represents the realization that the intellectual and literary culture tied to the models of the Resistance and neorealism had to come to an end. The neoavant-garde's shift toward the centrality of language aimed at transforming literature into an activity capable of producing its own communication – a production of forms and meanings and not an uncomplicated and dubious mirror of externality. *Poiesis* is recaptured in the meaning of its etymological roots: to make, to produce. For the poets of the neoavant-garde, the exploration of the materiality of language represented one of their major goals. Poetry, for them, was a journey into the material basis of the word, with the intention of opening up new paths of signification and inspiring life to rewrite itself. As has been emphasized, this encounter with language embodies phenomenological notions of the subject that subvert conventional concepts of writing and identity. The neoavant-garde poet worked in a laboratory experimenting with linguistic chemicals in search of new compounds. The objective is not to anchor conquered states of consciousness to the written word, but to activate new forms of consciousness through the act of writing. Consciousness becomes the result of a dynamic linguistic process that can follow the flux of the signifiers while also surfacing from a calculated montage of pre-existing materials. Unquestionably, one of the principal goals of the *neoavanguardia* was to demolish the lyrical foundation of poetry and thus the centrality of the 'I.' This does not exclude, however, the possibility that literature can construct a linguistic environment where new modalities of subjectivity are formed. There is no space in this poetry for lyrical effusions and declamations. The bracketing of the 'I' subverts conventional relationships between author and language and reader and language.

The neoavant-garde's objective to radicalize the role of the readers, in its proposal to make them an integral part of the construction of the text, evidences an awareness of a significant cultural shift that emphasizes the other and democratizes the relationship between author and reader. The destabilization of meanings and the effects of defamiliarization pursued by the neoavant-garde aimed at creating a hermeneutic tension that, on the one hand, envisions a culture that can subvert restraining and authoritarian models, and, on the other, is able to practise a critique of alienated forms of communication produced within the new mass society. Indeed, it is hardly an overstatement to submit that, for the neoavant-garde, reading is not so much an act of interpretation as an activity through which the text is produced. Writing and reading are complementary activities.

Detractors of the *neoavanguardia* have contended that its theoretical fervour did not translate in the production of significant creative texts. Analysis of the poets presented in this book, however, demonstrates the opposite: their texts are engaging and refreshing. Indeed, the diversity of styles and poetic projects is impressive. As a whole, the neoavant-garde did not write an obituary of avant-gardism. It re-evaluated, with intelligence and critical awareness, the possible role that innovative literary projects can perform within the intricate cultural space in which we live. Its abrupt demise confirms the unavoidable fate of every avant-garde, which is driven either by a conscious act of suicide or by an unconscious impulse of self-annihilation. There is no other way to escape the contradiction of prolonged survival without it becoming a manneristic expression of itself. However, it is equally undeniable that the upheaval caused by the neoavant-garde on the entire Italian literary landscape has had effects whose signs are visible on generations of younger poets and on the critical perspectives through which we approach the literary word. The linguistic nomadism of the neoavant-garde, together with its renewed tools for scrutinizing literature's intricate territory, reveal that there exist no metahistorical literary models, no transcendent literariness. Literature is an endless project that persistently denies any form of crystallization.

Notes

1 Poetry in Revolt: The Novissimi

1 It could be objected that Futurism finds in fascism its political expression. Undoubtedly, some elements of Futurism are absorbed by fascist mythology (glorification of war, courage, aggressiveness, nationalism – central aspects of the 1909 manifestos). However, it should be kept in mind that by 1922 – the year marking the advent of fascism – the Futurist movement had already lost its initial impact. Important protagonists like Boccioni and Sant'Elia had lost their lives during the first world war, while others, such as Carrà or Palazzeschi, were no longer taking part in the movement. The point here is that artistic projects tied to revolutionary social and political objectives – such as that represented by Surrealism – could not develop a cultural space under the repression and the censorship of fascism. By the end of Second World War, and through the late 1940s and early 1950s, the avant-garde's legacy, particularly within the literary context, had essentially been lost.

2 The anthology was first published by Rusconi and Paolazzi (Milan, 1961); rev. ed. with a new preface, Turin: Einaudi, 1965. All quotations are taken from this latter edition, reprinted in 1972. Hereinafter cited in the text as *IN*. English edition, *I Novissimi – Poetry for the Sixties* (Los Angeles: Sun and Moon Press, 1995) [prose and notes translated by David Jacobson; poetry: Pagliarani, translated by Luigi Ballerini and Paul Vangelisti; Giuliani, translated by Michael Moore; Sanguineti, translated by Bradley Dick; Balestrini, translated by Stephen Sartarelli; Porta, translated by Paul Vangelisti. Hereinafter cited in the text as *I Nov*.

3 In *Immagini e maniere*, a collection of critical studies (Milan: Feltrinelli, 1965), Giuliani writes: 'Poetry is done neither with good nor with bad sentiments,

and not even with good or bad ideologies' ('la poesia non si fa né con i buoni né con i cattivi sentimenti, e neppure con le buone o cattive ideologie' [146]).

4 Jaspers's philosophical works were introduced in Italy from the early 1940s by phenomenologists like Antonio Banfi and Enzo Paci. See, for instance, *La filosofia dell'esistenza*, introduction by Banfi (Milan: Bompiani, 1943), or *Ragione e esistenza*, trans. Paci (Milan: Bocca, 1942). A volume related to psychology, published in 1950, was *Psicologia delle visioni del mondo* (Roma: Astrolabio). For Binswanger cf. *Schizophrenie* (Tubingen: Neske, 1957), or *Der Mensch in der Psichiatrie* (Tubingen: Neske, 1957).

5 See *La schizophrénie: psychopathologie des schizoides et des schizophrènes* (Paris: Payot, 1927; 2nd ed., Paris: Desclée, 1953); *Le temps vecu: etudes phénoménologiques et psychopathologiques* (Paris: D'Artrey, 1933), trans. Nancy Metzel, *Lived Time: Phenomenological and Psychopathological Studies* (Evanston, Ill.: Northwestern University Press, 1970). All pages in the text refer to this latter volume. Minkowski, a Russian doctor with a background in phenomenology, started his training in psychiatry in Zurich, working as an assistant to Eugen Bleuler, a pioneer of modern research on these clinical conditions.

6 F.T. Marinetti, 'Manifesto tecnico della letteratura futurista,' [1912] in Luciano De Maria, ed., *Marinetti e il futurismo* (Milan: Mondadori, 1973), 81.

7 T.S. Eliot, ed., *Literary Essays of Ezra Pound, 1907–1941* (New York: New Directions 1954), 4, 5. In a letter dated 1916, Pound writes: 'I think there must be more, predominantly more objects than statements and conclusions, which latter are purely optional, not essential, often superfluous and therefore bad.' D.D. Paige, ed., *The Letters of Ezra Pound* (London: Faber and Faber, 1951), 141.

8 A disciple of Antonio Banfi (a pioneer in Italy of the studies on Husserl and phenomenology), Anceschi, beginning in the 1930s, applied phenomenological principles to aesthetics and literary criticism (*Autonomia e eteronomia dell'arte* [Florence: Vallecchi, 1936]). In the early 1950s, he brought together six poets from northern Italy in the anthology *Linea lombarda* (Varese: Editrice Magenta, 1952), in which he proposed a 'poesia in re,' a poetic tendency centred on the symbolic possibilities of objects and the silencing of direct statements of the 'I' (see in particular 22–4). For a concise overview of Anceschi's aesthetic background, see Peter Carravetta, 'Luciano Anceschi,' in Frank N. Magill, ed., *Critical Survey of Literary Theory* (Pasadena: Salem Press, 1987). For his relationship to Gruppo 63, see Alfredo Giuilani, 'Eravamo l'avanguardia,' (interview by Francesco Erbani), *La Repubblica*, 5 August 1997; and Luciano Nanni, 'Anceschi e l'europeismo epistemologico della neo-avanguardia degli anni 60,' *Poetiche* 2, 1996.

9 Olson's essay, published in 1950 in *Poetry New York*, no. 3, was translated into Italian in *Il Verri* 1 (1961). Some years later, Pagliarani, with William McCormick, translated Charles Olson's collection *The Distances* (1961): *Le lontananze* (Milan: Rizzoli, 1967). It should be added that Giuliani, in the years of gestation of *I Novissimi*, translated into Italian Eliot's *Sulla poesia e sui poeti* (Milan: Bompiani, 1960). Indeed, Giuliani's familiarity with Eliot's poetry and poetics is clearly shown in the essay included in the anthology's section 'Dietro la poesia,' in which metric and other formal aspects of poetic language are discussed.

10 It is interesting to note that in developing his own poetics, Olson had an Italian connection. In the 1940s the artist Corrado Cagli introduced him to non-Euclidean geometry and to the works in this field by the Italian physicist Roberto Bonola, which contributed to his poetic development. See Ralph Maud, *Charles Olson's Reading: A Biography* (Carbondale and Edwardville: Southern Illinois University Press, 1996), in particular 70–2.

11 See Luigi Russolo, 'L'arte dei rumori' [1913], in Luciano De Maria, ed., *Marinetti e il futurismo*, 91–9.

12 F. Gambaro, *Colloquio con Edoardo Sanguineti: quarant'anni di cultura italiana attraverso i ricordi di un poeta intellettuale* (Milan: Anabasi, 1993), 26–7. Sanguineti's first collection was written between 1951 and 1954. Sections appeared in a Florentine review of visual arts, *Numero*, in 1951, accompanied by reproductions of paintings by Klee and Kandinsky. It was published in its entirety in 1956 (Varese: Editrice Magenta), in the series 'Oggetto e simbolo' (Object and Symbol), edited by Anceschi.

13 The journal devoted an entire issue to Abstract Expressionism (1 [1961]), entitled 'L'Informale.' In various issues, dating back to 1958 and 1959, Barilli wrote on Klee and Dubuffet.

14 In 1961, at the 'Galleria del Naviglio' in Milan, Barilli organized an exhibit centred on Dubuffet, and the following year he published a volume on the painter, *Dubuffet materiologo* (Bologna: Alfa, 1962).

15 Cf. Eliot's works such as *The Rock* (1934), *Murder in the Cathedral* (1935), or *The Cocktail Party* (1950). Majakovskij's dramatic poetry dates to 1918 with *Misterija-Buff*. In his political poetry, everyday language and impersonal chronicles are dominant features, as, for instance, in the poem 'Vladimir Il'ich Lenin' (1925).

16 Porta's essay was originally published, with the title 'Dietro la poesia' (Behind Poetry), in the review *La Fiera letteraria* (10 July 1960); Calvino's text appeared in *Il Menabò* 2 (1960). The essay is reprinted in a collection of articles on literature, *Una pietra sopra: discorsi di letteratura e società* (Turin: Einaudi, 1980).

17 See R. Barthes, *Le degré zéro de l'écriture* (Paris: Editions du Seuil, 1954), trans. Annette Lavers and Colin Smith, *Writing Degree Zero* (London: Jonathan Cape, 1967), in particular the section entitled 'Writing and Silence' (80–4).

18 There is no doubt that Porta and the Novissimi showed an interest in the *école du regard*. In fact, *Il Verri* (2, [1959]) devoted an entire issue to the *nouveau roman*. Robbe-Grillet's novels, such as *Dans le labyrinthe* (Paris: Minuit, 1959), Michel Butor's *La modification* (Paris: Minuit, 1957), and Natalie Sarraute's *Le planétarium* (Paris: Gallimard, 1959), certainly provided a cultural and aesthetic reference, but their poetics and work on language revealed preoccupations that went beyond the search for a depersonalized form of writing, abolition of the plot, or adherence to the world of objects. Indeed, a novelist who provided a more significant point of reference for the Novissimi was Carlo Emilio Gadda (*Quer pasticciaccio brutto de via Merulana* [Milan: Garzanti, 1957]). Gadda's fragmented narration and iconoclastic plurilinguism attracted considerable attention among the Novissimi. In particular, a critic belonging to *Il Verri*'s circle, Angelo Guglielmi, showed significant interest in the Italian novelist beginning in the late 1950s. See, for instance, the article 'L'officina di Gadda,' *Il Verri* 2 (1958), reprinted in *Vero e falso* (Milan: Feltrinelli, 1968), 50–6.

2 The Neoavanguardia and the Theoretical Debate

1 See: *Il 'nuovo romanzo' francese* 2 (1959); *La fenomenologia* 1 (1960) and 6 (1961); *L'informale* 1 (1961); *La nuova poesia* 1 (1962). To publicize its aesthetic orientation, *Il Verri* published as well its own series of books: 'Le poetiche' (The Poetics), 'Biblioteca de Il Verri' (Il Verri's Library), 'Quaderni de Il Verri' (Il Verri's Notebooks).

2 The complete title of the volume is *Opera aperta: forma e indeterminazione nelle poetiche contemporanee* (Milan: Bompiani, 1962), trans. Anna Cancogni, *The Open Work* (Cambridge, Mass.: Harvard University Press, 1989). In 1967 and 1976 two revised Italian editions, with new essays added, were published. In the English translation, some chapters present in the first edition are omitted. Hereinafter cited in the text as *OA* and *OW* respectively. When no reference is made to the English translation, passages are taken solely from the Italian edition and the translations are mine.

3 See *Estetica: teoria della formatività* (Bologna: Zanichelli, 1960); 1st ed., 1954.

4 Some of Eco's first publications, including material utilized in *Opera aperta*, appear in a review edited by Berio, *Incontri musicali: quaderni internazionali di musica contemporanea.*

5 See particularly chapter 2, 'Apertura, informazione, comunicazione'
   (Openness, Information, Communication).
6 See Elio Vittorini, 'Industria e letteratura,' *Il Menabò* 4 (1962): 13–21.
7 If we adopt a Marxist perspective on the issue at hand, it can be added that
   all work under capitalism is always an alienated activity, including the
   work of writing. Indeed, working through an alienated language, objectifying that alienation in the act of writing, can be seen as a writer's only
   responsible choice.
8 'La sfida al labirinto,' *Il Menabò* 5 (1962). The essay is reprinted in Calvino's
   Una pietra sopra: discorsi di letteratura e società (Turin: Einaudi, 1980), 82. All
   quotations are taken from this publication. Hereinafter cited in the text as
   SL.
9 Calvino writes: 'It is now difficult ... to mark a clear demarcation between
   "tradition" and "avant-garde." I envy Umberto Eco's certainty in believing
   that "open forms" are newer than the "closed forms"' ('È difficile ormai ...
   tracciare una linea netta tra "tradizione" e "avanguardia." Invidio la
   sicurezza di Umberto Eco nel credere che le "forme aperte" siano più
   nuove delle "forme chiuse"' [*SL*, 91]).
10 An allusion is made to Renato Barilli, *La barriera del naturalismo* (The Barrier
   of Naturalism [Milan: Mursia, 1964]). This volume brings together a number of essays previously published in *Il Verri*. The writings directly related
   to the debate with Calvino and *Il Menabò* are; 'Il mare dell'oggettività,' *Il
   Verri* 2 (1960); 'Industria e letteratura,' *Il Verri* 5 (1961); and 'L'apertura a
   sinistra del *Menabò*,' *Il Verri* 3 (1962). They are published together in *La barriera del naturalismo* under the title 'Tre numeri del *Menabò*.' Hereinafter
   cited in the text as *BN*.
11 Giuliani, in his introduction to *I Novissimi*, also sides with Gadda in his
   opposition to Naturalism. Quoting Gadda's essay 'Belle lettere e contributi
   delle tecniche' (*I viaggi, la morte* [Milan: Garzanti, 1958]), Giuliani writes:
   'One becomes aware that representing is a useless action, inasmuch as life
   already independently writes itself, precisely in its living: "One must look
   at the world to be able to represent it: only, in so looking at it, one comes to
   notice that it has, to some extent, represented itself: already the soldier,
   ahead of the poet, has spoken of the battle, and the sail of the sea, and the
   new mother of childbirth"' ('ci si accorge che rappresentare è inutile in
   quanto già la vita si scrive da sé sola, appunto, vivendo: "Il mondo bisogna
   pur guardarlo, per poterlo rappresentare: e così guardandolo avviene di ril-
   evare che esso, in certa misura, ha già rappresentato se medesimo: e già il
   soldato, prima del poeta, ha parlato della battaglia, e il marinaio del mare, e
   del suo parto la puerpera"' [*I Nov*, 55, *IN*, 11]). As mentioned in chapter 1,

the Novissimi and the entire *Il Verri* group embraced the fragmentation, pastiche, and sense of instability of the self and of reality that pervade Gadda's writing. As for the *nouveau roman*, Barilli was its leading proponent. See, for instance, his preface to Robbe-Grillet's *Una via per il romanzo futuro* (Milan: Rusconi and Paolazzi, 1961) or his essays 'Robbe-Grillet e Butor' and 'Da Sartre a Robbe-Grillet,' written respectively in 1959 and 1963, later included in *L'azione e l'estasi* (Milan: Feltrinelli, 1967). Indeed, Barilli's interest in the *nouveau roman* was a lasting one, as demonstrated by his volume *Robbe-Grillet e il romanzo postmoderno* (Milan: Mursia, 1998).

12 'Il mare dell'oggettività,' *Il Menabò* 2 (1960), reprinted in *Una pietra sopra*, 44.

13 The essay is entitled 'Una sfida senza avversari,' *Il Menabò* 6 (1963), reprinted in Angelo Guglielmi, *Avanguardia e sperimentalismo* (Milan: Feltrinelli, 1964). Hereinafter cited in the text as *AS*.

14 The issue in question is no. 8. The topic was discussed again in no. 10 (October 1963).

15 The group, composed of over thirty writers, critics, visual artists, and musicians, met at Hotel Zagarella, located a few kilometres from Palermo. Readings of texts were followed by discussions. In the evenings, Luigi Gozzi and Ken Dewey directed theatre performances. Gruppo 63 met on four other occasions and founded a monthly newspaper, *Quindici*, in 1967; some of its members were involved with various other journals as well. The group lasted for about six years, from October 1963 to August 1969. Its demise, as will be discussed, coincided with the closing of *Quindici* and the student uprisings.

16 'Gli ultimi fuochi,' *La Repubblica*, 9 October 1984, 'Cultura,' n.p.

17 There is no doubt that the debate provoked by Gruppo 63 was vital in initiating a process of deprovincialization within post-war Italian culture. Indeed, a European and international cultural orientation was evident in the work of *Il Verri* and the Novissimi. Of all the members of the group, it was perhaps Alberto Arbasino who made the most critical observations on the narrowness and provincialism of the Italian culture of the times. His acute and rather sarcastic attacks appeared in particular in the newspaper *Il Giorno*. One of the most memorable was 'La gita a Chiasso,' *Il Giorno*, 22 January 1963.

The group brought into the debate on literature an innumerable array of international aesthetic models and theories. On the one hand, it drew from many foreign sources in an attempt to expand Italy's cultural boundaries, and, on the other, it was able to contribute – with an original and complex theoretical framework – to the renewal of cultural and aesthetic models.

As already done in chapter 1, whenever appropriate, references will be made to a number of artists and theorists operating outside Italy. The network of cultural affinities was indeed vast. The unconvetional and provocative spirit of the group encompassed broad cultural paradigms that included poets and writers of the 'Beat' generation, the Situationists, and the *Tel Quel* group. Guy Debord, editor of the review *L'internationale situationniste* (1958–69) and a central figure in the Situationist movement, developed a critique of capitalist society that can be aligned with the general views of Gruppo 63. He argued that, given the current conditions of production, all aspects of life have become an 'immense accumulation of *spectacles*' and thus the image is the final form of commodity reification. The spectacle, he writes, 'is not a supplement to the real world, an additional decoration. It is the heart of the unrealism of the real society': *Society of the Spectacle*, translator unnamed (Detroit: Black and Red 1983, n.p., sections 1, 6; originally published as *La société du spectacle* [Paris: Champ Libre, 1967]). Even though the Situationists were influenced by Marxist thought and championed a revolt against the social conditions created by late capitalism, they anticipated, at the same time, postmodern postures that will come to full bloom in the positions of Baudrillard and Lyotard in particular. The power of absorption (namely, the ability to co-opt any form of material) characteristic of 'spectacular' society, whose empty images are without control, undermines the possibility of an avant-garde movement – an issue addressed in a specific fashion by Gruppo 63.

Relations with the members of *Tel Quel* were more direct and intriguing. The review, headed by Philippe Sollers, was founded in 1960 (four years after the birth of *Il Verri*) and gathered together some of the most representative French intellectuals of the second half of twentieth century, from Barthes and Bataille to Derrida, Foucault, and Kristeva. Through the years, the *neoavanguardia* established contact with Jean-Pierre Faye, Marcelin Pleynet, Jean Thibaudeau, and Jacqueline Risset. When, in September 1963, the review organized a colloquium at the centre Cérisy-la-Salle on the theme of the new literature ('Une littérature nouvelle?'), Giuliani and Sanguineti were invited. The latter's Marxist orientation, however, sharply clashed with Foucault's position and that of the rest of the group. Indeed, in its first years, the *Tel Quel* group consistently rejected any form of social commitment or dialectics for literary activity. The notion of a literature disengaged from political and ideological stands and from canons of realism, as advocated by the *Telquelians*, is particularly close to that expressed by the postmodern wing of the neoavant-garde. The French group would experience a process of political involvement starting around 1967–68, when it became involved with the student movement and the Communist Party. (For an English translation of some of *Tel Quel*'s material, see Patrick ffrench and Roland-François Lack eds. *The Tel Quel Reader* (London and New York: Routledge, 1998). The review published texts by Eco, Balestrini, and Sanguineti, many translated by Thibaudeau and Risset. The latter, in collaboration with Giuliani, translated into Italian the poets involved with the review. See *Poeti di Tel Quel* (Turin: Einaudi, 1968).

18 A. Giuliani, 'Ma non è mai esistito,' *La Repubblica*, 9 October 1984, 'Cultura,' n.p. Eco's statement is reported by Giuliani in this same article. Eco poses the question of the existence of the group in an essay entitled 'Il Gruppo 63, lo sperimentalismo e l'avanguardia,' in his volume *Sugli specchi e altri saggi* (Milan: Bompiani, 1985), in particular 94–6.

19 Undoubtedly, the terms modernism/postmodernism, modernity/postmodernity have been widely abused and have created some confusion and numerous clichés. The situation becomes rather cloudy if we consider postmodern shifts in the readings of important authors like Becket, Pound, Yeats, Woolf, who were traditionally regarded as modernists. The decision to use here the two terms, for describing ideological and literary differences within the group, has not been taken without reluctance. In the end, particularly the term 'postmodern' has been adopted in the hope that it will help to orient the reader. Given the scope of the research, I do not consider it appropriate to engage in a detailed discussion of the terms in question. References are made to theorists, or to general postures associated with postmodernism, as a way of elucidating the literary debate conducted by Gruppo 63. This approach is also intended to draw attention to the fact that, as will be emphasized, issues and positions connected to postmodernism were central to the literary debate long before the labels became fashionable.

20 The debate during the first gathering of the group is reproduced with the title 'Il dibattito' (The Debate) in Nanni Balestrini and Alfredo Giuliani, eds., *Gruppo 63: la nuova letteratura* (Milan: Feltrinelli, 1964), 371–406. All pages indicated in the text within parentheses refer to this publication. The debate can also be read in Renato Barilli and Angelo Guglielmi, eds., *Gruppo 63: critica e teoria* (Milan: Feltrinelli, 1976), 264–88. It was opened with general remarks by Luciano Anceschi and the participants were Alfredo Giuliani, Angelo Guglielmi, Edoardo Sanguineti, Renato Barilli, Gillo Dorfles, Paolo Milano, Francesco Leonetti, and Enrico Filippini. The core issues were addressed by Giuliani, Guglielmi, Sanguineti, and Barilli. The analysis here revolves around their respective positions.

21 Reconnecting art with the everyday was an important objective of the his-

torical avant-garde. This goal, greatly undermined by the role of art under late capitalism, was not shared by the group as a whole. As will be discussed, this issue will take centre stage during the student uprising in 1968, and it will contribute to the disintegration of the group. Looking back at Gruppo 63 after about twenty years, Eco wrote that it is a 'very old aesthetic utopia ... to transport art into life. A very difficult thing to do, if not impossible' ('una utopia estetica antichissima ... trasportare l'arte nella vita. Il che è molto difficile, per non dire impossibile' ['Il Gruppo 63, lo sperimentalismo e l'avanguardia' (*Sugli specchi e altri saggi*, 95)]).

22 It is unlikely that in the early 1960s Sanguineti was familiar with Valentin Volosinov's study *Marxism and the Philosophy of Language*, trans. L. Matejka and I.R. Titunik (New York: Seminar Press, 1973). Still, this work, attributed to Mikhail Bakhtin – indeed, the French edition, with a preface by Roman Jakobson, *Le marxisme et la philosophie du langage* (Paris: Minuit, 1977), is published under the name of Bakhtin – has much in common with Sanguineti's position. Volosinov argues that signs and meanings are refractions of an ideology, and consciousness is not attainable without some semiotic material. 'The domain of ideology,' he writes, 'coincides with the domain of signs. They equate with one another. Wherever a sign is present, ideology is present, too. *Everything ideological possesses a semiotic value ... consciousness itself can arise and become a viable fact only in the material embodiment of signs* ... The individual consciousness is nurtured on signs' (10, 11, 13).

23 Sanguineti is referring to Walter Benjamin's volume *Angelus novus* which was published in Italy one year before the debate (Turin: Einaudi, 1962). English edition: *Illuminations* (New York: Harcourt, Brace and World, 1969).

24 Adorno's works were translated into Italian starting in the 1950s: *Minima moralia* (Turin: Einaudi, 1954); *Filosofia della musica moderna* (Turin: Einaudi, 1959); and *Dissonanze* (Milan: Feltrinelli, 1959).

25 The group gathered again on the following occasions: at Reggio Emilia (1–3 November 1964); in Palermo (3–6 September 1965); at La Spezia (10–12 June 1966); and, finally, at Fano (26–28 May 1967). As in 1963 these gatherings followed the format adopted by the German Group 47 (Hans Werner Richter, Heinrich Böll, Günther Grass, Hans Magnus Enzensberger, Uwe Johnson, and others). In fact, Enrico Filippini, a writer close to *Il Verri*, was invited in 1962 to take part in a gathering of Group 47. The debate's format, which Filippini observed in Germany, consisted of the reading of texts followed by discussion (see Filippini's 'Che cosa è il Gruppo 47,' *Corriere della Sera*, 7 April 1963).

    Members of the group – from its inception to its breakdown – were involved in the founding not only of *Quindici* but also of two literary and art reviews, *Malebolge* (1964–7) and *Grammatica* (1964–76). Another journal that supported Gruppo 63 was *Marcatré*. Two publishers in particular, Feltrinelli and Scheiwiller, both located in Milan, opened their doors to the group. The first inaugurated the series 'I materiali' (The Materials) and the second started the series 'Poesia novissima' (The Newest Poetry), both devoted exclusively to books written by members of the group. Other publishers, such as Mursia (Milan), Rusconi e Paolazzi (Milan), and Einaudi (Turin), welcomed, although less conspicuously, the creative and theoretical work associated first with the Novissimi and later with the larger Gruppo 63.

The confrontational cultural climate that Gruppo 63 created, and the urgency it placed on the questions that were being raised, drew attention and criticism from some of Italy's most prominent writers, critics, and intellectuals. Italo Calvino, Elio Vittorini, Pier Paolo Pasolini, Alberto Moravia, Franco Fortini, among others, contributed essays and newspaper articles. Indeed, although extremely critical of the theoretical positions of the group and of the texts it was producing, Moravia was present, as a observer, at the first gathering in Palermo. Vittorini, too, was present at the second gathering, in Reggio Emilia. The positions expressed by the group provoked negative reactions even in the Soviet Union. The critic Gheorgij Breitburd, in an article that first appeared in the review *Novyi Mir* and was reproduced in the section 'Documenti' in *Quindici* (1 [1967]), under the title 'La polemica di Novyi Mir contro il Gruppo 63,' accused the new avant-garde of being a neo-capitalist movement blind to the ideals of social commitment that literature should pursue. At the second gathering, a number of foreign intellectuals took part: François Wahl, Jean Thibaudeau, and Marcelin Pleynet from France (the latter two belonging to the *Tel Quel* group); Marc Slomin from England; Klaus Wagenbach from Germany; and Miguel Silva Otero from Cuba. (Some of their comments are reproduced in 'Gruppo 63,' *Malebolge* 2 [1965]). Foreign writers were also represented in *Il Verri* and *Quindici*. Both publications included articles by William Burroughs, Clement Greenberg, Jean Paulhan, Jean Starobinski, Octavio Paz, and Peter Brook.

26 Given the objectives of this book, discussions specifically related to the novel are omitted. Emphasis is placed on the general theoretical framework of the group and on issues pertaining directly to poetry.

27 For a discussion of the avant-garde's social antagonism, see the seminal work by Renato Poggioli, *Teoria dell'arte di avanguardia* (Bologna: Il Mulino, 1962) (*The Theory of the Avant-Garde*, trans. Gerald Fitzgerald [New York: Harper and Row, 1971]); and Charles Russel, *Poets, Prophets, and Revolution-*

aries: The Literary Avant-Garde from Rimbaud through Postmodernism (New York: Oxford University Press, 1985).

28 The controversy surrounding the terms 'postmodernity,' and 'postmodernism,' together with their cultural referents, has produced a vast literature. The goal here is not to address specific aspects of the debate but to suggest that essentially all the studies produced in English concentrate on American, British, and French sources. One of the few exceptions is Matei Calinescu's *Five Faces of Modernity: Modernism, Avant-garde, Decadence, Kitsch, Postmodernism* (Durham, N.C.: Duke University Press, 1987), in which Guglielmi's work is briefly mentioned and associated with a postmodern tendency.

Early in the 1960s, Guglielmi, Giuliani, and other members of Gruppo 63 had begun formulating a theoretical framework that displayed the core issues around which the controversy surrounding postmodernism would later revolve. Fundamental contributions to postmodernism (such as Ihab Hassan, *The Dismemberment of Orpheus: Toward a Postmodern Literature* [New York: Oxford University Press, 1971]; Charles Jenks, *The Language of Post-Modern Architecture* [London: Academy, 1977]; Jean-François Lyotard, *La condition postmoderne: rapport sur le savoir* [Paris: Minuit, 1979]; *The Postmodern Condition: A Report on Knowledge*, trans. Geoff Bennington and Brian Massumi [Manchester, U.K.: Manchester University Press, 1984]) were the result of research carried out in the 1970s. In North America, the postmodern theoretical turn started taking shape with the arrival of deconstruction, destructive hermeneutics, and reader-response criticism. The works of their main representatives, from Paul de Man, J. Hillis Miller, Geoffrey Hartman, and Harold Bloom to William Spanos and Stanley Fish, were all produced in the 1970s. The debate on post-structuralism launched the postmodern trend. In fact, seminal essays reflecting the new literary and cultural perspective were published in 1970 in Richard Mackesey and Eugenio Donato, eds., *The Structuralist Controversy: The Languages of Criticism and the Sciences of Man* (Baltimore, Md.: Johns Hopkins University Press). The large numbers of readers on postmodernism (such as Joseph Natoli and Linda Hutcheon, eds., *A Postmodern Reader* [Albany: State University of New York Press, 1993]) or collections of essays (such as Paul Bové, ed., *Early Postmodernism: Foundational Essays* [Durham, N.C.: and London: Duke University Press, 1995]) do not include any material predating the 1970s. (It should be added that one of the first books on American postmodernism was published in Italy in the 1980s, Peter Carravetta and Paolo Spedicato, eds., *Postmoderno e letteratura: percorsi e visioni della critica in America* [Milan: Bompiani, 1984].)

Unquestionably, as Hans Bertens argues in *The Idea of Postmodern: A History* (London and New York: Routledge, 1995) 20–36, by the mid-1960s a number of essays by Leonard Meyer, Leslie Fiedler, Robert Venturi, Erich Kahler, and the above-mentioned Ihab Hassan, among a few others, had foreshadowed critical perspectives on postmodernism. It must be underscored, however, that the Italian postmodern camp of the new avant-garde, as demonstrated both by the group's debates and by its publications, had articulated a decisive critical shift that, as discussed, encompassed subjectivity, language, ideology, and cognition, thereby challenging the entire humanistic paradigm. It is equally undeniable that the *neoavanguardia*'s debate on avant-garde culture, within the realm of late capitalism, was able to frame the fundamental aspects of the situation in such a mature fashion that subsequent investigations, in North America as elsewhere, did not take a substantially different form.

29 Peter Bürger's book *Theorie der Avantgarde* was first published in German in 1974 (Frankfurt am Main: Suhrkamp) and translated into English in 1984 by Michael Shaw (Minneapolis: University of Minnesota Press). He writes: 'Since now the protest of the historical avant-garde against art as institution is accepted as *art*, the gesture of protest of the neo-avant-garde becomes inauthentic' (53). In a note (109), he clarifies: 'If an artist sends a stove pipe to an exhibit today, he will never attain the intensity of protest of Duchamp's Ready-Mades. On the contrary, whereas Duchamp's *Urinoir* is meant to destroy art as an institution (including its specific organizational forms such as museums and exhibits), the finder of the stove pipe asks that his 'work' be accepted by the museum. But this means that the avant-gardist protest has turned into its opposite.' The contradictions of the new avant-garde were identified by Hans Magnus Enzersberger, 'Die Aporien der Avantgarde,' in *Einzelheiten: Poesie und Politik* (Frankfurt am Main: Suhrkamp, 1962); translated in Italian in 1965, 'Le aporie dell'avanguardia,' in *Questioni di dettaglio* (Milan: Feltrinelli). An obituary of the avant-garde was written by Leslie Fiedler in an essay dated 1964, 'The Death of Avant-Garde Literature,' in *Collected Essays* (New York: Stein and Day). For an overview of the debate on the avant-garde and its relationship with postmodernism, see Andreas Huyssen, *After the Great Divide: Modernism, Mass Culture, Postmodernism* (Bloomington: Indiana University Press 1986), in particular chapter 9, 'The Search for Tradition: Avantgarde and Postmodernism in the 1970s.' See also Paul Mann, *The Theory-Death of the Avant-Garde* (Bloomington and Indianapolis: Indiana University Press, 1991), and Wladimir Krysinski, 'Le avanguardie di ostentazione e le avanguardie del fare cognitivo: verso una descrizione dei linguaggi trasgressivi,' *Parol: quaderni d'arte* 12 (1996).

30 He writes: 'The historical avant-garde ... is an anachronistic movement that has at its disposal tools for action, both practical and ideological, that are no longer adequate or able to provide answers' (L'avanguardia storica ... è un movimento anacronistico, che dispone di strumenti di azione, tanto pratica che ideologica, non più rispondenti e adeguati' [61]). However, it must be pointed out that, even though Guglielmi and others proclaim the impossibility of reigniting the dialectical spirit associated with the avant-garde, Gruppo 63 represents, in its general objectives, an effort to reconnect with the aesthetic legacy of the historical avant-garde. Avantgardism meant searching for alternatives to dominant literary and cultural models. The group definitely shared with the historical avant-garde the so-called *pars destruens*, the goal of destroying or demystifying literary forms accepted as standard and indisputable. Some of its members also shared the precept that art is to be linked to a project of cultural revolt and that innovation of forms entails a new view of the world. This latter aspect can be designated as the *pars construens* of the avant-garde, namely, its aim of uncovering radical new ways to interact with the world on a sensorial and psychological plane.

31 Guglielmi underlines 'stylistic mixtures' ('impasti stilistici'), 'the boldest lexical contaminations' ('contaminazioni lessicali più ardite' [58]). He explains: 'Cultural recoveries carried out by the great experimentalists of our times are rather divided and irregular: it involves Dante, Homer, Rabelais, ancient Chinese texts, African masks' ('repêchages culturali effettuati dai nostri grandi sperimentali del nostro tempo è quanto mai fratto e irregolare: passa attraverso Dante, Omero, Rabelais, gli antichi testi cinesi, le maschere negre' [58]).

32 In one of the last issues of *Quindici* (17 [1969]), in an article entitled 'Il futuro della realtà' (The Future of Reality), Guglielmi reiterates that even though we live in a 'world that seems to absorb (neutralize) every challenge' ('un mondo che pare assorbire [neutralizzare] ogni sfida'), literature can 'still be a sign of disorder, a presence of provocation' ('essere ... ancora un segno del disordine, ancora una presenza di provocazione' [14]).

33 (Milan: Feltrinelli, 1965; revised edition, 1970); the volume includes essays written between 1963 and 1967. It can be seen not only as a rebuttal to Guglielmi's positions and those of the postmodern wing of the group but, as the title itself suggests, an antithesis to Pasolini's collection of essays *Passione e ideologia* (Passion and Ideology [Milan: Garzanti, 1960]); it is not 'passion' at the base of the ideological structure of literature, but language. All citations refer to the second edition.

34 The essay first appeared in the inaugural issue of *Quindici* (1 [1967]) and was later reprinted in the second edition of *Ideologia e linguaggio*. All quotations are taken from this latter publication.

35 Indeed, for Baudrillard, programs of revolt are an inherent part of the strategies of the system itself. In *For a Critique of the Political Economy of the Sign* [1972], trans. Charles Levin (St Louis, Mo: Telos Press, 1981), he writes: 'Modern art wishes to be negative, critical, innovative and a perpetual surpassing, as well as immediately (or almost) assimilated, accepted, integrated, consumed. One must surrender to the evidence: art no longer contests anything, if ever did. Revolt is isolated, the malediction "consumed" ... Modern art, midway between critical terrorism (ideological) and *de facto* structural integration, is quite exactly an *art of collusion vis-à-vis* this contemporary world' (110).

36 See, for example, the negative review by Renato Barilli, 'Lukács e gli scrittori dell'avanguardia,' *Il Mulino* 79 (1958), reprinted in *La barriera del naturalismo*.

37 For Benjamin's concept of allegory, cf. *The Origin of the German Tragic Drama* [1928], trans. John Osborne (London: Verso, 1985). For Benjamin, allegory exposes the illusion of a totality of meaning and calls for a mode of communication deprived of continuity, atemporality, or linear time. If the symbol aims at capturing univocal meanings, allegory enacts conflicting and polyvalent messages. For Benjamin, allegory and ruination go hand in hand. He writes: 'Allegories are, in the realm of thoughts, what ruins are in the realm of things' (178). Allegory as a sign of disintegration and decay is adopted by Sanguineti as a strategy for exposing the meaninglessness and alienation that dominate capitalist society. The mutilation of communication corresponds to the true conditions of the world. And, just as in Benjamin the allegorical gaze is placed in a dialectical position with that of redemption, so in Sanguineti it corresponds to the decay of capitalism and the hope of revolution. As will be made evident by Sanguineti's own poetic production, the allegorical construction becomes a disruptive element, thwarting codified expectations and stimulating critical distance and speculation. For postmodern fragmentation and the collapse of metanarratives, cf. Jean-François Lyotard, *The Postmodern Condition: A Report on Knowledge* [1979] (Minneapolis: University of Minnesota Press, 1984), and Fredric Jameson, *Postmodernism, or, The Cultural Logic of Late Capitalism* (Durham, NC.: Duke University Press, 1991). The opening and central chapter of Jameson's work was published as an article (with the same title as the book) in 1984 in *New Left Review* (146). It is interesting to note that Jameson's analysis of art within the confines of late capitalism (characterized by pastiche, schizophrenia, and the collapse of any illusion in accessing reality) presents innumerable correspondences with the debate surrounding

Gruppo 63. Jameson's critique of postmodernism, based on its devaluation of a political dimension, corresponds to Sanguineti's critique of Guglielmi's positions. Gruppo 63's debate encapsulates the controversy on postmodernism that will become the focus of theoretical investigation in North America during the 1970s and 1980s.

38 The address is published in Renato Barilli and Angelo Guglielmi, eds., *Gruppo 63: critica e teoria*. All pages in parentheses refer to this edition.

39 The article is reprinted in R. Barilli and A. Guglielmi, ed., *Gruppo 63: critica e teoria*. All pages in parentheses refer to this publication.

40 Horkheimer's *Eclissi della ragione* (*Eclipse of Reason*), was published in 1962, (Milan: Sugar) and his *Dialettica dell'illuminismo* (*The Dialectic of Enlightenment*), in collaboration with Theodore Adorno, in 1966 (Turin: Einaudi). One of Marcuse's most influential works, *One-Dimensional Man: Studies in the Ideology of Advanced Industrial Society* (Boston: Beacon Press, 1964), was translated into Italian in 1967 (*L'uomo a una dimensione* [Turin: Einaudi]). Marcuse devotes much attention to the condition of art and its commodification within capitalist society. He writes: 'The absorbent power of society depletes the artistic dimension by assimilating its antagonistic contents. In the realm of culture, the new totalitarianism manifests itself precisely in a harmonizing pluralism, where the most contradictory works and truths peacefully coexist in indifference' (61). As a result, Marcuse suggests that art can no longer express a state of alienation, namely, the 'unhappy consciousness' for an unrealized possible world, betrayed by the negativity of the present. He envisages a destructive dialectics, a negation of 'that-which-is' that, for truly avant-garde works of literature, means to 'communicate the break with communication' (68). The issue of the absorption of all opposition had already been anticipated by Marcuse's new preface, 'A Note on Dialectic,' to his volume *Reason and Revolution: Hegel and the Rise of Social Theory* [1941] (Boston: Beacon Press, 1960).

41 Cf. L. Althusser, *Pour Marx* (Paris: Maspero, 1965); P. Macherey, *Pour une théorie de la production littéraire* (Paris: Maspero, 1966).

42 Cf. L. Goldmann, *Le dieu caché: étude sur la vision tragique dans les pensées de Pascal et dans le théâtre de Racine* (Paris: Gallimard, 1955), and *Pour une sociologie du roman* (Paris: Gallimard, 1964); Sanguineti's critical studies, like, for instance, the one on Giovanni Pascoli ('Attraverso i *Poemetti* pascoliani,' *Ideologia e linguaggio*, 7–37), adopt the concept of homology as a fundamental guiding principle. The group's interest in Goldmann's theories is demonstrated also by Barilli's essay 'Le teorie di Goldmann sul romanzo,' written in 1965 and later included in *L'azione e l'estasi* (Milan: Feltrinelli, 1967).

43 Liala is the pen name of a successful Italian writer of sentimental and melo-
    dramatic romances.
44 For other dissenting voices, see Enzo Siciliano, 'Avanguardia italiana:
    band-wagon,' in *Prima della poesia* (Florence: Vallecchi, 1965); Gian Carlo
    Ferretti, 'Orientamenti e sviluppi della nuova avanguardia: l'ottavo
    Menabò,' *Rinascita* 35 (1965); and Gian Franco Venè, 'Le origini sociologiche
    della neo-avanguardia,' in the collective volume introduced by Giansiro
    Ferrata, *Avanguardia e neo-avanguardia* (Milan: Sugar, 1966). Numerous lit-
    erary and cultural reviews devoted special issues to the new avant-garde
    debate and tried to formulate a critical appraisal. Here are some of them:
    'Sulla lingua della neoavanguardia,' *La Fiera letteraria*, 21 February, 7 and 28
    March 1965; 'Un dibattito su linguaggio e ideologia,' *Rinascita*, 25 Septem-
    ber 1965; 'Inchiesta sulla letteratura di avanguardia,' *Letteratura* 73 (1965).
45 The interview is titled 'Lo scrittore prefabbricato' (The Prefabricated
    Writer), 20 October 1963. Reprinted in *Almanacco letterario Bompiani* (Milan:
    Bompiani, 1965). All quotations are taken from this latter publication.
46 The first article appeared in *Rinascita*, 26 December 1964, and the second in
    Nuovi argomenti 3–4 (1966). They are reprinted in *Empirismo eretico* (Milan:
    Garzanti, 1972); English edition: Louise K. Barnett, ed., *Heretical Empiricism*,
    trans. Ben Lawton and Louise K. Barnett (Bloomington: Indiana University
    Press, 1988). Hereinafter cited in the text as *EE* and *HE* respectively.
47 See, for example, poems like 'Le ceneri di Gramsci' and 'Il pianto della sca-
    vatrice,' in *Le ceneri di Gramsci* (Milan: Garzanti, 1957), 71–84 and 97–118
    respectively.
48 Y. Lotman, *Analysis of the Poetic Text*, trans. D. Barton Johnson (Ann Arbor,
    Mich.: Ardis, 1976), 19.
49 Cf. C. Metz, 'Le cinéma: langue ou langage?' *Communication* 7 (1964); this
    article forms the basis of his semiotic study of film, published a few years
    later, *Essais sur la signification au cinéma* (Paris: Klimcksieck, 1968).
50 Cf. M. McLuhan, *The Gutenberg Galaxy* (Toronto: University of Toronto
    Press, 1962); *Understanding Media* (New York: McGraw-Hill, 1964). For the
    relationship between cinema and reality, see 'Il cinema di poesia' in *Uccel-
    lacci e uccellini* (Milan: Garzanti, 1966). For further clarifications, see the
    interview with Oswald Stack, *Pasolini on Pasolini* (London: Thames and
    Hudson, 1969). In this interview, he declares: 'In my view the cinema is
    substantially and naturally poetic, for the reasons I have stated: because it
    is dreamlike, because it is close to dreams, because a cinema sequence and
    a sequence of memory or of a dream – and not only that but things in them-
    selves – are profoundly poetic: a tree photographed is poetic, a human face
    photographed is poetic because physicity is poetic in itself, because it is an

apparition, because it is full of mystery, because it is full of ambiguity, because it is full of polyvalent meaning, because even a tree is a sign of a linguistic system. But who talks through a tree? God, or reality itself. Therefore the tree as a sign puts us in communication with a mysterious speaker. Therefore, the cinema by directly reproducing objects physically, etc. etc., is substantially poetic' (153).

51 The clash between the two dates to the late 1950s when Sanguineti wrote a long and fiercely ironic poem entitled 'Una polemica in prosa' (*Officina*, November 1957), reprinted in *Segnalibro Poesie 1951–1981* (Milan: Feltrinelli, 1982). There he protests against Pasolini's decision to publish, without his consent, some of his poems in the same journal and for having described him as an 'epigone' writer. Sanguineti rejects Pasolini's notions of poetry and literature and accuses him of ignoring the difference between his work and that of other poets published in the same issue of the journal. In this poem, Sanguineti states that his intent is to 'turn the avant-garde into museum art' ('fare dell'avanguardia ... un'arte da museo'), meaning that the moment was ripe to channel the avant-garde's formal innovations towards their limits. He sarcastically excludes the possibility that there can be affinities between his poetry and that of Pasolini or the *Officina* group.

   Many members of Gruppo 63 launched fierce attacks on Pasolini's work. Perhaps the most memorable is Angelo Guglielmi's critique in 'Pasolini, maestro di vita,' *Il Verri* 3 (1960), reprinted in volume *Vero e falso* (Milan: Feltrinelli, 1968). More recently, Guglielmi has recalled his clashes with Pasolini in an interview conducted by Simonetta Fiori, 'Pasolini, mio amatissimo nemico,' *La Repubblica*, 31 October 2000.

52 Perhaps the most transparent example of a mythologized sub-proletariat – a spontaneous, instinctual, and non-alienated social class – emerges in his novel *Ragazzi di vita* (Milan: Garzanti, 1955).

53 Cf. U. Eco, 'The Death of The Gruppo 63,' *Twentieth Century Studies* 5 (1971), in particular 71. Alfredo Giuliani resigned as editor of *Quindici* in March 1969. In his last editorial, 'Perché lascio la direzione di *Quindici* (My Reasons for Leaving *Quindici*), *Quindici* 16, (1969), he insisted that the review had become victim of an 'orthodoxy of dissent' ('ortodossia del dissenso'), a 'consumption of dissent' ('consumo del dissenso' [3]), and that it was espousing strictly political ends which departed from the initial literary project of the group. In the same issue, Eco claimed that the review was experiencing an internal crisis because it was unable, as the platform of a group, to formulate any common message ('Pesci rossi e tigri di carta,' *Quindici* 16 [1969]). A few years later, commenting on the events that led to

the disintegration of the group, Balestrini declared: 'Its end, its burning itself out was already in its premises, it was the fundamental condition of its accomplishment and victory ... The blocking operation of bourgeois literature has ... succeeded, the new avant-garde has won, but destroying itself, inasmuch as it too was the literature of the bourgeoisie. Indeed, the literature of the most advanced stage of the bourgeoisie and of neo-capitalism ... It was for the purpose of renewing an outdated and paleocapitalist literature, like that produced by Moravia & Company, that the bourgeoisie supported, financed, and publicized the literature of the new avant-garde. It was a good investment, indeed a necessary one in order to bring poetry and the novel at least to the average level of the European Common Market: as they were renewing their machinery, Fiat and Iri could not afford not having their own Robbe-Grillet and Günter Grass, compared to whom Bassani and Cassola represented the hand loom' (La sua fine, il suo consumarsi era, già nelle premesse, la condizione fondamentale della sua riuscita, della sua vittoria ... L'operazione di blocco della letteratura della borghesia è ... riuscita, la neoavanguardia ha vinto, ma autodistruggendosi, in quanto anch'essa letteratura della borghesia. Anzi, letteratura dello stadio più avanzato della borghesia, del neocapitalismo ... Proprio per questo, per la necessità di svecchiare una letteratura arretrata, paleocapitalistica come quella di Moravia & C., la borghesia ha appoggiato, finanziato, propagandato la letteratura della neoavanguardia. Era un buon investimento, necessario anzi, quello di portare la poesia e il romanzo almeno a un livello medio del MEC: la Fiat e l'Iri, mentre rinnovavano il macchinario, non potevano permettersi di non avere il loro Robbe-Grillet e il loro Günter Grass, di fronte ai quali Bassani e Cassola facevano la figura del telaio a mano.' N. Balestrini, 'Intervento,' in *Prendiamoci tutto. Conferenza per un romanzo: letteratura e lotta di classe* [Milan: Feltrinelli, 1972] (16–17)). For a history of the events that led to the breakdown of the group, see the chapters 'Il gruppo 63' and 'Letteratura o rivoluzione,' in Nello Ajello, *Lo scrittore e il potere* (Roma-Bari: Laterza, 1974).

54 For some members of the group, like Balestrini, the fundamental issue is the fact that the literature produced by the new avant-garde is inseparable from bourgeois strategies and institutions. Even though this literature can represent an internal critique of the system, it is not a direct tool of the revolution. He declares: 'By now, it should be taken for granted that literature is of no use on the immediate level of praxis. It is an illusion believing that literature is in direct communication with revolution, that is, with the violent struggle with which the proletarian class demolishes the power of the bourgeoisie and seizes it. An entire left-wing ideological line, particularly the official one beginning from the post-war period, believed also that a

person of letters had an important active role to play in this struggle. To day, having become aware of the fact it is the metallurgical and machine workers who play an active and determinant role, with disappointment they choose to retreat in lamenting refusal. As a result, they reveal a late-Romantic and idealist position that believes literature can directly transform society or change it through its influence. Instead, its performance is necessarily always mediated and does not have controllable channels of action. I am convinced that many writers of the recent new avant-garde have also fallen prey to the same misunderstanding' ('Dovrebbe ormai essere acquisito che la letteratura non serve sul piano immediato della prassi, e che è illusorio credere che sia in diretta comunicazione con la rivoluzione, cioè con la lotta violenta con cui la classe proletaria abbatte il potere della classe borghese e se ne impadronisce. Tutta una linea ideologica di sinistra, e soprattutto quella ufficiale dal dopoguerra in poi, ha creduto che in questa lotta anche il letterato avesse un ruolo attivo importante. Oggi, resisi conto che il ruolo attivo determinante ce l'ha solo il metalmeccanico, i letterati scelgono di ritirarsi delusi in un lamentoso rifiuto. Rivelano così una posizione tardo romantica, idealistica, quella che crede che la letteratura possa direttamente trasformare la società o modificarla col suo influsso. Mentre il suo intervento è necessariamente sempre mediato, non ha canali di azione controllabili. Sono convinto che anche molti scrittori della recente neoavanguardia abbiano patito lo stesso equivoco.' [N. Balestrini, 'Intervento,' *Prendiamoci tutto*, 16]). However, against the position of the postmodern wing of the group, which insisted on strictly literary action, Balestrini urged direct participation in the class struggle of the times. For him, the 'populist-humanitarian' ideology of the left-wing intellectuals, who are content in identifying their social commitment with words or with the signing of manifestos, is a form of 'mystification.' At the same time, he condemns members of the group who identified opposition to the system solely with their revolutionary aesthetic forms. In fact, he arrives at the conclusion that 'it is clearly impossible that the system, namely a class in power, can ever be conquered by *its* literature. At the most, literature can become its critical awareness, the dissent, that is a beneficial and stimulating process of renewal, an adaptation to the system's new necessities of development and efficiency' ('è chiaramente impossibile che il sistema, cioè una classe al potere, possa essere mai vinto dalla *sua* letteratura. Che tutt'al più arriva a esserne la coscienza critica, la contestazione, cioè un benefico e stimolante processo di rinnovamento, di adeguamento alle nuove necessità di sviluppo e di efficienza del sistema stesso.' [N. Balestrini, 'Intervento,' *Prendiamoci tutto*, 18]).

55 It should be emphasized that the demise of Gruppo 63 did not mean the

end of the literary, cultural, or political activities of its members. On the contrary, their activities continued unabated. Indeed, for all of them, their ties with the group confirmed their influence within the Italian cultural world. Through the years, Barilli, Giuliani, Sanguineti, and Eco continued their carreers in the academic field, teaching at various universities (the latter three were to be engaged both in research and in creative work and, as we all know, Eco was to become a world-renowned novelist; Barilli, as a major art critic, became a curator of significant art exhibits both in Italy and abroad). Guglielmi became the director of one of the RAI stations, the Italian state television network, and Porta and Balestrini continued their work with leading publishers. After the 1960s, practically all of them received prestigious literary prizes and their writings appeared in the most influential Italian newpapers and weekly magazines, from *Corriere della Sera* to *L'Unità* and *La Repubblica*, from *L'Espresso* to *Panorama* and *Il Giorno*. In 1979 Porta, Balestrini, and Eco founded a monthly periodical, *Alfabeta*, which was a pivotal point of reference for Italian culture until it ceased publication in 1988. After 1969, the group never gathered again, but some of its members were busy organizing cenferences such as the 'Conevegno Internazionale degli Scrittori' (International Conference of Writers), held in Orvieto in 1976 under the auspices of the Cooperativa Scrittori (a publishing house managed by Pagliarani and Balestrini). Porta, on the other hand, became one of the founders, in 1981, of Cooperativa Intrapresa, a cultural association through which he organized the most successful poetry festival held in Italy in the 1980s, 'Milanopoesia.' The critical attention the group attracted is noteworthy. Articles on the neoavant-garde have appeared in practically all Italian journals, encyclopedias, literary dictionaries, and publications dealing with twentieth-cenntury italian literature. For a bibliography up to the mid-1970s, see Renato Barilli and Angelo Guglielmi, ed., *Gruppo 63: critica e teoria* (Milan: Feltrinelli, 1976), and Fabio Gambaro, *Invito a conoscere la neoavanguardia* (Milan: Mursia, 1993). For critical overviews, see Fausto Curi, *Ordine e disordine* (Milan: Feltrinelli, 1965); Giuliano Manacorda, 'Le neoavanguardie,' in *Storia della letteratura italiana contemporanea* (Rome: Editori Riuniti, 1967); Gianni Poli, *La sperimentazione come assoluto: letteratura della neoavanguardia italiana* (Messina and Florence: Editrice D'Anna, 1975); Walter Siti, *Il realismo dell'avanguardia* (Turin: Einaudi, 1975); Roberto Esposito, *Ideologie della neoavanguardia* (Naples: Liguori, 1976); Alberto Asor Rosa, 'Avanguardia,' in *Enciclopedia Einaudi*, vol. 2 (Turin: Einaudi, 1977); Maria Corti, 'Neoavanguardia,' in *Il viaggio testuale: le ideologie e le strutture semiotiche* (Turin: Einaudi, 1978); Romano Luperini, 'Gli altri novissimi e poeti del Gruppo 63,' in *Il Novecento* (Turin: Loescher,

1981); Thomas Harrison, ed., *The Favorite Malice: Ontology and Reference in Contemporary Italian Poetry* (New York and Milan: Out of London Press, 1983); Christopher Wagstaff, 'The Neo-avantgarde,' in Michael Caesar and Peter Hainsworth, eds., *Writers & Society in Contemporary Italy* (Leamington, U.K.: Berg Publishers, 1984); Francesco Muzzioli, *Teoria e critica della letteratura delle avanguardie italiane degli anni sessanta* (Rome: Istituto della Enciclopedia Italiana, 1982); Ciro Vitiello, *Teoria e tecnica dell'avanguardia* (Milan: Mursia, 1984); Gianni Grana, *Novecento: le avanguardie letterarie* (Milan: Marzorati, 1986); Lucio Vetri, *Letteratura e caos: poetiche della 'neo-avanguardia' italiana degli anni Sessanta* (Milan: Mursia, 1992); Renato Barilli, *La neoavanguardia italiana* (Milan: Mursia, 1995).

The above represents only a few of the critical studies on the phenomenon of the neoavant-garde as a group. For a bibliography on individual poets, see, for instance, Maurizio Cucchi and Stefano Giovanardi, eds., *Poeti italiani del secondo Novecento: 1945–1995* (Milan: Mondadori, 1996). A number of monographs also have been published. On Pagliarani, see Gabriella Di Paola, *La ragazza Carla: linguaggio e figure* (Rome: Bulzoni, 1984). On Giuliani, see Ugo Perolino, *La poesia divisa: dalla neoavanguardia alle figure immaginarie di Alfredo Giuliani* (Naples: Edizioni Scientifiche Italiane, 1995); Corrado Bologna, Paola Montefoschi, and Massimo Vetta, ed., *Chi l'avrebbe detto: arte, poesia e letteratura per Alfredo Giuliani* (Milan: Feltrinelli, 1994). On Sanguineti, see Gabriella Sica, *Sanguineti* (Florence: La Nuova Italia, 1974); Armando La Torre, *La magia della scrittura: Moravia, Malerba, Sanguineti* (Rome: Bulzoni, 1984); Antonio Pietropaoli, *Unità e trinità di Edoardo Sanguineti: poesia e poetica* (Naples: Edizioni Scientifiche Italiane, 1991); Beate Sprenger, *Neoavantgardistische Theorienbildung in Italien und Frankreich: das emanzipatorische Literaturkonzept von Edoardo Sanguineti und Philippe Sollers* (New York: Peter Lang, 1992); Fausto Curi, ed., *Edoardo Sanguineti: opere e introduzione critica* (Verona: Anterem, 1993). On Porta: Luigi Sasso, *Antonio Porta* (Florence: La Nuova Italia, 1980); Mario Moroni, *Essere e fare: l'itinerario poetico di Antonio Porta* (Rimini: Luisè, 1991); John Picchione, *Introduzione a Antonio Porta* (Rome and Bari: Laterza, 1995).

Essays and introductions to the poets of the new avant-garde appear in virtually all publications dealing with the history of Italian literature, such as *Letteratura italiana: i contemporanei*, edited by Gianni Grana (Milan: Marzorati, 1974/1989). See also Niva Lorenzini, *Il laboratorio della poesia* (Rome: Bulzoni, 1978), with essays on the five Novissimi.

For introductions in English, see, for instance, Giovanna Wedel De Stacio, Glauco Cambon, and Antonio Iliano, ed., *Twentieth-Century Italian Poets* (Detroit and London: Bruccoli Clark Layman, 1993), with profiles of Balestrini by Enesto Livorni, Pagliarani by Fausto Pauluzzi, Pignotti by Corrado Federici, Rosselli by Pietro Frassica, Giuliani, Sanguineti, and Porta by John Picchione, Spatola by Elena Urgnani. See also John Picchione and Lawrence R. Smith, ed., *Twentieth-century Italian Poetry: An Anthology* (Toronto: University of Toronto Press, 1993), with profiles of Pagliarani by Christopher Wagstaff, Giuliani by Thomas Harrison, Balestrini and Sanguineti by Lawrence R. Smith, Porta and visual poets by John Picchione, Rosselli by Lucia Re, Cacciatore by Pasquale Verdicchio, and Niccolai by Rebecca West.

The extensive critical attention the neoavant-garde has received in the years following its demise is testimony to its significant impact on Italian culture.The neoavant-garde has changed in many respects the perception of literary language, particularly its ideological functions and its clashes with the social system of communication. Indeed, the influence of the new avant-garde is felt by a number of younger poets, such as Cesare Viviani and the ones belonging to Gruppo 93 (Tommaso Ottonieri, Biagio Cepollaro, Marcello Frixione, Lorenzo Durante, Mariano Baino, Gabriele Frasca, and Lello Voce). These and other poets, including Alessandra Berardi, Paolo Gentiluomo, and Marco Berisso, pursue an innovative poetic language whose strongest point of reference is grounded in the experience of the neoavant-garde (not in the sense of a passive return to its modes of expression). These poets have absorbed the notion that the exploration of language is at the centre of any meaningful poetic work. Literature must, first and foremost, rely on its formal creations if it is to navigate the unchartered territories of human imagination and become a medium of otherness, *vis à vis* the conventional systems of communication. A number of these poets are part of an anthology edited by a member of Gruppo 63, Roberto Di Marco, together with Filippo Bettini: *Terza ondata: il nuovo movimento della scrittura in Italia* (Bologna: Synergon, 1993). See as well Renato Barilli, *È arrivata la terza ondata: dalla neo alla neo-neoavanguardia* (Turin: Testo and Immagine, 2000), and Renato Barilli et al., *63/93 trent'anni di ricerca letteraria: convegno di dibattito e di proposta* (Reggio Emilia: Elytra, 1995). For further readings on Gruppo 93, see the review *Baldus* (0 and 1, 1990 and 1991 respectively), edited by Mariano Baino, Biagio Cepollaro, and Lello Voce, and *Terra del Fuoco*, nos. 18–19–20 (n.d.), with articles grouped under the title 'Terza ondata' by Roberto Di Marco, Filippo Bettini, Marcello Carlino, Aldo Mastropasqua, Francesco Muzzioli, Giorgio Patrizi, and Iolanda Capotondi. An article by Voce is available in English: 'Avant-Garde and Tradition: A Critique,' in K. David Jackson, Eric Vos, and Joanna Drucker, eds., *Experimental Visual Concrete: Avant-Garde Poetry since the 1960s*

(Amsterdam and Atlanta: Editions Rodopi, 1996); this same volume includes writings by William Anselmi, Wladimir Krisinski, John Picchione, Enzo Minarelli, and Lamberto Pignotti on the Italian avant-garde. See also the volume edited by Filippo Bettini and Francesco Muzzioli, *Gruppo 93: la recente avventura del dibattito teorico letterario in Italia* (Lecce: Manni, 1990). A Bettini article is available in English: 'Gruppo 93: The Birth of a Movement,' in Luigi Ballerini ed., *Shearsmen of Sorts: Italian Poetry 1975–1993, Forum Italicum*, 1992 (Italian Poetry Supplement).

The linguistic and theoretical influence of the neoavant-garde can be traced also in poets who are definitively removed from its general orientation. The drastic linguistic shifts that emerge in works by poets such as Andrea Zanzotto, or even Eugenio Montale, can certainly be viewed in light of the climate of renewal engendered by Gruppo 63. This, however, is a vast issue that lies outside the objectives of this volume.

3 The Gestural and Schizoid Language of Alfredo Giuliani

1 Born in Mombaroccio, near Pesaro, in 1924, Giuliani has spent most of his life in Rome, where he studied and obtained a degree in philosophy in 1949. Two years after the publication in 1955 of his first collection of poetry, *Il cuore zoppo* (The Lame Heart), Giuliani became a member of the editorial staff of *Il Verri*. Later, as a member of Gruppo 63, he was the editor of *Quindici* from its foundation (June 1967) to January 1969, when he resigned. In the following years, as a militant critic, Giuliani contributed to such newspapers as *Il Resto del Carlino, Mondo operaio*, and *La Repubblica*. He was also active as a translator: he translated, among other writers, William Empson, T.S. Eliot, James Joyce, and Dylan Thomas. Giuliani taught Italian literature at the University of Bologna for many years. In the last period of his teaching career, he taught at the University of Chieti.

2 With the exception of a few early poems, Giuliani's entire poetic production, from the 1950s to the 1980s, is collected in the volume *Versi e nonversi* (Verses and Nonverses [Milan: Feltrinelli, 1986]). Whenever possible, all quotations are taken from this collection. Hereinafter cited in the text as *VN*.

3 A number of poems written in the 1970s make direct reference to Jarry's character Ubu-Roi; see *Nostro padre Ubu* (Our Father Ubu) [Rome: Cooperativa Scrittori, 1977]).

4 It is significant that an anonymous reviewer of *I Novissimi*, in one of the first commentaries to appear in English, perhaps recalling Hamlet's 'Though this be madness, yet there is method in 't,' speaks of method and

madness 'Method, Madness, or Both?' *Times Literary Supplement*, 3 September 1964).

5 In a statement of poetics, 'Teatro nudo' (*Marcatré* 3 [1964]), Giuliani declares: 'I seize my dialogues wherever I find them; I listen to talks at cafés and at shops' doorsteps, I consider great opportunities telephone 'conversations' ... In my practices there is undoubtedly more than one analogy with those followed by some painters of Pop Art. I am not sure if this is a way ... to redeem the degradation of the logos to a utensil' ('prendo il mio dialogo dovo lo trovo, ascolto i discorsi al caffé e sulle porte dei negozi, considero una fortuna i 'contatti' telefonici ... Nel mio procedimento c'è senza dubbio più di un'analogia con quello che seguono certi pittori della pop art. Non so se sia un modo ... per riscattare la degradazione del logos a utensile' [3]).

6 Indeed, Bataille's name appears both in the introduction to the second edition of *I Novissimi* (*IN* 3; *I Nov* 43) and in Giuliani's essays. In *Immagini e maniere* (the essay is titled 'La poesia, che cosa si può dire' [What Can You Say about Poetry]), he cites this revealing passage by Bataille taken from *La haine de la poésie* (Paris: Minuit, 1962, 2nd edition): 'La poésie qui ne s'élève pas au non-sens de la poesie n'est que le vide de la poésie, que la belle poésie.' (146).

7 A. Giuliani, *Autunno del Novecento* (Milan: Feltrinelli), 243; these comments were made in connection with the Italian translation of a 1934 work by Vygotsky, *Pensiero e linguaggio* (Florence: Giunti-Barbera, 1966).

8 In the first edition of *The Novissimi*, the poem in question is entitled 'Prologo' (Prologue). It was later changed to 'La cara contraddizione' (The Dear Contradiction). The English edition of *The Novissimi* has kept the original title.

9 In the essay 'Nuove poesie' [1973], in *Le droghe di Marsilia* (Milan: Adelphi, 1977), Giuliani writes: 'Language is a clown, mixes up what understands and what doesn't know, it does somersaults with misunderstandings, it invents everything from top to bottom' ('Il linguaggio è un clown, mescola ciò che capisce e ciò che non sa, fa capriole sui fraintendimenti, inventa da cima a fondo' [342]).

10 Here is the text: 'gutter leucocytibond, furfunnel of the stuffme, / your cuntboiled slaverplays and sneers alldelicacy / the skinnyautumn: oh slimthin dungs twisteyes / presticerebrations, the stranganguish you pulping moist / superstriking the voraciousslock oldwoman, your sweetness / that stupefies very very sofa-like the itchbum; / shitharlot witheredacts the barbark scratched: / your blackbirdy angrybond and life' (trans. Enzo Minarelli, in R. Barilli, *Voyage to the End of the Word*, 62) ('Sgrondone leuco-

citibondo, pellimbuto di farcime, / la tua ficalessa sbagioca e tricchigna tut-
tadelicatura / la minghiottona: oh sottilezze cacumini torcilocchi /
presticerebrazioni, che ti strangosci polpando mollicume, / arcipicchiando
la voraciocca passitona, la tua dolcetta / che allucchera divanissimamente
il pruggiculo; / cagoscia vizzosaggini il bàrlatro grattoso: / la tua merlosa
irabondaggine e vita' [VN, 99]). Barilli's volume contains also a section of
'Nuove predilezioni' (New Predilections), translated by Minarelli, belonging to the same collection.
11 For Ludwig Wittgenstein, see *Tractatus Logico-Philosophicus* [1922] (London:
   Routledge and Kegan Paul, 1961), in particular sections 4.121, 5.6, 5.61, and
   5.62.
12 Appropriately, this collection was later included in the volume *Versi e nonversi* (Verses and Nonverses).

4 Collage, Multilingualism, and Ideology: Elio Pagliarani's Epic Narratives

1 Elio Pagliarani was born at Viserba di Rimini, in the Emilia Romagna
  region, on 25 May 1927. He comes from a working-class family and he had
  to support himself through school at an early age. At eighteen he moved to
  Milan, where he worked at various jobs, including one in an import-export
  company. He was able to attend university and, in 1951, he received a political science degree from the University of Padua. He taught for some years
  in private schools and vocational night schools. In 1956 he joined the editorial staff of the Socialist Party newspaper *Avanti!*. In 1960 he moved to
  Rome, where a few years later he became theatre critic of the daily *Paese
  Sera*. He took part in all gatherings of Gruppo 63 and contributed to
  Quindici, as well as to a number of other journals (*Officina, Il Verri, Il
  Menabò, Nuova corrente, Nuovi argomenti*), and in 1970 he became editor of
  Periodo ipotetico. He was one of the founders of a writers' co-op, the publishing house Cooperativa Scrittori.
2 The *Scapigliatura* is a movement that has its origins in the period immediately following Italian unification (1861) and comprises mainly Milanese
  writers such as Emilio Praga and Arrigo Boito. It features an anarchic revolt
  against bourgeois social norms and values. *Verismo* is a movement similar
  to French Naturalism and includes writers like Giovanni Verga and Luigi
  Capuana. It, too, is a literary phenomenon of Italian post-unification and
  stresses the social conditions of the poor and marginalized classes. One *ver-
  ista* in particular, Emilio De Marchi, who wrote of the squalid life of the
  oppressed in Milan in the second half of nineteen century, can be seen as a
  distant influence on Pagliarani.

3 (Florence: Solaria, 1936); enlarged edition (Turin: Einaudi, 1943); trans. William Arrowsmith, *Hard Labor* (New York: Grossman, 1976).

4 'Realtà e tradizione formale nella poesia del dopoguerra,' *Nuova corrente* 16 (1959): 95.

5 Whenever texts are included in the anthology *I Novissimi* (and thus translations are available in the English edition), all quotations come from this latter publication. This applies also to the long poem *La ragazza Carla*, of which a few sections are included in the anthology.

6 The poems in *Inventario privato* were later included in Alberto Asor Rosa, ed., *La ragazza Carla e nuove poesie* (Milan: Mondadori, 1978). All page references are from this latter publication.

5 Edoardo Sanguineti and the Labyrinth of Poetry

1 Edoardo Sanguineti was born in Genoa on 9 December 1930 and spent his formative years in Turin where, in 1956, he graduated from the University of Turin after defending a thesis on Dante. He then remained at this university, beginning his teaching career as a lecturer in Italian literature. He later moved to the University of Salerno where he taught for several years. He returned to his native city in the early 1970s to hold the chair in Italian literature. Sanguineti's intellectual activity has taken many forms. Besides writing novels and plays, he has translated works by Euripides, Seneca, and Sophocles, written the script for Luca Ronconi's successful theatre adaptation of Ariosto's *Orlando Furioso*, and collaborated with the musicians Luciano Berio and Globokar Vinko in producing opera libretti and other texts for music. Sanguineti has also been engaged in constant journalistic activity. His articles dealing with a wide range of subjects – not only literary – have appeared in newspapers, particularly *Paese Sera* and *Il Giorno*, and in magazines like *L'Espresso*. In 1979 he was elected a member of the Italian parliament. Sanguineti has often claimed that autobiographical elements are present in his works and that the fundamental events of his life are his marriage to Luciana in 1954 and the birth of their four children. 'All the rest' – he states – 'is nothing but psychology' ('Il resto non è che psicologia').

2 The interpretation of Sanguineti's poetry as a manifestation of a nervous breakdown is suggested by the poet Andrea Zanzotto, 'I Novissimi,' *Comunità* 99 (1962): 89–91.

3 For sections of *Laborintus* included in the anthology *I Novissimi*, translations are taken from the English edition.

4 The title is reminiscent of Teofilo Folengo's *Chaos del Triperuno* (1527).

5 *T.A.T* was first published by a small press (Verona: Sammaruga, 1968). *Wir-*

rwarr was later included in *Catamerone* (Milan: Feltrinelli 1974), a collection in which all of Sanguineti's poetic works written between 1951 and 1971 are reprinted.

6 The movement of *Crepuscolarismo* (Twilight Poets) arose around 1905 and comprises poets like Sergio Corazzini, Guido Gozzano, and Marino Moretti. This poetry features a weary, melancholic tone and a sense of exhaustion. Sanguineti's references to a street-organ (sec. 7) or to rubbish (sec. 11) are direct recollections of objects present in the poetry of Corazzini and Gozzano. In one poem (sec. 10), a poet watching television in a lonely hotel room re-creates the sad atmosphere of Crepuscular poetry.

7 The onomatopoeic word *bisbidis* is related to the verb *bisbigliare* (to whisper). As pointed out on the collection's back cover, the term is derived from the work of a medieval poet, Immanuel Romano.

8 *Scartabello* comprises a series of poems written in 1980. It is included in *Segnalibro* (Milan: Feltrinelli, 1982), a volume that gathers together all of Sanguineti's poetry written between 1951 and 1981.

6 The Poetic Nomadism of Antonio Porta

1 Antonio Porta (pseudonym of Leo Paolazzi) was born in Vicenza in 1935 but lived all his life in Milan. After graduating in Italian literature, he worked in the publishing industry (at Bompiani and Feltrinelli in particular) while also being involved with journals like *Il Verri* and *Malebolge*. In 1967 he was one of the founders of *Quindici* and in later years, as a literary critic, he contributed to newspapers such as *Corriere della Sera*, *Il Giorno*, *Tuttolibri*, *L'Unità*, and *Comunicare*. In the 1960s he participated in various exhibits of visual poetry both in Italy and abroad; in 1979 he was among the founders of one of Italy's most innovative reviews, *Alfabeta*; and in 1981 he contributed to the activities of Cooperativa Intrapresa, a cultural association of Milan. One of the major events organized by Porta was an annual festival of poetry, 'Milanopoesia.' In the 1980s he was in charge of a television (RAI) cultural program and was also active as a novelist and playwright. He died in Rome in 1989 as a result of a heart attack.

2 The two collections in question were later reprinted in *I rapporti* [Milan: Feltrinelli, 1966], which includes all his poetic production from 1958 to 1964. All quotations related to this period are taken from this volume. Hereinafter cited in the text as *IR*.

3 The collection *Aprire* derives its title from this poem.

4 *Zero* was first published in 1963 in a limited edition comprising five sheets of paper of about 40 x 60 cm. A second and enlarged edition is included in *I rapporti*.

5 The expression 'al riparo' should be translated more appropriately as 'sheltered,' literally 'under cover.'

6 All quotations are from 'Utopia del nomade' (Utopia of the Nomad), *Weekend*, 29–4.

7 Pasquale Verdicchio provides translations of selection of poems belonging to this collection in *Passenger* (Montreal: Guernica, 1986). A selection of Porta's epistolary poems, including 'Brevi lettere' (Brief Letters), is contained in the volume *L'aria della fine* (Catania: Lunarionuovo, 1987). Anthony Molino translates some of the poems in *Kisses from Another Dream* (San Francisco: City Lights, 1987).

8 Porta makes this statement in the introduction to a selection of texts from *Passi passaggi* for his anthology *Nel fare poesia* (Florence: Sansoni, 1985), 93.

7 Nanni Balestrini and the Invisibility of the Poetic 'I'

1 Nanni Balestrini was born in Milan in 1935. He attended university in his native city, enrolling first in the faculty of engineering and later in political science. In 1956 he became a member of *Il Verri*'s editorial board. Balestrini was the principal organizer of the first gathering of Gruppo 63, in Palermo, and was one of the founders of the group's newspaper, *Quindici*. Following its demise, he established the political periodical *Compagni* and was responsible for the formation of the radical extraparliamentary left-wing group 'Potere Operario' (Workers' Power). For a period he lived in Rome, working in film and publishing. In 1979 he was accused of terrorist activities and a group of magistrates issued a warrant for his arrest. He fled to Paris where he lived for many years, earning a living in the publishing industry. He returned to Italy when the charges were dropped.

2 Norbert Wiener's work on cybernetics (*Cybernetics: or Control and Communication in the Animal and the Machine* [New York: Wiley, 1948]) was translated into Italian in 1958 as *Introduzione alla cibernetica* (Turin: Einaudi). It is possible that Balestrini was familiar with the works of Max Bense and Abraham A. Moles, who were applying information theory to the aesthetic field in the late 1950s; M. Bense, *Asthetik und Zivilisation: Theorie der asthetischen Kommunikation* (Krefeld/Baden-Baden: Agis, 1958); A. Moles, *Théorie de l'information et perception esthétique* (Paris: Flammarion, 1958). On the concept of entropy, see Gillo Dorfles, 'Entropia e relazionalità del linguaggio letterario,' *Aut Aut* 18 (1958). Umberto Eco devotes a whole chapter of *Opera aperta* (Open Work) to information theory and aesthetic messages.

3 As already discussed, for Balestrini, poetry is not able to change the social and political realities of the world. Rather, poetry's revolution rests in its language. In an interview conducted by Mario Lunetta, Balestrini states:

'Independently of whether poetry possesses an explicit or obscure discourse, it has always represented and still represents the highest degree of awareness and of transformation of society's language. For this reason, which is its only function and meaning, poetry always collides with reality and changes it: that is, precisely, the reality of language. Not the reality of the world, this has never been transformed nor it will ever be transformed by poetry. But why this bizarre idea, why should exactly poetry do it? Why not sculpture, ballet, or gardening?' ('Indipendentemente dal fatto che la poesia abbia un discorso esplicito o oscuro, essa ha sempre rappresentato e rappresenta tuttora il grado più alto di consapevolezza e di trasformazione del linguaggio della società. Per questo, che è la sua unica funzione e il suo significato, la poesia sempre investe e modifica la realtà: quella del linguaggio appunto. Il mondo no, quello non l'ha mai trasformato né mai lo trasformerà la poesia. Ma perché quest'idea bizarra, perché proprio lei dovrebbe farlo? Perché non la scultura, il balletto o il giardinaggio?' (N. Balestrini, *Prendiamoci tutto. Conferenza per un romanzo: letteratura e lotta di classe* [Milan: Feltrinelli, 1972], 20).

4 In 1976 Balestrini published *Poesie pratiche 1954–1969* (Practical Poems [Turin: Einaudi]), which contains a selection of all preceding collections. Only one text was unpublished, 'Senza lacrime per le rose' (Without Tears for the Roses), composed in 1969. The title is taken from a passage of the book *Operai e capitale* (Workers and Capital [Turin: Einaudi, 1966]), by Mario Tronti, a Marxist intellectual who, together with Toni Negri, was a central figure in the radical movement Autonomia operaria (Workers' Autonomy)] and a contributor to the influential reviews of the new left, *Quaderni rossi* and *Classe operaia*. The poem, in fact, evinces Balestrini's attention to direct political praxis, referring to the social and political violence that, in 1969, followed the student revolts. During the so-called *Autunno caldo* (Hot Autumn), workers organized a series of long strikes and engaged in violent clashes with the police. The poem is constructed through an account of events that shaped that year and through a series of its major slogans. The initial part of the slogan 'we want it all and now' ('vogliamo tutto e subito'), a succinct statement of the workers' demands (sec. 4), will later become the title of one of Balestrini's most successful novels, *Vogliamo tutto* (We Want It All [Milan: Feltrinelli, 1971]).

8 Other Poets, Other Subversions

1 Edoardo Cacciatore, born in Palermo in 1912, lived in Rome most of his life and started publishing his poetry in the early 1950s in the review *Botteghe oscure*. He never associated with any specific group and remained distant

throughout his life from all schools and movements. For translations in English of some of his poems, see Luigi Ballerini, Beppe Cavatorta, Elena Coda, and Paul Valgelisti, eds., *The Promised Land: Italian Poetry after 1975* (Los Angeles: Sun and Moon Press, 1999); for Cacciatore and a few other poets the anthology includes texts that date to the 1950s and 1960s. Hereinafter cited in the text as *PL*.

2 Amelia Rosselli was born in Paris in 1930. Her father, Carlo Rosselli, was assassinated in 1937 for anti-fascist activities, together with his brother Nello. Her mother, Marion Cave, was British. Rosselli spent her childhood in France, England, and the United States. She returned to Italy in 1946 and lived in Rome. A student of music and philosophy, she contributed to reviews like *Botteghe oscure*, *Nuovi argomenti*, *Civiltà delle macchine*, *Il Menabò*, and *Tabula*. She suffered a nervous breakdown, spent long periods in psychiatric hospitals, and committed suicide in 1996.

3 See the poems grouped under the title 'Palermo '63' in Amelia Rosselli, *Poesie*, edited by Emmanuela Tandello (Milan: Garzanti, 1997), 133–7.

4 'The only poet I felt close to and influenced me,' she declared, 'was Antonio Porta. I liked his first books, I was curious about his elegant way for abstraction' ('L'unico poeta a cui mi sentii vicina, e che mi influenzò, fu Antonio Porta. I suoi primi libri mi piacevano, m'incuriosiva la sua astrazione elegante' [A. Rosselli, *Antologia poetica*, edited by G. Spagnoletti (Milan: Garzanti, 1987)]), 159.

5 Giuseppe Guglielmi was born in Bari in 1923 and, for most of his life, worked in Bologna as a cultural activist. A contributor to *Il Verri*, he died in 1995.

6 *Panglosse*, containing poems written between 1953 and 1966, together with other texts, was later reprinted in *Ipsometrie (Le stasi del sublime)* (Rome: Savelli, 1980). All pages refer to this edition.

7 Adriano Spatola was born in Sapjane (Yugoslavia) in 1941. He studied in Bologna with Luciano Anceschi and contributed to *Il Verri*, *Malebolge*, and *Quindici*. Together with Giulia Niccolai, he founded the poetry review *Tam Tam*. He was editor of the visual-poetry review *Doc(k)s*. As a sound poet, he performed in Europe, North America, and Australia. Along with Paul Vangelisti, he edited the anthology *Italian Poetry, 1960–1980: From Neo to Post Avant-garde* (San Francisco and Los Angeles: Red Hill Press, 1982). He died in 1988.

8 'Il breve quanto schematico editoriale del primo numero,' *Tam Tam* 2 (1972); translated by Paul Vangelisti with the title 'A Vaguely Ontological Aspiration,' in *Majakovskiiiiiij* (Los Angeles: Red Hill Press, 1975), n.p.

9 Giulia Niccolai was born in Milan in 1934. For some years she worked as a

photographer. Active in both visual and sound poetry, she exhibited and performed her work in Italy and abroad. She was Spatola's companion for some years and founded with him the review *Tam Tam*. She was editor of *O/E*.

10 Patrizia Vicinelli was born in Bologna in 1943. A contributor to the reviews *EX*, *Malebolge*, *Marcatré*, and *Ana etcetera*, she was active as a sound poet and partcipated in projects of experimental film and theatre. She died in 1991.

11 Giorgio Celli was born in Bologna in 1935. He is an expert of entomology and teaches at the university of his native city. For some years he has hosted a television program on the life of animals. He contributed to reviews like *Il Verri* and *Niebo* and was editor of *Malebolge*.

12 For these aspects of Celli's poetics, see the appendix 'L'operazione poetica: il grande trasparente' (The Poetic Operation: The Great Transparency), *Il pesce gotico* (Turin: Geiger, 1968), n.p.

13 Corrado Costa was born in Mulino di Bazzano, near Parma, in 1929 and lived in Reggio Emilia where he worked as a lawyer. He was editor of *Malebolge* and *Il caffè* and contributed to *Il Verri*, *Quindici*, and *Nuova corrente*. He died in 1991. Besides the collection *Our Positions*, a series of poems with the title *The Complete Films* has been translated into English by Paul Vangelisti (San Francisco and Los Angeles: Red Hill Press, 1983).

9 Crossing the Boundaries of the Word: The Visual Poets

1 Cf. A. Lora-Totino, 'Poesia concreta,' *Presenza Sud* 1 (1968): 45. Arrigo Lora-Totino was born in Turin in 1928. In the mid-1960s he founded the reviews *Antipiugiù* and *Modulo*, devoted exclusively to concrete poetry. In later years, he became one the Italy's major representatives of sound poetry. He is the editor of *Futura* (Cramps Records), an anthology of this genre.

2 Mirella Bentivoglio was born in Klagenfurt (Austria) in 1922. She has exhibited her work at the Venice Biennale and in art galleries both in Italy and abroad.

3 For biographical data on Spatola, see chapter 8. Emilio Isgrò was born at Barcellona Pozzo di Gotto (Sicily) in 1937 and moved to Milan in the late 1950s. His works have been exhibited in galleries throughout Italy and he has participated in the Venice Biennale and the Biennale in São Paulo, Brazil.

4 Both Carrega's and Accame's statements appear in Eugenio Giannì, *Pòiesis* (Arezzo: Istituto Statale d'Arte, 1986), 197. Ugo Carrega was born in Genoa in 1935. In the late 1950s he came into contact with Anna and Martino Oberto and started contributing to *Ana etcetera*. He is the founder of cul-

tural centres devoted to poetry and visual arts ('Centro Tool' and 'Mercato del Sale,' both located in Milan). Vincenzo Accame was born in Loano (Liguria) in 1932 and died in Milan in 1999. He is the author of *Il segno poetico* (Samedan: Munt Press, 1977), an extensive study of visual and interdisciplinary practices in poetry.

5 Ketty La Rocca was born in La Spezia in 1938 and died in 1976. She moved to Florence to study music and spent most of her life there. Her works have been exhibited both in Europe and North America (Venice Biennale, Philadelphia Art Museum, Columbia University). The art gallery Emi Fontana (Milan) has produced a CD of her works.

6 Luciano Ori was born in Florence in 1928. In the 1960s he was also involved in experimental theatre. After the activities of Gruppo 70 came to an end in 1968, he became one of the founding members of the International Group of Visual Poetry.

7 On this subject, see Lamberto Pignotti, *Istruzioni per l'uso degli ultimi modelli di poesia* (Rome: Lerici, 1968), in particular 78–81, 86. Motivated by Max Bense's research on technological styles (cf. *Plakatwelt* [Stuttgart: Deutsche Verlags-Anstalt, 1952]), Pignotti started adopting the term 'technological poetry' (poesia tecnologica) in the early 1960s. See also the volume written in collaboration with Stefania Stefanelli, *La scrittura verbo-visiva* (Rome: L'Espresso, 1980).

8 E. Miccini and M. Perfetti, 'Poesia visiva,' in E. Miccini, ed., *Poesia e/o poesia* (Brescia-Firenze: Edizioni Sarmic, 1972), 3–4. Hereinafter cited in the text as *P/P*. The volume contains an anthology of visual poems and a number of theoretical texts, both in Italian and English, by most members of Gruppo 70.

9 Lamberto Pignotti was born in Florence in 1926. He participated in the first gathering of Gruppo 63 and became a leading figure in Gruppo 70. In 1965 he edited the first anthology of visual poetry *Antologia della poesia visiva* (Bologna: Sampietro). He taught at the universities of Florence and Bologna. For a profile, see Corrado Federici, 'Lamberto Pignotti,' in Giovanna Wedel De Stasio, Glauco Cambon, and Antonio Iliano, eds., *Twentieth-Century Italian Poets* (Detroit and London: Bruccoli Clark Layman, 1993), and, by the same author, 'The Technological Poetry of Lamberto Pignotti,' in Rocco Capozzi and Massimo Ciavolella, eds., *Scrittori, tendenze letterarie e conflitto delle poetiche in Italia (1960–1990)* (Ravenna: Longo, 1993). Lucia Marcucci was born in Florence in 1933. Her theoretical writings have been published in reviews such as *Il Ponte, La Battana, Arte oggi*, and her works have been exhibited at the Venice Biennale and at the Spoleto's Festival of Two Worlds.

10 Eugenio Miccini was born in Florence in 1925. One of the most active members of Gruppo 70, Miccini is the founder of the cultural centre 'Centro Téchne,' which published a review of visual poetry. In the 1970s he was involved with the review *Lotta poetica.*

11 Sarenco (pseudonym of Isaia Mabellini) was born at Vobarno (Lombardy) in 1945. He began his activity as a visual poet in the mid-1960s. Active in Brescia, he founded in that city a number of cultural centres and art galleries that devote particular attention to visual practices in poetry (Galleria Sincron, Galleria Amodulo, Centro La Comune).

12 Sarenco, 'Museo,' in E. Miccini and Sarenco, eds., *Poesia visiva 1963-1988: 5 maestri* (Paris: Henri Veyrier, 1988), 170. The volume contains an anthology of poetic works by Carrega, Stelio Maria Martini, Miccini, Pignotti, and Sarenco, as well as critical texts, in Italian and English, by Giulio Carlo Argan, Renato Barilli, Aldo Rossi, Luciano Nanni, Luigi Ballerini, Achille Bonito Oliva, and Umberto Eco, among others. For an overview of visual practices in poetry centred on the Italian experience, from the early twentieth century to the 1970s, see Luigi Ballerini, *La piramide capovolta* (Venice: Marsilio, 1975); Luciano Nanni, 'Lo sperimentalismo poetico novecentesco e la crisi dell' 'aesthetica' borghese,' in Renato Barilli et al., *Estetica e società tecnologica* (Bologna: Il Mulino, 1976); Giuseppe Morrocchi, *Scrittura visuale: ricerche ed esperienze nelle avanguardie letterarie* (Messina-Florence, 1978). See also the chapter 'La poesia totale,' in Lucio Vetri, *Letteratura e caos: poetiche della neo-avanguardia italiana degli anni Sessanta* (Milan: Mursia, 1992). In 1973 an exhibit of Italian visual poets was organized in New York at the Finch College Museum. See Luigi Ballerini, ed., *Italian Visual Poetry: 1912-1972* (New York: Istituto Italiano di Cultura, 1973); the volume contains a number of works presented at the exhibit together with statements of poetics translated into English. For a bibliography on visual poetry in Italy until the mid-1970s, see Matteo D'Ambrosio, *Bibliografia della poesia italiana d'avanguardia: poesia visiva, visuale, concreta e fonetica* (Rome: Bulzoni, 1977).

Works Cited

Accame, Vincenzo. *Il segno poetico*. Samedan: Munt Press, 1977.

Adorno, Theodor W. *Minima moralia*. Turin: Einaudi, 1954.

– *Filosofia della musica moderna*. Turin: Einaudi, 1959.

– *Dissonanze*. Milan: Feltrinelli, 1959.

Adorno, Theodor W., and Max Horkheimer. *La dialettica dell'illuminismo*. Turin: Einaudi, 1966.

Ajello, Nello. *Lo scrittore e il poere*. Laterza: Rome-Bari, 1974.

Althusser, Louis. *Pour Marx*. Paris: Maspero, 1965.

Anceschi, Luciano. *Autonomia e eteronomia dell'arte*. Florence: Vallecchi, 1936.

– ed. *Linea lombarda*. Varese: Editrice Magenta, 1952.

– *Poetica americana*. Pisa: Nistri Lischi, 1953.

Anonymous. 'Method, Madness, or Both?' *Times Literary Supplement*, 3 September 1964.

Arbasino, Alberto. 'La gita a Chiasso.' *Il Giorno*, 22 January 1963.

Asor Rosa, Alberto. 'Avanguardia.' In *Enciclopedia Einaudi*, vol. 2. Turin: Einaudi, 1977.

Baino, Mariano, Biagio Cepollaro, Lello Voce, et al. [Gruppo 93]. *Baldus* 0 and 1 (1990 and 1991).

Balestrini, Nanni. *Il sasso appeso*. Milan: Scheiwiller, 1961.

– *Come si agisce*. Milan: Feltrinelli, 1963.

– *Altri procedimenti*. Milan: Scheiwiller, 1965.

– ed. *Gruppo 63: il romanzo sperimentale*. Milan: Feltrinelli, 1966.

– *Ma noi facciamone un'altra*. Milan: Feltrinelli, 1968.

– *Vogliamo tutto*. Milan: Feltrinelli, 1971.

– 'Intervento.' In *Prendiamoci tutto. Conferenza per un romanzo: letteratura e lotta di classe*. Milan: Feltrinelli, 1972.

– *Poesie pratiche 1954–1969*. Turin: Einaudi, 1976.

– *Osservazioni sul volo degli uccelli*. Milan: Scheiwiller, 1988.

Balestrini, Nanni, and Alfredo Giuliani, eds. *Gruppo 63: la nuova letteratura*. Milan: Feltrinelli, 1964.

Ballerini, Luigi. *La piramide capovolta*. Venice: Marsilio, 1975.

– ed. *Italian Visual Poetry: 1912–1972*. New York: Istituto Italiano di Cultura, 1973.

Ballerini, Luigi, Beppe Cavatorta, Elena Coda, and Paul Valgelisti, eds. *The Promised Land: Italian Poetry after 1975*. Los Angeles: Sun and Moon Press, 1999.

Barilli, Renato. *Dubuffet materiologo*. Bologna: Alfa, 1962.

– *La barriera del naturalismo*. Milan: Mursia, 1964.

– *L'azione e l'estasi*. Milan: Feltrinelli, 1967.

– *Viaggio al termine della parola*. Milan: Feltrinelli, 1981. Trans. Teresa Fiore and Harry Polkinhorn. *Voyage to the End of the Word*. San Diego: San Diego State University Press, 1997.

– *La neoavanguardia italiana*. Milan: Mursia, 1995.

– et al. *63/93 trent'anni di ricerca letteraria: convegno di dibattito e di proposta*. Reggio Emilia: Elytra, 1995.

– *Robbe-Grillet e il romanzo postmoderno*. Milan: Mursia, 1998.

– *È arrivata la terza ondata: dalla neo alla neo-neoavanguardia*. Turin: Testo and Immagine, 2000.

Barilli, Renato, and Angelo Guglielmi, eds. *Gruppo 63: critica e teoria*. Milan: Feltrinelli, 1976.

Barthes, Roland. *Le degré zéro de l'écriture*. Paris: Édition de Seuil, 1954. Trans. Annette Lavers and Colin Smith. *Writing Degree Zero*. London: Jonathan Cape, 1967.

Bataille, Georges. *La haine de la poésie*. Paris: Minuit, 1962, 2nd edition.

Baudrillard, Jean. *Pour une critique de l'economie politique du signe*. Paris: Gallimard, 1972. Trans. Charles Levin. *For a Critique of the Political Economy of the Sign*. St Louis, Mo.: Telos Press, 1981.

Benjamin, Walter. *Illuminations*. New York: Harcourt, Brace and World, 1968. Italian translation, *Angelus novus*. Turin: Einaudi, 1962.

– *The Origin of the German Tragic Drama* [1928]. Trans. John Osborne. London: Verso, 1985.

Bense, Max. *Plakatwelt*. Stuttgart: Deutsche Verlags-Anstalt, 1952.

– *Asthetik und Zivilisation: Theorie der asthetischen KommuniKation*. Krefeld/Baden-Baden: Agis, 1958.

Bertens, Hans. *The Idea of Postmodern: A History*. London and New York: Routledge, 1995.

Bettini, Filippo. 'Gruppo 93: The Birth of a Movement,' in Luigi Ballerini, ed. *Shearsmen of Sorts: Italian Poetry 1975–1993. Forum Italicum*, 1992. [Italian Poetry Supplement]

Bettini, Filippo, and Francesco Muzzioli, eds. *Gruppo 93: la recente avventura del dibattito teorico letterario in Italia*. Lecce: Manni, 1990.

Bettini, Filippo, and Roberto Di Marco, eds. *Terza ondata: il nuovo movimento della scrittura in Italia*. Bologna: Synergon, 1993.

Binswanger, Ludwig. *Schizophrenie*. Tubingen: Neske, 1957.

– *Der Mensch in der Psichiatrie*. Tubingen: Neske, 1957.

Bologna, Corrado, Paola Montefoschi, and Massimo Vetta, eds. *Chi l'avrebbe detto: arte, poesia e letteratura per Alfredo Giuliani*. Milan: Feltrinelli, 1994.

Bové, Paul, ed. *Early Postmodernism: Foundational Essays*. Durham, N.C., and London: Duke University Press, 1995.

Bürger, Peter. *Theorie der Avantgarde*. Frankfurt am Main: Suhrkamp, 1974. Trans. Michael Shaw. *Theory of the Avant-Garde*. Minneapolis: University of Minnesota Press, 1984.

Butor, Michel. *La modification*. Paris: Minuit, 1957.

Cacciatore, Edoardo. *La restituzione*. Florence: Vallecchi, 1955.

– *Lo specchio e la trottola*. Florence: Vallecchi, 1960.

– *Tutti i poteri*. Milan: Feltrinelli, 1969.

Calinescu, Matei. *Five Faces of Modernity: Modernism, Avant-garde, Decadence, Kitsch, Postmodernism*. Durham, N.C.: Duke University Press, 1987.

Calvino, Italo. 'Il mare dell'oggettività.' *Il Menabò* 2 (1960). Reprinted in *Una pietra sopra: discorsi di letteratura e società*. Turin: Einaudi, 1980.

– 'La sfida al labirinto.' *Il Menabò* 5 (1962). Reprinted in *Una pietra sopra*.

– 'Gli ultimi fuochi.' *La Repubblica*, 9 October, 1989.

Carravetta, Peter. 'Luciano Anceschi,' in Frank N. Magill ed., *Critical Survey of Literary Theory*. Pasadena, Calif.: Salem Press, 1987.

Carravetta, Peter, and Paolo Spedicato, eds. *Postmoderno e letteratura: percorsi e visioni della critica in America*. Milan: Bompiani, 1984.

Celli, Giorgio. Il pesce gotico., Turin: Geiger, 1968.

– *Morte di un biologo*. Bologna: Centro Duchamp, 1970.

Corti, Maria. 'Neoavanguardia,' in *Il viaggio testuale: le ideologie e le strutture semiotiche*. Turin: Einaudi, 1978.

Costa, Corrado. *Pseudobaudelaire*. Milan: Scheiwiller, 1964.

– *Inferno provvisorio*. Milan: Feltrinelli, 1970.

– *Le nostre posizioni*. Turin: Edizioni Geiger, 1972. Trans. Paul Vangelisti. *Our Positions*. Los Angeles: Red Hill Press, 1975.

– *The Complete Films*. Trans. Paul Vangelisti. San Francisco and Los Angeles: Red Hill Press, 1983.

Cucchi, Maurizio, and Stefano Giovanardi, eds. *Poeti italiani del secondo Novecento: 1945-1995*. Milan: Mondadori, 1996.

Curi, Fausto. 'Proposte per una storia delle avanguardie.' *Il Verri*, 8 (1963).

– *Ordine e disordine*. Milan: Feltrinelli, 1965.
– ed. *Edoardo Sanguineti: opere e introduzione critica*. Verona: Anterem, 1993.
D'Ambrosio, Matteo. *Bibliografia della poesia italiana d'avanguardia: poesia visiva, visuale, concreta e fonetica*. Rome: Bulzoni, 1977.
Debord, Guy. *La société du spectacle*. Paris: Champe Libre, 1967. Trans. unnamed. *Society of the Spectacle*. Detroit: Black and Red, 1983.
Della Volpe, Galvano. *Critica del gusto*. Milan: Feltrinelli, 1960.
De Stasio Wedel, Giovanna, Glauco Cambon, and Antonio Iliano, eds. *Twentieth-Century Italian Poets*. Detroit and London: Bruccoli Clark Layman, 1993 (profiles of Balestrini by Ernesto Livorni, Pagliarani by Fausto Pauluzzi, Pignotti by Corrado Federici, Rosselli by Pietro Frassica, Spatola by Elena Urgnani, Giuliani, Sanguineti, and Porta by John Picchione).
Di Marco, Roberto, Filippo Bettini, Marcello Carlino, Aldo Mastropasqua, et al. 'Terza ondata.' *Terra del Fuoco*, 18–19–20 (n.d.).
Di Paola, Gabriella. *La ragazza Carla: linguaggio e figure*. Rome: Bulzoni, 1984.
Dorfles, Gillo. 'Entropia e relazionalità del linguaggio letterario.' *Aut Aut*, 18 (1958).
Eco, Umberto. *Opera aperta*. Milan: Bompiani, 1962. Trans. Anna Cancogni. *The Open Work*. Cambridge, Mass.: Harvard: Harvard University Press, 1989.
– 'Per una indagine sulla situazione culturale.' *Rinascita*, 5 and 12 October 1963.
– 'Pesci rossi e tigri di carta.' *Quindici* 16 (1969).
– 'The Death of Gruppo 63.' *Twentieth Century Studies* 5 (1971).
– 'Il Gruppo 63, lo sperimentalismo e l'avanguardia.' In *Sugli specchi e altri saggi*. Milan: Bompiani, 1985.
Eliot, Thomas Stearn. *The Sacred Wood: Essays on Poetry and Criticism*. London: Methuen, 1920. Translated into Italian by Luciano Anceschi. *Il bosco sacro*. Milan: Muggiani, 1946.
Enzersberger, Hans Magnus. 'Die Aporien der Avantgarde.' In *Einzelheiten: Poesie und Politik*. Frunkfurt am Main: Suhrkamp, 1962. Italian translation, 'Le aporie dell'avanguardia.' In *Questioni di dettaglio*. Milan: Feltrinelli, 1965.
Erba, Luciano. *Il male minore*. Milan: Mondadori, 1960.
Esposito, Roberto. *Ideologie della neoavanguardia*. Naples: Liguori, 1976.
Federici, Corrado. 'The Techological Poetry of Lamberto Pignotti.' In Rocco Capozzi and Massimo Ciavolella, eds. *Scrittori, tendenze letterarie e conflitto delle poetiche in Italia (1960–1990)*. Ravenna: Longo, 1993.
Ferrata, Giansiro, ed. *Avanguardia e neo-avanguardia*. Milan: Sugar, 1966.
Ferretti, Gian Carlo. 'Orientamenti e sviluppi della neoavanguardia.' *Rinascita* 35 (1965).
ffrench, Patrick, and Roland-Françõis Lack. *The Tel Quel Reader*. London and New York: Routledge, 1998.

Fiedler, Leslie. 'The Death of Avant-Garde Literature.' In *Collected Essays*. New York: Stein and Day, 1964.

Filippini, Enrico. 'Che cosa è il Gruppo 47.' *Corriese della Sera*, 7 April 1963.

Gadda, Carlo Emilio. *Quer pasticciaccio brutto de via Merulana*. Milan: Garzanti, 1957.

– 'Belle lettere e contributi delle tecniche.' In *I viaggi, la morte*. Milan: Garzanti, 1958.

Gambaro, Fabio. *Invito a conoscere la neoavanguardia*. Milan: Mursia, 1993.

– *Colloquio con Edoardo Sanguineti: quarant'anni di cultura italiana attraverso i ricordi di un poeta intellettuale*. Milan: Anabasi, 1993.

Giannì, Eugenuio. *Pòiesis*. Arezzo: Istituto Statale d'Arte, 1986.

Giudici, Giovanni. *L'intelligenza col nemico*. Milan: Scheiwiller, 1957.

Giuliani, Alfredo. *Il cuore zoppo*. Varese: Magenta, 1955.

– [Trans. of T.S. Eliot.] *Sulla poesia e sui poeti*. Milan: Bompiani, 1960.

– ed. *I Novissimi – Poesie per gli anni '60*. Milan: Rusconi and Paolazzi, 1961; rev. ed., Turin: Einaudi, 1965; English trans. Luigi Ballerini, Bradley Dick, David Jacobson, Michael Moore, Stephen Sartelli, and Paul Vangelisti. *I Novissimi – Poetry for the Sixties*. Los Angeles: Sun and Moon Press, 1995.

– 'Teatro nudo.' *Marcatré*, 3 (1964).

– *Immagini e maniere*. Milan: Feltrinelli, 1965.

– *Povera Juliet e altre poesie*. Milan: Feltrinelli, 1965.

– *Il tautofono*. Milan: Feltrinelli, 1969.

– 'Perché lascio la direzione di Quindici.' *Quindici*, 16 (1969).

– *Chi l'avrebbe detto*. Turin: Einaudi, 1973.

– 'L'avventura dentro i segni.' In *Le droghe di Marsilia*, Milan: Adelphi, 1977.

– *Le droghe di Marsilia*. Milan: Adelphi, 1977.

– *Nostro padre Ubu*. Rome: Cooperativa Scrittori, 1977.

– *Autunno del Novecento: cronache di letteratura*. Milan: Feltrinelli, 1984.

– 'Ma non è mai esistito.' *La Repubblica*, 9 October 1984.

– *Versi e nonversi*. Milano: Feltrinelli, 1986.

– 'Eravamo l'avanguardia' (interview by Francesco Erbani). *La Repubblica*, 5 August 1997.

Giuliani, Alfredo, and Jacqueline Risset, eds. *Poeti di Tel Quel*. Turin: Einaudi, 1968.

Goldmann, Lucien. *Le dieu caché: étude sur la vision tragique dans la pensée de Pascal et dans le théâtre de Racine*. Paris: Gallimard, 1955.

– *Pour un sociologie du roman*. Paris: Gallimard, 1964.

Grana, Gianni, ed. *Letteratura italiana: i contemporanei* Milan: Marzorati, 1974/ 1989.

– *Novecento: le avanguardie letterarie*. Milan: Marzorati, 1986.

Guglielmi, Angelo. 'L'officina di Gadda.' *Il Verri* 2 (1958). Reprinted in *Vero e falso*. Milan: Feltrinelli, 1968.
- *Avanguardia e sperimentalismo*. Milan: Feltrinelli, 1964.
- 'Il futuro della realtà.' *Quindici* 17 (1969).
- 'Pasolini mio amatissimo nemico' (Interview by Simonetta Fiori). *La Repubblica*, 31 October 2000.
Guglielmi, Giuseppe. *Essere e non avere*. Varese: Editrice Magenta, 1955.
- *Panglosse*. Milan: Feltrinelli, 1967.
Harrison, Thomas, ed. *The Favorite Malice: Ontology and Reference in Contemporary Italian Poetry*. New York and Milan: Out of London Press, 1983.
Hassan, Ihab. *The Dismemberment of Orpheus: Toward a Postmodern Literature*. New York: Oxford University Press, 1971.
Horkheimer, Max. *Eclissi della ragione*. Milan: Sugar, 1962.
Huyssen, Andreas. *After the Great Divide: Modernism, Mass Culture, Postmodernism*. Bloomington: Indiana University Press, 1986.
Jameson, Fredric. *Postmodernism, or, the Cultural Logic of Late Capitalism*. Durham, N.C.: Duke University Press, 1991.
Jaspers, Karl. *Ragione e esistenza*. Milan: Bocca, 1942.
- *La filosofia dell'esistenza*. Milan: Bompiani, 1943.
- *Psicologia delle visioni del mondo*. Rome: Astrolabio, 1950.
Jenks, Charles. *The Language of Post-Modern Architecture*. London: Academy, 1977.
Krysinski, Wladimir. 'Le avanguardie di ostentazione e le avanguardie del fare cognitivo: verso una descrizione dei linguaggi trasgressivi.' *Parol: quaderni d'arte*, 12 (1996).
La Torre, Armando. *La magia della scrittura: Moravia, Malerba, Sanguineti*. Rome: Bulzoni, 1984.
Lora-Totino, Arrigo. 'Poesia concreta.' *Presenza Sud* 1 (1968).
Lorenzini, Niva. *Il laboratorio della poesia*. Rome: Bulzoni, 1978.
Lotman, Yuri. *Analysis of the Poetic Text* [1970]. Trans. D. Barton Johnson. Ann Arbor, Mich.: Ardis, 1976.
Lukács, Georg. *The Meaning of Contemporary Realism*. Trans. Johnand Necke Mander. London: Merlin Press, 1962. Italian trans. *Il significato del realismo critico*. Turin: Einaudi, 1957.
- *History and Class Consciousness* [1922]. Trans. Rodney Livingstone. Cambridge, Mass.: MIT Press, 1971.
Luperini, Romano. 'Gli altri novissimi e poeti del Gruppo 63.' In *Il Novecento*. Turin: Loescher, 1981.
Luzi, Mario. *L'inferno e il limbo*. Marzocco: Florence, 1949.
Lyotard, Jean François. *La condition postmoderne: rapport sur le savoir*. Paris:

Minuit, 1979. Trans. Geoff Bennington and Brian Massumi. *The Postmodern Condition: A Report on Knowledge*. Manchester, U.K.: Manchester University Press, 1984.

Macherey, Pierre. *Pour une théorie de la production littéraire*. Paris: Maspero, 1966.

Mackesey, Richard, and Eugenio Donato, eds. *The Structuralist Controversy: The Languages of Criticism and the Sciences of Man*. Baltimore: Johns Hopkins University Press, 1970.

Manacorda, Giuliano. 'Le neoavanguardie.' In *Storia della letteratura italiana contemporanea*. Rome: Editori Riuniti, 1967.

Manganelli, Giorgio. *Letteratura come menzogna*. Milan: Feltrinelli, 1967.

Mann, Paul. *The Theory-Death of the Avant-Garde*. Bloomington and Indianapolis: Indiana University Press, 1991.

Marcuse Herbert. 'A Note on Dialectic.' In *Reason and Revolution: Hegel and the Rise of Social Theory*. Boston: Beacon Press, 1960.

– *One-Dimentional Man: Studies in the Ideology of Advanced Industrial Societies*. Boston: Beacon Press, 1964.

Marinetti, Filippo Tommaso. 'Manifesto tecnico della letteratura futurista' (1912). In Luciano De Maria, ed., *Marinetti e il futurismo*. Milan: Mondadori, 1973.

Maud, Ralph. *Charles Olson Reading: A Biography*. Carbondale and Edwardville: Southern Illinois Press, 1996.

McLuhan, Marshall. *The Gutemberg Galaxy*. Toronto: University of Toronto Press, 1962.

– *Understanding Media*. New York: McGraw-Hill, 1964.

Metz, Christian. 'Le cinéma: langue ou language?' *Communication* 7 (1964).

– *Essais sur la signification au cinéma*. Paris: Klimcsieck, 1968.

Miccini, Eugenio, et al. 'Arte e tecnologia.' *Marcatré* 11–12–13 (1964).

– Miccini, Eugenio, ed. *Poesia e/o poesia*. Brescia-Firenze: Edizioni Sarmic, 1972.

Miccini, Eugenio, and Sarenco, eds. *Poesia visiva 1963–1988: 5 maestri*. Paris: Henri Veyrier, 1988.

Minkowski, Eugène. *La schizophrénie: psichopathologie des schizoides et des schizophrènes*. Paris: Peyot, 1927; 2nd ed. Paris: Desclée, 1953.

– *Les temps vecu: etudes phénoménologiques et psychopathologiques*. Paris: D'Artrey, 1933. Trans. Nancy Metzel, *Lived Time: Phenomenological and Psychopathological Studies*. Evanston, Ill.: Northwestern University Press, 1970.

Moles, Abraham. *Théorie de l'information et perception esthétique*. Paris: Flammarion, 1958.

Montale, Eugenio. *La bufera e altro*. Venice: Neri Pozza, 1956

Moravia, Alberto. 'Lo scrittore prefabbricato' (Interview). *L'Espresso*, 20 October 1963. Reprinted in *Almanacco letterario Bompiani*. Milan: Bompiani, 1965.

- 'Illegibilità e potere.' *Nuovi argomenti* 7–8 (1967).
- 'Metaavanguardia e manierismo.' *Nuovi argomenti* 6 (1967).
Moroni, Mario. *Essere e fare: l'itinerario poetico di Antonio Porta*. Rimini: Luisè, 1991.
Morrocchi, Giuseppe. *Scrittura visuale: ricerche ed esperienze nelle avanguardie letterarie*. Messina-Florence: Editrice D'Anna, 1978.
Muzzioli, Francesco. *Teoria e critica della letteratura delle avanguardie italiane degli anni sessanta*. Rome: Istituto della Enciclopedia Italiana, 1982.
Nanni, Luciano. 'Lo sperimentalismo poetico novecentesco e la crisi dell' 'aesthetica' borghese.' In Renato Barilli et al., ed., *Estetica e società tecnologica*. Bologna: Il Mulino, 1976.
- 'Anceschi e l'europeismo epistemologico della neo-avanguardia degli anni 60.' *Poetiche*, 2 (1996).
Natoli, Joseph, and Linda Hutcheon, eds. *A Postmodern Reader*. Albany: State University of New York Press, 1993.
Niccolai, Giulia. *Humpty Dumpty*. Turin: Geiger, 1969.
- *Greenwich*. Turin: Geiger, 1971.
- *Harry's Bar e altre poesie 1969–1980*. Milan: Feltrinelli, 1981.
Niccolai, Giulia, and Paul Vangelisti. *Substitution*. Los Angeles: Red Hill Press, 1975.
Olson, Charles. 'Projective Verse.' *Poetry New York* 3 (1950). Reprinted in Robert Creely, ed., *Selected Writings of Charles Olson*. New York: New Directions, 1966. [This edition includes the essay 'Human Universe.']
Pagliarani, Elio. *Cronache e altre poesie*. Milan: Schwarz, 1954.
- *Inventario privato*. Milan: Veronelli, 1959.
- 'Realtà e tradizione formale nella poesia del dopoguerra.' *Nuova corrente*, 16 (1959).
- *La ragazza Carla e altre poesie*. Milan: Mondadori, 1962.
- *Lezione di fisica e fecaloro*. Milan: Feltrinelli, 1968.
- *La ragazza Carla e nuove poesie*. Alberto Asor Rosa ed. Milan: Mondadori, 1978.
- and William McCormich, trans., Charles Olson, *Le lontananze*. Milan: Rizzoli, 1967.
Pareyson, Luigi. *Estetica: teoria della formatività*. Bologna: Zanichelli, 1960.
Pasolini, Pier Paolo. *La meglio gioventù*. Florence: Sansoni, 1954.
- *Ragazzi di vita*. Milan: Garzanti, 1955.
- *Le ceneri di Gramsci*. Milan: Garzanti, 1957.
- 'La libertà stilistica.' *Officina* 9–10 (1957).
- *Passione e ideologia*. Milan: Garzanti, 1960.
- *La religione del mio tempo*. Milan: Garzanti, 1961.

- 'Notizia su Amelia Rosselli.' *Il Menabò* 6 (1963).
- 'Il cinema di poesia.' In *Uccellacci e uccellini*. Milan: Garzanti, 1966.
- *Empirismo eretico*. Milan: Garzanti, 1972. Trans. Ben Lawton, and Louise K. Barnett. *Heretical Empiricism*. Bloomington: Indiana University Press, 1988.
Pavese, Cesare. *Lavorare stanca*. Florence: Solaria, 1936; 2nd, enlarged edition. Turin: Einaudi, 1943. Trans. William Arrowsmith, *Hard Labor*. New York: Grossman, 1976.
Pecora, Elio. 'Un incontro con Amelia Rosselli,' *Galleria*, January–August 1997.
Perolino, Ugo. *La poesia divisa: dalla neoavanguardia alle figure immaginarie di Alfredo Giuliani*. Naples: Edizioni Scientifiche Italiane, 1995.
Picchione, John. *Introduzione a Antonio Porta*. Rome and Bari: Laterza, 1995.
Picchione, John, and Lawrence R. Smith, eds. *Twentieth-century Italian Poetry: An Anthology*. Toronto: University of Toronto Press, 1993 (profiles of Pagliarani by Christopher Wagstaff, Giuliani by Thomas Harrison, Balestrini and Sanguineti by Lawrence R. Smith, Porta and visual poets by John Picchione, Rosselli by Lucia Re, Cacciatore by Pasquale Verdicchio, and Niccolai by Rebecca West).
Pietropaoli, Antonio. *Unità e trinità di Edoardo Sanguineti: poesia e poetica*. Naples: Edizioni Scientifiche Italiane, 1991.
Pignotti, Lamberto. *Antologia della poesia visiva*. Bologna: Sampietro, 1965.
- *Istruzioni per l'uso degli ultimi modelli di poesia*. Rome: Lerici, 1968.
- 'Poesia concreta e visiva.' *I problemi di Ulisse* 11 (1972).
Pignotti, Lamberto, and Stefania Stefanelli. *La scrittura verbo- visiva*. Rome: L'Espresso, 1980.
Poggioli, Renato. *Teoria dell'arte di avanguardia*. Bologna: Il Mulino, 1962. Trans. Gerald Fitzgerald. *The Theory of the Avant-Garde*. New York: Harper and Row, 1971.
Poli, Gianni. *La sperimentazione come assoluto: letteratura della neoavanguardia italiana*. Messina and Florence: Editrice D'Anna, 1975.
Porta, Antonio. *La palpebra rovesciata*. Milan: Azimuth, 1960.
- *Zero, posie visive*. Milan: Numbered Edition, 1963.
- *Aprire*. Milan: Scheiwiller, 1964.
- *I rapporti*. Milan: Feltrinelli, 1966.
- *Cara*. Milan: Feltrinelli, 1969.
- *Metropolis*. Milan: Feltrinelli, 1971. Trans. Pasquale Verdicchio. *Metropolis*. Kobenhavn and Los Algeles: Green Integer, 1999.
- *Week-end*. Rome: Cooperativa Scrittori, 1974.
- *Quanto ho da dirvi. Poesie 1958–1975*. Milan: Feltrinelli, 1977.
- *Passi Passaggi*. Milan: Mondadori, 1980. Trans. (selected texts) Pasquale Verdicchio. *Passenger*. Montreal: Guernica, 1986.

– *Invasioni*. Milan: Mondadori, 1984. Trans. (selected texts) Paul Vangelisti. *Invasions & Other Poems*. San Francisco: Red Hill Press, 1986.
– *Nel fare poesia*. Florence: Sansoni, 1985.
– *L'aria della fine*. Catania: Lunarionuovo, 1987. Trans. (selected texts) Anthony Molino. *Kisses from Another Dream*. San Francisco: City Lights, 1987.
– *Il giardiniere contro il becchino*. Milan: Mondadori, 1988.
Pound, Ezra. *The Letters of Ezra Pound*. D. D. Paige, ed. London: Faber and Faber, 1951.
– *Literary Essays of Ezra Pound 1907–1941*. T.S. Eliot, ed. New York: New Directions, 1954.
Quasimodo, Salvatore. *Giorno dopo giorno*. Milan: Mondadori, 1947.
– *La vita non è sogno*. Milan: Mondadori, 1949.
– *Il falso e il vero verde*. Milan: Mondadori, 1956.
Risi, Nelo. *Pensieri elementari*. Milan: Mondadori, 1961.
Robbe-Grillet, Alain. *Dans le labyrinth*. Paris: Minuit, 1959.
– *Una via per il romanzo futuro*. Milan: Rusconi and Paolazzi, 1961.
Rosselli, Amelia. *Variazioni belliche*. Milan: Garzanti, 1964.
– *Serie ospedaliera*. Milan: Il Saggiatore, 1969.
– *Documento 1966–1973*. Milan: Garzanti, 1976.
– *Antologia poetica*. Giacinto Spagnoletti, ed. Milan: Garzanti, 1987.
– *Poesie*. Emmanuela Tandello, ed. Milan: Garzanti, 1997.
Russel, Charles. *Poets, Prophets and Revolutionaries: The Literary Avant-Garde from Rimbaud through Postmodernism*. New York: Oxford University Press, 1985.
Russolo, Luigi. 'L'arte dei rumori' (1913). In Luciano De Maria, ed., *Marinetti e il futurismo*. Milan: Mondadori, 1973.
Sanguineti, Edoardo. *Laborintus*. Varese: Editrice Magenta, 1956.
– *Erotopaegnia*. Milan: Rusconi and Paolazzi, 1961.
– *Esposizione* (libretto). Milan: Universal Edition, 1963.
– *Passaggio* (libretto, 1961–1962). *Sipario*, 224 (December 1964).
– *Triperuno*. Milan: Feltrinelli, 1964.
– *Ideologia e linguaggio*. Milan: Feltrinelli, 1965. Revised, Milan: Feltrinelli, 1970.
– *Laborintus II* (libretto, 1965). Vienna: Universal Edition, 1976.
– *T.A.T.* Verona: Sammaruga, 1968.
– *Wirrwarr*. Milan: Feltrinelli, 1972.
– *Catamerone*. Milan: Feltrinelli, 1974.
– *Postkarten*. Milan: Feltrinelli, 1978.
– *Stracciafoglio*. Milan: Feltrinelli, 1980.
– *Segnalibro: Poesie 1951–1981*. Milan: Feltrinelli, 1982.
– *Novissimum testamentum*. Lecce: Manni, 1986.

– *Bisbidis*. Milan: Feltrinelli, 1987.

Sarraute, Nathalie. *Le planétarium*. Paris: Gallimard, 1959.

Sasso, Luigi. *Antonio Porta*. Florence: La Nuova Italia, 1980.

Sereni, Vittorio. *Diario d'Algeria*. Vallecchi: Florence, 1947.

– *Gli strumenti umani*. Turin: Einaudi, 1965.

Sica, Gabriella. *Sanguineti*. Florence: La Nuova Italia, 1974.

Siciliano, Enzo. 'Avanguardia italiana: band-wagon.' In *Prima della poesia*. Florence: Vallecchi, 1965.

Siti, Walter. *Il realismo dell'avanguardia*. Turin: Einaudi, 1975.

Smith, Lawrence, R. *The New Italian Poetry*. Los Angeles: University of California Press, 1981.

Spatola, Adriano. *L'ebreo negro*. Milan: Scheiwiller, 1966. Trans. (selected texts) Paul Vangelisti. *Various Devices*. Los Angeles: Red Hill Press, 1978.

– *Zeroglifici*. Bologna: Sampietro, 1966. Trans. Giulia Niccolai and Paul Vangelisti. *Zerogliphics*. Los Angeles: Red Hill Press, 1977.

– *Verso la poesia totale*. Salerno: Rumma, 1969.

– *Majakovskiiiiiiij*. Turin: Geiger, 1971. Trans. Paul Vangelisti. *Majakovskiiiiiiij*. Los Angeles: Red Hill Press, 1975.

– *La composizione del testo*. Rome: Cooperativa Scrittori, 1978.

Spatola, Adriano, and Paul Vangelisti, eds. *Italian Poetry, 1960–1980: From Neo to Post Avant-garde*. San Francisco and Los Angeles: Red Hill Press, 1982.

Sprenger, Beate. *Neoavantgardistische Theorienbildung in Italien und Frankreich: das emanzipatorische Literaturkonzept von Edoardo Sanguineti und Philippe Sollers*. New York: Peter Lang, 1992.

Stack, Oswald. *Pasolini on Pasolini*. London: Thames and Hudson, 1969.

Tagliaferri, Aldo. 'La superstizione della crudeltà.' *Quindici* 8 (1968).

Tronti, Mario. *Operai e capitale*. Turin: Einaudi, 1966.

Vetri, Lucio. *Letteratura e caos: poetiche della 'neo-avanguardia' italiana degli anni Sessanta*. Milan: Mursia, 1992.

Vicinelli, Patrizia. *à, a. A*. Milan: Lerici, 1967.

Vitiello, Ciro. *Teoria e tecnica dell'avanguardia*. Milan: Mursia, 1984.

Vittorini, Elio. 'Industria e letteratura.' *Il Menabò* 4 (1962).

Voce, Lello. 'Avant-Garde and Tradition: A Critique.' In K. David Jackson, Eric Vos, and Joanna Drucker, eds., *Experimental Visual Concrete: Avant-Garde Poetry since the 1960s*. Amsterdam and Atlanta: Editions Rodopi, 1996.

Volosinov, Valentin. *Marxism and the Philosophy of Language*. Trans. L. Matejka and I.R. Titunik. New York: Seminar Press, 1973. Published in French under the name of Mikhail Bakhtin *Le marxisme et la philosophie du langage*. Paris: Minuit, 1977.

Vygotsky, Lev. *Pensiero e linguaggio*. Florence: Giunti-Barbera, 1966.

Wagstaff, Christopher. 'The Neo-avantgarde.' In Michael Caesar and Peter Hainsworth, ed., *Writers & Society in Contemporary Italy*. Leamington, U.K.: Berg Publishers, 1984.

Wiener, Norbert. *Cybernetics: or Control and Communication in the Animal and the Machine*. New York: Wiley, 1948. Italian trans. *Introduzione alla cibernetica*. Turin: Einaudi, 1958.

Wittgestein, Ludwig. *Tractatus Logico-Philosophicus* [1922]. London: Routledge and Kegan Paul, 1961.

Zanzotto, Andrea. 'I Novissimi.' *Comunità* 99 (1962).

Index